Non-Binary Lives

NON-BINARY LIVES

An Anthology
of Intersecting Identities

Edited by JOS TWIST, BEN VINCENT,
MEG-JOHN BARKER and KAT GUPTA

Jessica Kingsley Publishers
London and Philadelphia

Epigraph on p. 101 is reprinted with kind permission of Wipf and Stock.

First published in 2020
by Jessica Kingsley Publishers
73 Collier Street
London N1 9BE, UK
and
400 Market Street, Suite 400
Philadelphia, PA 19106, USA

www.jkp.com

Library of Congress Cataloging in Publication Data
A CIP catalog record for this book is available from the Library of Congress

British Library Cataloguing in Publication Data
A CIP catalogue record for this book is available from the British Library

ISBN 978 1 78775 339 6
eISBN 978 1 78775 340 2

Printed and bound in Great Britain

For Lizette, thank you for being part of my story

– Jos

Contents

SECTION 2: COMMUNITIES

SECTION 3: THE LIFE COURSE

SECTION 4: BODIES, HEALTH AND WELLBEING

Acknowledgements

Before naming specific people we would like to thank, it is important to say that we would not be here, editing this book, living our lives as we do, if it were not for those who came before us. Not just the queer and trans heroes that most academics and/or activists know, but those who we don't, whose names haven't made it into the history books, documentaries, journals, blogs, comics or songs. We may well have a long road left to travel, but the path is safer for those of us who walk it now because of the risks that others have taken.

We would also like to thank all of those who contributed to this collection: for sharing your stories, stepping into vulnerability and standing proud.

Jos: I would like to thank all of those who have either inspired me to start, or persevere when things got tricky, with this project. I would like to first thank Ben Vincent for being there at the beginning with me, for helping me with both the practical challenges and some emotional decisions, and the longest Skype call I have ever made! To MJ Barker and Kat Gupta for coming on board when Ben needed to take a back seat. If it were not for the support from you two, I don't think we would have got this far. I am also grateful to Dang Nguyen for further editorial support. And to Andrew James and Sean Townsend from Jessica Kingsley Publishers for answering my never-ending list of questions.

I am immensely grateful to my friends Liz, Stacey (and now Finley), Sebastian, Al and Colin, who are always there for me when needed and have tolerated my lateness and cancelled plans whilst I have been working on this book. I would like to express my gratitude to all past and present inhabitants of Room 317, as well as Claudia and Pippa, for the giggles and joy, as well as kindness, wisdom and grounding that you have all offered me. Lastly, to Adam, my partner and my rock. We have been through many transformations together, adapted and grown, and still we are the same. Thank you for standing with me through the uncertainty, for holding me and loving me.

Ben: I remain very grateful to Jos for initially inviting me to work with them on this collection. We worked hard, and it's so rewarding to see what it's become. I took the very difficult decision part way through to step back due to the weight of other commitments, so it's an unexpected privilege to be able to write this after coming back onto the team in the eleventh hour. To MJ I owe a great amount: for their inspiring, nuanced, and prolific work, but also the many opportunities and collaborations they've gently directed my way in the early years of my academic career. It's also such a pleasure to get to know Kat, who has such an incredible mind complemented by such brilliant humour. I'd like to thank all the contributors who I worked closely with, for giving of their time and opening up their stories for all of us. Further, thank you to my dear friends Sonja Erikainen, Stuart Lorimer and Ruth Pearce. Thanks to Amby, John and Kat, of course, and always, thanks to Mum.

MJ: I would like to thank Jos for bringing me on board to co-edit this book. It was an anchor for me through a tough year as I went through a number of (further) transitions: from city to coast, from academic/ therapist to self-employed writer, from living-together to living-solo. During a period when I didn't have much capacity for my own writing (other than a whole lot of journaling), it meant a lot to be part of this awesome project, bringing non-binary voices together, including those of some of my closest people as well as new friends and colleagues.

During this time of trans moral panic, so many of us are in fragile places, confronting our trauma, sometimes sadly bashing up against and bruising ourselves and each other in the process. I'm deeply grateful to those who've been alongside me through this time in all kinds of ways: supporting, sustaining, and sometimes struggling together. In addition to Jos, Ben and Kat, particular thanks from me go out to H, Alex, Juz, Ed, Rowan, Jess, Bee, Kimwei, Ellis, Michael, Max, Tania and Arianne.

Kat: I would first like to thank Jos and MJ. At a time when the trans community has been under attack, this book has been a source of joy and hope. Knowing that such a diversity of voices exist – such a range of experiences, all with their own strength and courage and insights – has meant a huge amount to me.

Several specific people have been a source of support, kindness and wisdom: I would especially like to thank Laura, Ruth, Em-Ben, Iona and Kirsty for all the conversations and tea; my sister Jen, my most staunch ally; and my parents, who don't always understand but who have always supported me.

non-binary
is varied
unexpected
unique

non-binary
is beautiful

Introduction

THE POWER OF STORIES

As a species, we humans love stories. Stories have been told, shared, and remembered in many ways and forms over time and across cultures. Stories are performed in art, pottery, poems, and stained-glass windows. They entertain us in films, plays, comedies, and operas. They are passed down through generations by oral traditions, books, photo albums, quilts, and museums. Stories have many purposes: they entertain and they help us bond, they enable us to let off steam and to make sense of things, they help us to learn about our pasts and to put foundations down for our futures.

We tell stories about ourselves: where we have been, what we have done, and where we are going. We tell stories about others: those who interest us, those who annoy us, those who we daydream about. Others tell stories about us: what kind of people they believe us to be and how they see us. These stories form part of our relationships. Wider culture tells stories about groups, about people who have a shared history, identity, or culture: those who we're told should be praised and admired and those who we're told should be feared or blamed.

The stories that we tell, and those that are told about us, help us to form an understanding of who we are. They support the formation of our identities. Are we the helpful child? The diligent worker? The creative cook? The lazy student? The messy partner? The faithful friend? The stories we are part of give us roles, a place in the world, a space where we're allowed to be. Not only do stories tell us who we are and how we are seen, but they inform boundaries of our lives too: what we are not, where our limits are, and what we are restrained from doing, or being.

Stories are told about us as individuals, but also as pairs, units, groups, families, and communities. The stories that we claim for ourselves relate to broader identities: the groups and communities we are part of and where we belong. Yet, like our own individual stories, wider group narratives can also place limits and boundaries on us: how we are expected to think, behave, dress, and be in order to be part of one group and not another. We have some autonomy over how the stories of our group identities are told. Yet, other individuals and institutions hold powerful influences over these narratives too.

GENDER STORIES

When it comes to gender diverse people, many powerful forces determine the stories and broader narratives that are told about us: medical systems, historians, the media, religious leaders, film makers, and politicians, to name but a few. Yet, we also have the power to tell our own stories with music, blogs, books, our own films, vlogs, zines, community events, activism, and more.

In the last ten years or so, more stories of non-binary, genderqueer and agender individuals have started to be told within Western cultures – see Meg-John Barker, Ben Vincent, and Jos Twist (2018), for more on this and for a sense of the far older stories that have been told globally about gender. In accordance with the cultural context of our times, many of these stories are told through the images and headlines that we consume through screens and often share with our friends. However, these tend to tell limited stories of what it means to be gender diverse in the early part of the 21st century, with those who hold multiple privileges being far more visible than those who don't.

Non-binary people exist in multiple forms, many of which are not represented in the thin narratives that we are currently presented with. The aim of this book is to broaden out the ideas of what it means to be non-binary. We want to show that non-binary people come in multiple forms, shapes, sizes, backgrounds, and ages; that we come from various communities, countries, histories, and families; that there is no right or wrong way to be non-binary; that no one person or way of being is more legitimate than another; that we are all valid and real; and that our communities are more vibrant and nourished when they embrace the diversities within them. As the hashtag has it: *This* is what non-binary looks like.

Over the course of this book we present a collection of essays in which a range of non-binary people from a diversity of backgrounds share their experiences of their intersecting lives. We cannot think about our genders in isolation: they are impacted by our life histories, the cultures, countries, and communities we are born into, the people we meet, the places we go, and the way others and the world see us. The authors detail how these multiple aspects of their lives have impacted on their experiences of their genders, and how their gendered experiences and identities have impacted on other aspects of their lives.

We hope that this collection will offer you an insight into the diversity of non-binary people's lives. If you are reading this book as you are non-binary yourself, we hope that you can connect with the stories that are told and you find elements of your own story within them.

Before we get on with the stories, we want to say a bit more about the concept of intersections, and the language used through the book. Then we'll introduce the four sections of the volume to give you a taste of what is to come.

INTERSECTIONS

The focus of this book is on telling the stories of the ways other aspects of experience intersect with being non-binary. What is it like to be a non-binary person who is also mixed race, for example, or to be non-binary and neurodiverse in various ways, or a non-binary survivor?

The concept of intersectionality comes from the Black feminist legal scholar Kimberlé Crenshaw (Crenshaw 1990), although it draws upon earlier ideas and concepts within Black feminism as well (Hill-Collins and Bilge 2016). Crenshaw developed intersectionality to describe the experiences of Black women in the criminal justice system, and how they differed from those of White women or Black men because of the intersection of gender and race. Applying lenses and legislation relating to gender, or relating to race, was not enough to capture the way that Black women were specifically discriminated against and the impact this had on them. It's vital to acknowledge that while the theory of intersectionality is useful for understanding multiple kinds of intersections, it was born from Black feminism due to the marginalisation of Black voices within a largely White, Anglo-American feminist movement. It's vital to honour its roots and to keep hold of the impact of the combined forces of patriarchy and White supremacy, even as we broaden our horizons to consider other forms of privilege and oppression.

Intersectionality helps us to reflect on how we're all located in relation to cultural binary identity categories such as male/female, gay/straight,

Black/White, working/middle class, disabled/non-disabled, trans/cis, rich/poor, urban/rural, old/young, etc. It helps us to understand where our position in these binaries puts us in relation to power and privilege. People often misunderstand intersectionality as referring to the ways in which different aspects of our individual identities operate together to shape our experience, but actually it's about how interlocking systems of power impact us through patterns of privilege and oppression. Important intersectional thinkers like Patricia Hill-Collins (Hill-Collins and Bilge 2016), Audre Lorde (2007), and bell hooks (2014) point out that binary either/or thinking is a key aspect of oppression which intensifies dominance and marginalisation, privileging one side of the binary over others. In this book you'll find many examples of people exploring multiple, overlapping, non-binary experiences beyond gender, and how these resonate with, and inflect, each other.

Across this book many authors address the ways in which their intersections relate to wider axes of power and oppression. For example, some examine the ways in which their privilege in some areas protects them from some of the overt transphobia and cisgenderism experienced by other non-binary people. Many explore how the numerous ways in which they are regarded as 'other' in wider culture interweave and influence each other, thereby marginalising them in additional and often specific ways.

Several authors dig into the complexities of the various ways in which they are privileged and oppressed and how these have shifted over time and in different contexts.

Other authors hold the notion of an intersection more lightly – not necessarily drawing on intersectionality theory explicitly, but rather focusing in on the ways in which one aspect of their lived experience (being non-binary) relates to another. We've tried to be open to multiple ways of engaging with the concept of intersection (e.g. in terms of power structures, lived experiences, backgrounds, identities) rather than imposing one particular understanding. However, we hope that, taken as a collection, the chapters stay true to the spirit of intersectionality theory that has inspired us, and that – even where not explicitly stated – the reader can reflect on the multiple axes of power and privilege operating through all the lives included in this book.

Many authors herein offer nuanced understandings of the ways in which their experiences – and the ways in which they are positioned across axes of power and privilege – open up and close down their possibilities.

Reading across the different chapters offers a complicated picture, whereby quite similar positions or experiences may be a cause for celebration for one person but pain for another, and often both. Further binaries are troubled in this way, such as good and bad, positive and negative feelings, and gender dysphoria and gender euphoria – see Meg-John Barker and Alex Iantaffi (2019) for more on expanding our notion of non-binary.

LANGUAGE AND DEFINITIONS

Any discussion or conversation about non-binary gender brings up questions around language and definitions. So, before we go any further, we think it is important to clarify some of the decisions we've made around language use in this book.

The first challenge is how to talk about gender diverse people in a broad, inclusive way that captures common experiences, without excluding, invalidating, erasing, or marginalising others. In some ways this is an impossible task: language often fails us, and nuance and complexity can become lost in shorthand terms.

Non-binary

To reflect the current preferred terminology in UK/European conversations about gender, we employ the words 'non-binary' as an umbrella term for anyone who doesn't currently identify with the binary notion of being exclusively male or female. 'Non-binary' can include those who conceptualise gender as a spectrum, rather than two discrete categories. Some people experience themselves as existing at a point between these two poles, and some experience their gender as shifting between these poles at different times and/or in different contexts. 'Non-binary' can also include those who feel that gender is more complicated than one single spectrum, or those who disagree with the notion that gender is a spectrum at all. It can also include those who experience themselves as not having a gender or who take a political stance against the concept of gender.

At the heart of our position is the belief that it is up to the individual to decide whether the term 'non-binary' is useful for them or not. There will be those whom our broad definition has not captured, but who use the term 'non-binary' to describe an aspect of their gendered experiences. There will also be those whose gender experiences are captured here, but who for a variety of reasons do not feel that the term 'non-binary' works for them. Moreover, there will be those who have not yet encountered the term at all, thus it has not been available for them to claim.

Under the non-binary umbrella sit an array of different words that describe a diversity of gendered experiences. The ones that we come into contact with more frequently include: genderqueer, genderfluid, bigender, trans masculine, trans feminine, demi-boy, demi-girl, and agender. It is not possible to provide a list of all the identities that sit under the non-binary umbrella as this is evolving all of the time, with people coining new terms that capture the individuality of their experiences and some employing words that include further aspects of their identities, such as sexuality, ethnicity, or spirituality. It's also impossible to provide exact definitions of these terms, as many people differ in regard to what these mean to them, including unique understanding of how the multiple aspects of gender (roles, identity, expression, bodies, social gender, etc.) come together, intersect, and overlap.

There are other words that are currently employed as umbrella terms for those who do not identify with or experience themselves as exclusively female or male. These include genderqueer, gender creative, gender diverse, gender radical, enby, and other gender. We have chosen the use of 'non-binary' over these other terms as, for us, some of these other terms have additional meanings and 'non-binary' is the most common umbrella term in the UK, where we are based, at the time of writing. If we were embarking on this book ten years ago, or ten years into the future, we may have used a different term.

Trans

We've outlined our decisions around the use of the term 'non-binary', but how do we talk about the broader group of people who do not identify with their birth-assigned sex? The phrase 'trans and non-binary people' is often used to encompass all of those who do not identify with the sex they were assigned at birth (with those who do identify with the sex they were assigned at birth often being referred to as cis, or cisgender). However, the critique of this phrasing is that it risks implying that non-binary people are a discrete category separate to trans – or transgender – people. Whilst some non-binary people do not also identify as trans, many non-binary people do.

In an attempt to remedy this, some have extended the phrase to 'binary trans and non-binary people'. You may not be surprised to hear that this phrasing has also been challenged, with critics arguing that use of the phrase 'binary trans' reinforces the notion of a binary gendered system which is oppressive to those who do not experience themselves in this way. Yet, by denying the existence of the binary categories of male and female that do exist in our social worlds, we risk erasing or invalidating many people's lived gendered experiences. Moreover, it is also possible to critique the term 'non-binary' itself from this perspective. Using the word 'binary' in the descriptor risks reinforcing that which we aim to challenge: the centrality of a binary gendered system. Words fail us, meaning becomes blurred and contradictory; we end up risking going around in circles.

The term 'gender diverse' is often used as a catch-all term for all of those who do not identify with their birth-assigned sex. However, we are not keen on using this term given that everybody is diverse in terms of gender, not just trans and/or non-binary people. Applying gender diversity only to trans and/or non-binary people obscures the diversity within cisgender identities, and also the damage that the current gender system does to people across gender diversity, not just trans and non-binary people (see Iantaffi and Barker 2017).

As editors, we have considered whether to have consistency in language and definitions across all of the chapters to assist the reader. However, due to some of the arguments outlined here, and also the fact that each contributor has their own individual preferences and meanings attached to words, you will notice some differences in choice of phrasing in terms of how those who do not identify with their birth-assigned sex are collectively referred to.

More than gender

Gender is not the only identity category that comes up against complications when we try to talk about it and find words that accurately, inclusively, and unproblematically capture what we mean. When we think about intersecting marginalised identities, one other area that stands out above others – perhaps appropriately, given the origins of intersectionality – is race/ethnicity. It is not possible to do justice to the complexities involved in this, but we'll attempt to outline some of the key challenges as we see them.

First off, what is the difference between race and ethnicity? Are they easy to separate out into neat, discrete categories? Do we have agreed definitions about what they mean, or do different disciplines, people, and places hold different understandings? Have their meanings changed over time? Does the way they are used have historical and political implications? We are left with more questions than answers. We also have to consider how we talk collectively about people who are marginalised because of the colour of their skin, or their racial heritage. Some people prefer the phrasing 'people of colour' (PoC) over 'Black and Minority Ethnicity' (BAME), others the reverse. Some would add 'NB' in front of 'PoC' to stand for 'non-Black', but others would argue that this erases the different experiences between these groups. Some argue against using umbrella terms to collectively group all of those who are non-White together, as this also risks erasing the diversities of experiences across groups and individuals.

The mechanics of language and words become significant when we talk about race/ethnicity, cultures, and locations. The use of capitals or lower-case letters for words such as Black, White, Asian, Western, etc. has political meanings and histories, and these words also hold different meanings depending on who is writing and reading them.

Like when we thought about the terminology for talking about gender diversity, we are left with no simple and easy answers. We considered employing some kind of consistency across the chapters, yet we do not believe that it is our place, as editors situated in the UK, to tell people of different racial backgrounds from ourselves, who live in different countries, how to talk about themselves. One does not need to be well read in political and geographical history to see what we risk reproducing here. Thus, you may notice different authors making different choices in this regard.

Following these reflections, we decided to take very few hard lines in the editing process, as we wanted contributors to be able to talk about their own lived experiences without being censored. The main exception to this is any use of direct or indirect expressions of oppressive positions and terminology, including, but not limited to: racism, sexism, ableism, transphobia, biphobia, homophobia, classism, xenophobia, whorephobia, and fatphobia. Due to contributors writing about their own perspectives and experiences, and us taking this approach, there may be times where authors express opinions that are somewhat different from our own as editors. We welcome the expression of a diversity of beliefs, experiences, ideas, and values, whilst acknowledging the responsibility that comes with this freedom.

INTRODUCTION TO THE REST OF THE BOOK

As is the case with any book about intersecting identities, experiences, and dynamics, it is not possible to cover every combination of intersections, or every aspect of diversity. There is simply not the physical space to do so.

For a variety of reasons, there are also further restrictions on whom we've been able to include in this volume. One of our aims for the book was to include authors who come from a variety of countries, including those from the Global South. However, there have been limitations in whom our call for contributions has reached, in part due to our location in the UK and our personal connections being more likely to be situated in the UK, Europe and Western English-speaking countries. Our call for contributions was written in English and distributed around English-speaking non-binary communities and networks; thus, it will have mainly reached those who read English, and probably those who understand gender diversity in this current, Western way. It's important to acknowledge this up front and to commit to working with others in ways that address these biases over time.

There are further challenges in terms of who has the opportunity to contribute to this kind of collection and those who do not, which are related to privilege and intersectionality. The requirement of essays to be written in English and the related likelihood that those who have contributed to this collection have completed secondary education and, in many cases, will have had some kind of further or university education, excludes a considerable number of people from having the opportunity to be involved. Not everyone has the privilege of having enough time and/or energy to spend some of their resources writing for free. This includes those who have a variety of different caring responsibilities and/or those who have health conditions or disabilities that mean their energy is a precious resource that needs to be conserved and prioritised elsewhere. The reality is that for many gender diverse people the world continues to be unsafe, and contributing to a collection of this kind (even under a pseudonym) would not be an option for them due to the risk it may pose to their personal safety.

We are committed, as editors, to continuing to address these biases in our future projects, whilst also being mindful of our own limited resources, which form part of the reason why further outreach and payment of more marginalised authors wasn't possible in this case. We have therefore decided to donate any royalties that we would have received for our work on this book to Transgender Europe: https://tgeu.org.

As well as acknowledging these restrictions around equality of opportunity, we want to say that we are incredibly proud of the collection of essays that we have here to share with you. We're immensely grateful to those who have given their time, energy, and stories to this project, many of whom have entered into places of vulnerability and taken leaps of courage in doing so. We're excited to present to you the range of experiences, intersections, writing styles, and narratives that we have had the joy of bringing together over the last couple of years. Reading through these chapters ourselves has been a moving and powerful experience, and often one of personal affirmation, or of opening our eyes to experiences we weren't familiar with in ways that will, we hope, enable us to be more mindful of them in future. We hope it has a similar impact on you as a reader.

We have made the decision to organise the book into four parts, collecting overarching themes of narratives into sections. Most authors have not focused on their gendered experiences in relation to just one other area of their lives. At times, deciding which section to put a particular chapter into has not been straightforward. You may feel when reading them that you would have made different decisions.

We have named the four sections: Cultural Context; Communities; The Life Course; and Bodies, Health and Wellbeing. As the written word is not the only form of storytelling, we have also had the pleasure of introducing each section with a cartoon from the non-binary artist Lee-Anne Lawrence.

We will now briefly introduce each section before we leave you to enjoy the book.

In the first section, '**Cultural Context**', the writers detail how physical locations, spirituality, religion, skin colour, and language have enhanced, complicated, or placed restrictions on their relationship with their non-binary gender.

The book opens with a beautiful chapter from Kat Gupta, describing some of their experiences of stillness and fluidity in terms of how their age, race, and gender come together to shape how they are read by others in different contexts and countries. Next, Jespa Jacob Smith also draws on ideas of fluidity in talking about language and the instability of identity categories, sharing how their concept of softness has offered them strength. After this, Vynn describes some of their experiences of growing up in Borneo. They detail how language, religion, media, online conversations, and moving countries impacted on how they understand the concept of gender and how this related to their own experiences of gender. We turn next to Ynda Jas, who details their journey to increased visibility as a transfemme genderqueer/non-binary person in the UK, and the barriers and challenges they have faced in this quest. This is followed by LJ, who describes some of their experiences of the restrictive nature of gender and how this relates to narratives of being 'woman enough', 'man enough', and 'trans enough'. They detail how exhausting gender can be for them and share several stories of how gender functions in different contexts of their life. After this, twins Ludo and Mina Tolu reflect on some of their experiences of living in different countries. They also discuss the topics of relationships, activism, and careers, drawing on the emotions that are provoked when considering these topics, such as guilt, shame, belonging, and strength. This is followed by Kimwei McCarthy, who describes how the concept of non-binary reflects how he views and experiences not only his gender, but also his sexuality, ethnicity, and spirituality. Annelyn Janib then details how growing up in a Hispanic family, speaking Spanish, impacted on their experiences of gender, and discusses how the gendered nature of Spanish places limitations on how they can speak of themselves. Our first section closes with a chapter from Dang Nguyen, who reflects on how his understanding of masculinity has been influenced by his family history, growing up in a Vietnamese Confucian household. He also shares how his sense of being an outsider – as an immigrant living in Australia – was an experience that followed him as he began to explore his sexuality.

In the second section, '**Communities**', the writers discuss the themes of belonging, visibility, safety, and inclusion/exclusion, in reflecting on the spaces and groups they are part of.

Fred Langridge begins this section by sharing their experiences of being non-binary within their Quaker community. Fred details how the values associated with being a Quaker resulted in their process of coming out as non-binary in this space being relatively straightforward. This is followed by Reverend Rowan Bombadil, who discusses three layers of context, or rather circles, where their genderqueer identity intersects with their spirituality. They detail some of their experiences of being part of an interfaith ministry community as well as the work that they have done within queer communities. Calvin Hall next reflects on their process of finding their place in the world. They discuss how their ethnicity and gender overlap by sharing stories from their childhood, university, academia, and activism. Further stories of school, university, and career are detailed in our next chapter by Edward Lord. Edward shares how masculinity is performed in these spaces and the challenges this has posed for them. The topic of gender-defined spaces is also explored in the following chapter by the play writer Eli Effinger-Weintraub. They reflect on their process of coming to identify as agender and the question of whether they can still be part of women's theatre and playwriting communities when they no longer identify as a woman. Next, Al Head details the impact that feminism has had on que's life. Al discusses how politics, spirituality, activism, and sexuality have all influenced how que has understood que's gender at different points in time. The final chapter in this section is by Joel Korn. The first half of their chapter details how their overlapping identities around gender, sexuality, health, and disability play out for them within their Jewish communities and family contexts. The second half further discusses the relevance of these identities within their work as a therapist.

The third section of the book is titled 'The Life Course'. In this section, the writers explore how they have expressed a non-binary identity over the course of their life, have come to realise their non-binary identity later in life, and detail the experience of parenting in a non-binary way.

Karen Pollock opens this section with the beautiful philosophical metaphor of the trireme. Just as the ship is built and rebuilt but remains the same ship, Karen weaves the different identities they have had at different points in their life into a chain linking their past, present, and future selves. Next, Igi Moon writes about how they came to understand themselves as non-binary, and particularly how their gendered experience was shaped through being working class, involvement with the leather-clad lesbian scene, research, work as a therapist, and experience of rheumatoid arthritis. Like Igi, Meg-John Barker reflects on their class background: they explain how coming from a mixed-class background, and being hard-of-hearing, bisexual, and non-binary shaped their identity as a child. They describe the feeling of gender euphoria that they found as an adult, and explore the different masculinities they inhabit. Meg-John ends their chapter by inviting you, the reader, to think about your own experience of gender and the selves you may have learnt to suppress. The next chapter, by Lucy/Luc Nicholas, is an account of their exploration of their non-binary identity in terms of their class background, their generation and their political beliefs. They vividly describe the fear of being seen as inauthentic; however, like Meg-John, they describe the deep joy of liberation and of expanding possibilities. Our transitions can have profound effects on our families: in the next chapter, mud howard reflects on the deals they made with their blood family, and their sometimes difficult and non-straightforward process towards familial understanding. The final three chapters in this section focus on parenting. Eli explores their experiences of parenting as a queer, black, Muslim, disabled parent. In particular, they describe the challenges of pregnancy as a non-binary person: from their changing body, to finding suitable clothes, to being pregnant without being a 'mother'. They describe exposing their child to wide-ranging ideas about what gender is and their efforts to resist gender normative culture. This latter idea is explored further by Cal Orre in the next chapter. Cal, a non-binary parent themselves, describes parenting their non-binary child, Rio. Through Rio's experiences, Cal observes the way that society genders children, and the strategies Rio uses to resist these. In the final chapter of this section, Daniel Morrison reflects on the questions, comments, and responses he receives as he parents his children.

The book's final section is about 'Bodies, Health and Wellbeing'. Specifically, this section focuses on the intersection between non-binary experience and disability, various forms of physical and mental health struggles, neurodiversity, body shape, and size, 'feminine' or 'masculine' gender expressions, and working with other gender – and otherwise – diverse bodies (in the contexts of jobs like therapy and nursing, for example).

Alex Iantaffi opens this section with reflections on the intersections of gender non-normativity and disability, as well as touching on the way other aspects of their life, like being an immigrant, a therapist, and a person with complex post-traumatic stress disorder (cPTSD), inflect their experiences and how they are treated by others. After this, S. W. Underwood reflects on their experience of being 'gender chaotic', and particularly how different gender possibilities – and forms of femininity – were opened up and closed down across their life through their various relationships, relationship styles, and contexts. Like Alex earlier, in their chapter H Howitt explores the intersections of disability and transness, troubling binaries between physical and mental health. They highlight how the wider world (and its systems and structures) rarely allows people to occupy both disability and gender non-normativity simultaneously, and the restricting and painful position this frequently puts them and others in. Following H, Sam Hope's chapter explores intersections between non-binary, neurodiversity, and trauma, as well as the linked experiences of trying to mask such things in our lives, and the impact this has on us. Sam draws on increasing evidence that 'when human beings are divergent in one way, this increases the statistical odds of them being divergent in other ways', which may be useful knowledge to many readers, and which is explored more in Sam's book on counselling trans and non-binary people. Francis Ray White's contribution to this section considers the intersection between fat and being non-binary, particularly the contributions that fat activism and trans activism can make to each other and to our understanding in this area. They conclude that the experiences are completely intertwined: that fatness has enabled them to be non-binary and that non-binaryness has enabled them to be fat. Finally, in this section of the book, Drew Simms, tells their story of 'nursing whilst non-binary', including how working with gender diverse people as a trainee impacted their own gender, and how they have navigated outness and self-disclosure in their work with patients and colleagues.

As with many authors across this book, several of the authors in this section explore the common experience of imposter syndrome or not feeling X-enough (where X might equal disabled, mad, trans, queer, sick, masculine, feminine, androgynous, or any number of other categories), and how such feeling are exacerbated by normative systems and structures, and often within our own communities. We return to this, among other themes, in the conclusions to the book, where we also reflect on self-care and our experiences of editing this collection during the ongoing trans moral panic in the UK.

CULTURAL CONTEXT

But no matter where I am,
I am still non-binary.

Chapter 1

The Me I Am When I Am Not Me

Kat Gupta

> I am nine and I am in India. I have my sister and three cousins near my age. We go everywhere as a pack of five – hiking up hills, reading comics, putting on plays for our relatives, running around in the woods. We buy bamboo peashooters and lie on a wall in the sun, shooting dried peas so they ping off the neighbour's corrugated metal roof, and she comes out and yells at us. I am surrounded by people who look like me, who are me, where I can roam with my cousins and not attract a second glance, and I feel at home.

When I am small – no, smaller than that – I somehow hear the science fiction trope of existing as a brain in a vat, and am immediately intrigued. My body is a confusing thing: medicalised, examined, subject to baffling, painful procedures, mapped, charted, measured. I am regularly compared against a standard which I now realise was never meant for me. My body is awkward, confining, my skin too small, and my hands and legs lagging behind the sparking dart of my thoughts and imagination. For years, I come home from school bruised and frustrated, tearful with fury. If being a brain in a vat was an option, I'd take it.

> I don't know how old I am. I do know that my parents' phone number is not in the phonebook, and I know it's because people would find a non-British family name in the phonebook, ring it and

hurl racist abuse down the phone. And that is why our number has been ex-directory since before I was born.

Scientific reality notwithstanding, being a brain in a vat would have been the easier option. Learning to live in my body – to accept its flaws and to see its possibilities – was far harder.

I am in Borneo. I am fascinated by how easily I blend in, how my skin and hair and epicanthal folds are entirely unremarkable.

There is a broad swathe of the world where I look just local enough to blend in. I do not necessarily look like I could come from that region, but I look familiar enough to be read, perhaps, as mixed race, or coming from a different part of the country. As far as I can discern, based on travels and questions, this swathe encompasses parts of the following: South and Central America, the Caribbean, southern Europe and northern Africa, the Middle East, central Asia, China, Japan, the Philippines and the Pacific Islands, South-East Asia.

I am in Liverpool, and a friend is introducing me to a friend of hers. He peers at me, asks, 'Where are you from?'

'Ah, the accent?' I say. 'My parents live down south.'

'But where are you *really* from?'

'I was born in Carlisle,' I say, shutting down the conversation. I wonder if he realises what he was asking. He either does realise and is a racist, or does not realise that and is another ignorant white person, blundering into something he doesn't even know is offensive. It annoys me that I have had to develop a response to this line of questioning that smilingly shuts it down.

It means that people often address me in their language, and I have to apologise and explain that I don't speak it. It's an acknowledgement that I could be from there, that they see some kind of similarity in my brown skin and black hair, see some kind of kinship in my dark eyes and epicanthal folds. There are these little bits of sweetness and acceptance that are extended to me, little spaces that we open up to each other, inviting the other to step in.

> I am in Egypt and am wandering around the bazaar. A seller gets too pushy with one of the white women in the group. I am aware that here I am read as a young brown man. I am playing a different part and have different options open to me, so I tell him that she's not interested. All he does is smirk in response: no challenge, no pushback.

Sometimes I'm aware that it puts me in danger, and that I may not even be aware that I am in danger. I'm aware that I become the target of both more and less scrutiny due to being read as male, young and not obviously a white tourist. On the one hand, people tend to ignore me in markets; I am not immediately obvious as a wealthy tourist to call out to. On the other hand, I worry that my inevitable transgressions are not immediately attributable to my unfamiliarity with local life, as they might be if I was white and obviously a tourist. Brown boys do not always get to make mistakes.

> I am seventeen and the Twin Towers have fallen. The four or five brown kids in my tiny sixth form are not all friends with each other, but we check in regularly with each other: our cars keyed, bricks hurled through our windows, insults and threats shouted at us in the street. Our differences – Gujarati, Pakistani, Sikh, Muslim, Catholic, Hindu – dissolve. We are simply brown, and because we are brown, we are dangerous.

Brown boys do not always get to make mistakes. It is a strange thing to inhabit this exoticised Othered body, a body on which desires and fears and anxieties are projected. I cannot exist outside my brown skin. I cannot peel it off, cannot scrub away my brownness, cannot conceal it in any way from all those who look at me. My brown skin and black eyes conjure fantasies: a docile, subservient, sexually submissive femininity, or an aggressive, unpredictable masculinity. Over the years my gender expression tipped towards a flat chest and buzzed hair. I find myself less wary of strange men approaching me. I find myself more wary of the police. I carry a rucksack on the Tube less often these days.

> I am walking hand in hand with a boy I am perhaps seeing. We are in that nebulous phase of flirting and kissing and reluctance to examine our interactions too closely. A car drives past, the occupants yelling something homophobic at us. I find it hilarious – everyone, regardless of their gender, is perceived to be more gay, simply by holding hands with me! He finds it less amusing and is clearly cool with the kissing but less cool with the ramifications of being perceived as gay in public, the consequences of being seen in public with me. We end things shortly after that.

I learn how to navigate space differently, learn the careful chin-tilts of acknowledgement that men give to each other. I learn how they talk about women when there are no women present. I wonder if I – suspiciously small and skinny and beardless – am being tested, that my belonging to this club I never asked to be part of is contingent on laughing along. I wonder what would happen if I didn't huff a laugh out. I learn how to gently challenge these things. I come to relish what an ex-partner calls 'boy chats' at the barber's, where the young guy who clips my hair back into an undercut tells me about his nights out and his weekends away with the lads and how much he adores his girlfriend. I find men opening their fragile hearts to me in the most unexpected places.

My body allows for spaces to open up, for connections to be made, for sweetness and danger and softness and transgression.

> I am in my early twenties, and walking through Liverpool at night. A boy asks me for directions, so I tell him which way he should be going, then he falls into step with me. 'Are you Turkish? Spanish?'

he asks. I am tired of people treating my ethnicity as a game. 'You should turn left here,' I tell him, and walk on.

My body is stubbornly different, stubbornly itself, stubbornly Other: it is a racialised body, a gendered body, a body to which people attach meanings and readings. It is a body that is always being interpreted, with or without my input. I realise that my body will always be both different and familiar, evading easy categorisation. I move within race and gender and age, somehow becoming a shape-shifter in my stillness.

I am in my mid-twenties and working as an invigilator for English language exams. The candidates' guesses about my ethnicity are much better: one even asks if I am Nepali. I find that I don't mind their curiosity, their desire to seek a connection, their ability to recognise something of themselves in me.

It is an odd thing to inhabit this fluidity. I consider my internal sense of gender fairly stable. It is not static – no living thing is entirely static. Instead there is a steadiness to it: my gender feels like the rhythmic push and rise of bicycle pedals, the tender reaching of a plant towards light, the thump of a heartbeat, the space between breaths. My sense of gender does not rush or cartwheel or soar; it quietly unfurls, seeking a place to grow and be well.

I am in my early teens, in Disney World, and have somehow been separated from my family. I feel a rising sense of panic – the crowd has flowed to fill the space between them and me, and I am too short to see over it and the crowd is too dense to offer a gap to peer through. I push through the crowd, apologising and explaining. 'Let him through!' a woman shouts, and I feel a bright flash of joy, a spark of being seen. Oh, I think.

It is strange, then, that my gender, my race, even my age should be perceived by others as so chameleon. I am able to inhabit a galaxy of possibilities, to swoop between male and female, child and teenager and adult, and any number of ethnic or racialised identities in the space of a conversation. My body becomes a resistant body, a defiant body, an illegible body. It is a strange thing to be a shape-shifter, a shape-changer, being mentally mapped, charted, measured, but never quite recognised.

> I am dancing in a gay club with my friends. The dance floor is cramped, the air is humid, the place smells of spilled lager and sweat and cigarette smoke. Much to my surprised delight, I find myself kissing a girl. She pulls back. 'I just want to check – you do speak English, don't you?'

Where does mutability reside? Who has ownership of my body if it is a body that is constantly challenged – whether I am old enough to be allowed in a space, whether I am in the wrong gendered space, whether I am white enough or British enough to be in a space, whether I am some transgressive mixture of all of these things and definitely not welcome in a space? What does it mean to be a body that is read as something to challenge, and which issues a challenge of its own?

> I am an older teenager and in Tanzania. Someone is talking to my parents about their son, and they are confused before they realise that their son is me. They are annoyed, but I am secretly pleased. I befriend one of our guides and talk about tracking with him. We peer at marks in the dust and he says that if I was staying longer he'd teach me to track properly.

What does it mean to 'pass'? To 'pass' places the burden of intelligibility on the person who seeks to 'pass': if we are not interpreted correctly, it is because we have failed to make our meaning clear. I reject that. I reject that there is one meaning that we can make of our bodies. I reject that we have such a degree of control over the ways in which people interpret us. I reject the implication that failure to be read – failure to be *seen* – is our fault. Instead, all we can offer is ourselves. We can guide an interpretation but we cannot control it. My other selves – the selves that people see in me but who I am not – say this with one voice.

Who is allowed to inscribe a meaning on my body, to draw a border around it rather than to let it fly apart into a thousand darting sparks?

> I am in Istanbul. My girlfriend has asked me to buy us some water, so I nip to the shop across the road from our hotel. The man at the counter greets me and asks me what I'd like. I apologise and explain that I don't speak Turkish. He manages, 'But, you…?' before he gestures at his face. In his gestures, I see a welcome.

It is both terrifying and exciting, like plunging into a swirling galaxy of other lives, an array of lives not your own but which you temporarily inhabit. Like trying on new clothes, like acting a part, like conducting some kind of grand social experiment in perception. Which 'I' am I today? It is both freedom and recklessness and danger and love, love, love for every life you could have led.

My body is not a border.
My body is not a boundary.
My body is not.
My body is.

BIOGRAPHY

Kat Gupta (they/them) is a queer, genderqueer, British-Indian academic and researcher living in the UK. They have researched and written about the British suffrage movement, newspaper representation of transgender people, and online erotica. Their activism focuses on LGBTQ+ Black and minority ethnic inclusion. They are interested in too many things, including but not limited to bodies, consent, minority representation, and how we use language to create, sustain and communicate identities.

Website: http://mixosaurus.co.uk

Twitter: @mixosaurus

Chapter 2

The Soft Line In-Between

Jespa Jacob Smith

THE POWER OF FLUIDITY

Miles away from the shore, giant rocks are touched by the soft current that caresses them.

Their size and shape do not matter, it is the persistence of the gentle whisper of the sea that gives them their form.

From my diary, ca. 1998

My mom once told me that my first word was not '*Mama*' (Mum), or '*Papa*' (Dad), but '*Wasser*' (water).

There is a soft hum. I look up and see a fan, rotating slowly above my head. I wonder how I didn't notice it before. Its sound now is so prominent in my attention. My forehead is glistening with a fine band of sweat. The two chairs next to me are empty and my hands wrestle with a piece of paper. It is my first day at my new job in Canada, and I am waiting for the project manager to pick me up from the waiting area and show me my work station.

I am more nervous than usual, because for the first time in my life I have requested that my correct name and pronoun be used at work. I know it will create some confusion, or even rejection from my colleagues. But I am willing to go through with it. I will never be the person they expect me to be, anyway.

* * *

When I started living in Canada I made a promise to myself: to not be afraid to stand up for myself, and to see how it would change me. One simple-sounding task I gave myself was to stop hiding 'me'. To use my name full-time. To ask for my pronouns to be used correctly. I had been given this opportunity, and even though it might not have been the best time in my life to go, maybe it was the only time.

Before, in Germany, I had been out to my friends and the closest people in my biological family, but never at work, in school, at uni. I found it hard to talk to people about how I wanted to be addressed. I stumbled over words to explain how I felt. The feeling of invisibility had become my constant emotional companion.

I grew up speaking German. I love this language. It has lyrical depth at unexpected moments, it is versatile and yet so concise. At the same time this language requires so much effort to bend it, to make it flexible enough to find cracks and nooks to get through or hide in. Its harsh, bureaucratic vocabulary, its unwillingness to play around, to even be dismissive of playing around, its emotional flatness and cold 'stick to the rules' manner oftentimes render you at a loss for self-expression.

My way of speaking has always been called 'peculiar'. Even before studying philosophy had given me a thousand new ways of expressing myself, I had been told that I have an 'interesting way of saying things'. In a way this statement felt at least like some recognition of how I see the world. Language presented me with the tools to change things right away, to bring awareness to details, to the unseen, to the little glitches reality offers that usually languages try to rope in and control. I wanted to express these glitches as I felt somehow I was creating one myself. But when I was younger I couldn't yet express how. In German it is difficult to be gender 'neutral'. It requires a level of skill that even native speakers do not usually have, the use of a lot of passives and workarounds. We are not trained to speak that way.

* * *

I started learning English by mouthing the words of the Tina Turner, Harry Belafonte and Simply Red songs my mum would listen to in the car. Something about it, its grammar, its sounds, tickled my interest. The feeling of ease while speaking. I could never put my finger on it, but something really just drew me in.

I very distinctly remember that moment when – I was about 16 – I realised that I could talk about myself and did not have to use a gender specific word. That it could just be me and the things I did, I liked, I wanted. I discovered the subtlety of the use of 'they' when talking about a person of unknown gender. What I didn't know at that time was that there were actually people who used this pronoun for themselves.

* * *

When I met E in my mid-twenties I didn't know that this interaction would change my life. I attended a music and theatre camp in Canada, and E was part of the workshop I took part in to create a 'Haunted Sukkah' for the final night of the camp. There was something about E, something that made me very curious.

When we were introduced to each other, E casually said, 'By the way, I use "they"-pronouns.' Without thinking too much about it, I responded, 'Me too.' E looked at me and I was sure that they would say something like, 'Yeah, sure,' and laugh, because when I registered what I had just said, I immediately thought they must have felt like I was making fun of them. But E just nodded in appreciation. My body had just gone with the flow of the language and the wave of self-recognition was thunderous.

Through an accident, my unconscious mind had found itself reflected in the words of another person and for the first time, just by chance, language had finally managed to manifest myself in my body.

* * *

RESUME POSITION

In the introduction to her book *Queer Phenomenology: Orientations, Objects, Others*, Sara Ahmed wrote:

> What does it mean to be oriented? How is it that we come to find our way in a world that acquires new shapes, depending on which way we turn? If we know where we are, when we turn this way or that, then we are oriented. We have our bearings. We know what to do to get to this place or to that. (Ahmed 2006, p.1)

The way we position ourselves in the world influences our perspectives. The opportunities we have to shift our gaze are endless – but they are definitely increased by the number of times we get to experience ourselves in a different setting, an unknown framework, a new surrounding, and give in.

I have been part of different, mostly leftish, activist groups, from environmental causes to intersectional queer activism, for more than a decade. In my early years of activism there was a lot of competition and a pressure to perform your 'radicality' within and outside the groups. Chauvinism and ableist behaviour, such as working too much, sleeping too little (sometimes helped by drugs) and the pressure to always simply 'do' more than everybody else, were part of many people's 'activist philosophy'.

I never survived in these groups for very long. My insecurities about my presentation and the ignorance of most people towards everything related to mental health and gender normativity made me sad and very angry at the same time. I grew more tired of it the more I experienced the same ignorance over and over again, especially in groups that claimed feminism and 'awareness' of social issues as part of their politics. I was called stubborn for not letting go of the casual sexism of many cis men (and women) in these groups. I was laughed at because I was serious about it. I was made fun of because they could not 'place' me, so they sought to make me irrelevant.

* * *

The way we position ourselves in the world influences our perspectives. The opportunities we have to shift our gaze are endless – but they are definitely increased by the number of times we get to experience ourselves in a different setting, an unknown framework, a new surrounding, and give in.

Reflections of the things known to us show up everywhere. It is never the case that they might need a re-coding, a new structure, and it might seem like we need a new dictionary for ourselves. It is a moment of shapeshifting, of letting go of old ideas and giving ourselves permission to be re-formed.

Coming to appreciate the idea of softness, the readiness to be touched by the world around me, has been an important learning process for me. It has been a struggle to let go of the idea of myself as hard and stable and to be able to show vulnerability within groups that do not necessarily value this as an important trait. Being able to say, 'I need a break,' and to let go and still feel okay. To make visible that most trans people – binary or non-binary – are never getting a break from advocating for themselves in any context, except maybe in the sanctuary of their own home (but some not even there).

The idea of softness as a strategy for my activism has given me a tool to be gentle and persistent at the same time. To not be too hard on myself and others. To save energy in the right places. To let go of this ridiculous idea of competition and look for solidarity – for myself and others. To fight at the right frontiers instead of within my own community, where many of us unconsciously recreate the stress and oppression we experience in our everyday lives.

For me, being queer and non-binary in the context of activism does not only concern my identity. It is a position I relate to in the face of this world, and it includes more than just my gender or sexuality. Positioning myself as trans and queer is necessary for me and others to be seen when we would otherwise be erased by labels that other people assign(ed) to us. It feels necessary for me to actively resume other labels, as long as these oppressive categories are still so strong and used against us.

My queerness shows in the way I act out my politics in my everyday practices. To me it means being willing to learn about things that I do not know about and that I may never experience. It encourages me to accept difference instead of trying to tolerate it, or trying to forcefully include things into my concept of the world.

Staying soft and vulnerable is a vital part of that. By reading and listening to a lot of femme and trans feminine people (particularly of colour), I learned that being vulnerable is not a weakness but is actually a strength to pursue, a shield in the face of the people who hold pretensions to power when your position is already at the margins. A random act of kindness can be a more powerful way to politicise someone than a thousand speeches. It is there that I see strength.

To me, softness is a tool to reveal a multiplicity of realities and to raise awareness of their existence within and around each other. To be vulnerable means to question not only the categories other people use for me, but also the ones I use for other people, and how much unreflected structural oppression I promote through my own actions.

It is not only to see myself the way I want to be seen, but to provide the space and time and opportunity for others as well.

* * *

A GENDER OF ONE'S OWN

Why, if it was an illusion, not praise the catastrophe, whatever it was, that destroyed illusion and put truth in its place?

Virginia Woolf, *A Room of One's Own* (1928/2004, p.17)

An important part of my strategy to survive school was daydreaming. So many times I saw myself running down the steep hill the school buildings were scattered against, lifting off and just flying away. I thought that nobody noticed. But of course it was noticed by my teachers and peers and I was teased by both for that.

In 1998, when a total eclipse of the sun took place, I brought a portable radio to the schoolyard because one of my favourite bands, Einstürzende Neubauten, who wrote a song about the event, was going to be played at the exact moment of the eclipse. If my taste in music wasn't already weird enough, the whole act of me being so peculiar about this moment was what really made people furrow their brows. Most of them thought I was trying to connect to alien life forms. Maybe in a way I was: I was desperately trying to find people who understood.

* * *

One common idea about identity is that it gives us a frame to exist in – a gender, a nationality, a job, a background, a religion, etc. The concept of identity in most Western societies is focused on identity as being constant and unchanging. When applied to people, this strict pattern never fits: either you spill out at one end, produce too much excess; or you can't fill it, you are too small, too 'weak'.

It wasn't simply that I just didn't fit the patterns people deemed appropriate for me. At some point I actively refused to try anymore. I sought to explore the world without them being forced onto me, finding names and ideas that actually applied to me. But the thing that seemed to be most important to me was my way of communicating.

* * *

In his book *Cruising Utopia* José Esteban Muñoz writes:

> We may never touch queerness, but we can feel it as the warm illumination of a horizon imbued with potentiality. We have never been queer, yet queerness exists for us as an identity that can be distilled from the past and used to imagine a future. The future is queerness's domain. (Muñoz 2009, p.1)

As I try to navigate the space of identity, the concept of 'being queer' or 'being trans' points me towards the potential to make a difference in the present, to break the patterns and to reclaim the past from a different point of view. Undermining the one-sided narrative in Western European societies of 'how things are' is a very specific way of producing knowledge, consciously and wilfully. It has the power to provide a reflection of our actual reality in a fabulous futuristic mirror. I want to live inside the distortion, because it is the soft line in-between, a magnifying glass to look at the details of the world, a never-ending rite of passage to oneself.

BIOGRAPHY

Jespa Jacob Smith (they/them) is a DIY artist and activist that lives between Germany and Canada. They are the author of several zines (*Soft Boy Chronicles*, *Ta(l)king It Out*) and part of a queer feminist collective in Cologne, Germany. In their work and activism they focus on Transformative Justice and Radical Softness as tools for change. They love language, their parents, and their community-family, especially for being welcoming and ever evolving in the face of all the difficulties this world places before us.

Chapter 3

Coming Out of Borneo, Coming Into Non-Binary

Vynn

Growing up in Borneo, gender was always either male or female. This was implemented in schools as I was growing up, where mandated crewcuts for boys were enforced by unskilled teachers equipped with electric razors. It was considered a disgrace for boys to appear feminine. The colloquial term *pondan*, meaning 'sissy' or 'effeminate boy', was used with the harshest derision against boys who behaved outside the codified gender norms. There was a strong moral element attached to it as well. Going against what was 'normal' was a sign of moral deviancy. *Ayu* was another word in Malay which carried varying connotations, depending on whom it was applied to. Lacking a precise English equivalent, it can roughly be translated as 'tender', 'pretty', 'soft', gentle', 'elegant', 'beautiful', 'polite', 'civil', or even 'cultivated'. *Ayu* had a strange quality because it was received so differently, depending on one's background.

Ayu was received favourably by some of my friends who had grown up in a more traditional Malay setting where *ayu* is also associated with the word *santun*. *Santun* was used to describe someone who was virtuous in character, whose mannerisms were polished and smooth. Gentleness, compassion, and refined etiquette were all part of the polite culture that epitomises the pinnacle of Malay cultural refinement and civility. However, local customs are coloured not only by traditional indigenous values but also by the arrival of relatively recent non-native religions. Islam, which was spread by Arabic and Indian traders during the 16th to 18th centuries, would infuse their views with those of local Malay culture. Christianity, which would come later, also left its mark on local attitudes towards gender, suffusing religiosity with local belief systems.

Those who were more religious, whether Muslim or Christian, tended to view *ayu*-ness as an effete, or even decadent quality when applied to boys. This might be because of the strong association of *ayu*-ness with homosexuality, which coupled with a religiously fuelled homophobia might lead to a moral colouring of femme-males as 'sexual and moral deviants'. Their perceptions would change if *ayu*-ness was displayed by a girl, deeming it 'proper' and 'refined'. On the other hand, non-religious households were more tolerant of unconventional gender expression. My childhood self, much to the chagrin of my adult self, had been raised by a devout Catholic mother and a Christian convert of a father, so *ayu*-ness was viewed with derision by both my parents. This hostility, instilled from a young age, would remain with me into my late adolescence.

I never questioned these attitudes while I was growing up – or at the very least, I did not probe too deeply into them. I was very feminine growing up. And I remember this very distinct memory of when I was accused of being 'too sensitive' by my brother, and that he didn't like the tone in my voice because it sounded 'too feminine'. I was sharply reprimanded by my father. This was not how a 'real boy' was supposed to behave. I must have internalised that misogyny, because I then began to resent all the *pondans* in school. They were bullied by the other boys and I would sit on the sidelines and think to myself, 'If I had to learn the hard way, then they should too. They deserved what they had coming.' My notions of masculinity were warped. It wouldn't be until my late teens that I would begin to seriously question gender norms and how pervasive they were.

As a result of a strict upbringing, access to the internet was restricted until I was 15, as it was viewed as a distraction. Online was where I would explore my identity and stake my ground in what I would come to know as 'Identity Politics'. Terms like 'political correctness', 'Social Justice Warriors', 'feminists', and 'feminazis' were all very new to me at the time. Having a thousand genders seemed like a joke to me, a trend that started on Tumblr and was now being frivolously perpetuated throughout the internet. Parodies of Apache helicopter genders were rife during this period, and they biased my early perceptions of genderqueer identities. I couldn't take them seriously.

Then came *Steven Universe*. *Steven Universe* is a children's animation series created by Rebecca Sugar that centres around the young protagonist, Steven, who is raised by The Crystal Gems – a team of extra-terrestrial beings who are the self-appointed guardians of Steven.

The gems are sexless beings that typically use she/her pronouns. Up until that point, I hadn't even considered the possibility of there being an identity that could not be neatly categorised into the binary. 'You were either one or the other,' or so I thought. Yet, here was *Steven Universe*, a speculative fiction (SF) that opened up that conceptual gendered possibility with the Crystal Gems. The Gems are an alien race which expresses femininity without having it grounded in biology. Stevonnie – an explicitly non-binary character – was my first encounter with a person (albeit a fictional one) that I could not pigeonhole neatly into either one of the two gender categories that I had been conditioned to believe were supposed to be exhaustive of all gender identities. This was not a life-changing epiphany. It had been planted very surreptitiously, slowly growing in my mind to dislodge entrenched ideas about gender. At the same time, I discovered that one of the episodes that featured a kiss scene between two of the female-presenting characters in the show was censored in the Malaysian airing of the show by the National Film Bureau, which deemed it a 'vulgar' display of lesbianism. The censorship did not pose much of a problem for me since I could watch the uncensored episode online, but this was one of the many instances where I realised how pervasive the government's hold on gender and sexuality narratives was.

Gender, sex, genitals, gonads, chromosomes – I had been taught to believe that there was a 'natural' relationship between these things. I had been taught that gender is synonymous with sex; that gender was determined by biology. The narrative was that being genderqueer is just a bunch of trendy Tumblr teens going through a phase. 'Transtrenders', I believe, was the pejorative that was used to describe them (and still is in some contexts now); and somehow, people who identified as a different gender were simply denying their biology and 'making it up'. But slowly, these ideas were being eroded; if not among my immediate family members, then at least in the cyberspaces I also call home. The two cultures I was part of – the geographic culture in Borneo and the digital culture of Twitter and YouTube – intermingled in complex ways.

Discourses about gender in the government-sponsored mass media were confined to the Malay language. Sex and gender were conflated in a single word: *jantina*. The discussions held in Malay also reflected this simple understanding of gender. Rafidah Hanim Mokhtar, who is the Vice President of Muslim Practitioners of Medicine and Health Association Malaysia (I-MEDIK) with a PhD in Health Sciences from the International Islamic University of Malaysia, often appears on national television to spout her ideology of biological essentialism. She is known for her bigoted pronouncements, such as 'Homosexuality is a psychological health problem' or 'It's just a simple biological fact that there are only two genders', while citing how holy scripture dictates that Allah created the animals of the earth in pairs and justifying it with a simplistic understanding of sex chromosomes. Her institution, the I-MEDIK, receives funding from JAKIM, the Prime Minister's Office of Islamic Development in Malaysia.

The Malaysian government has a long history of regulating the practice of Islam among its citizens. The creation of institutions of Islamic governance throughout the latter half of the 20th century by the UMNO-led Malaysian government can aptly be described as the 'bureaucratisation' of a government-sanctioned Islam. When asked by the German media whether Malaysia will welcome gays, Datuk Mohamaddin Ketapi, the Tourism Minister, said, 'I don't think we have anything like that in our country.'

The contemporary Malaysian government's wide-ranging efforts to institutionalise policies of heterosexism and homophobia, and the cultural sensibilities associated with them, had the effect of disciplining all individuals involved in transgressing gender norms, including those who do not necessarily engage in 'deviant sexual practices' but are nonetheless tarred as 'gay' or 'lesbian'. The long-term sociopolitical developments contributed to a further stigmatisation and criminalisation of all forms of transgressing gender norms. This is especially evident in the enactment in recent years of ostensibly Islamic laws proscribing 'cross-dressing', sodomy, and sexual relations among women. This is coupled with the rise of concomitant discourses and 'volunteer' (vigilante) organisations that serve to increase the purview, consciousness, surveillance, and disciplining modes of both Islamic and secular courts with respect to allegedly Western 'perversions' of 'gender waywardness'.

However, with many of my English-speaking friends who were just as much a part of the digital sphere as I was, there was a rapid acceptance of LGBT identities and sympathy for their struggle. Gender nonconformity felt simply like an extension of gay rights. Gay rights, gender nonconformity, and local politics interlinked in interesting ways. Because the anti-gay agenda was associated with central government, Borneans' resistance to the anti-gay agenda was also seen as a protest against the Malaysian government's policing of our bodies. Gay rights were vehemently opposed at the national level (even still today), going so far as to say that LGBT ideology was a 'plague on civilisation' and would spell the doom of 'Asian values' as it did for the West. However, at the sub-national level, the vast majority of Borneans that I knew, although not in outright support of LGBT individuals, were more tolerant of behaviour that ran counter to state-defined 'decent conduct', seeing as 'decent conduct' also meant suppression of local languages, cultural practices, and indigenous identities. Central government pursued a number of policies that stoked the ire of Borneans, such as issuing hair-grooming standards for boys in school (which was seen as an affront to local traditions), the deportation of Catholic priests, and the systematic erasure of indigenous languages. Central government's attempt at policing homosexual behaviour and its suppression of gay rights appeared as another way the government was trying to regulate the bodies of Borneans, which only served to antagonise Borneans to the government's anti-gay agenda.

I can think of many instances where Roman Catholicism, rather than being used to morally police sexuality, was used as a safeguard against such policing. For example, I-MEDIK classifies homosexuality as a mental illness and considers it to be an inherently medical condition that must be rectified. Local priests have taken a stand against such overt medicalisation of homosexuality by citing the 2,358th Catechism of the Catholic Church, which states that being homosexual is not inherently a sin whereby:

> They must be accepted with respect, compassion, and sensitivity. Every sign of unjust discrimination in their regard should be avoided. These persons are called to fulfil God's will in their lives and, if they are Christians, to unite to the sacrifice of the Lord's Cross the difficulties they may encounter from their condition.

This could be interpreted as your typical 'hate the sin, not the sinner' cliché that one would normally encounter among Christian apologists. However, here in this specific Bornean context, the citing of one religious scripture to counter the pathologisation of homosexuality by I-MEDIK which is informed by the Malaysian government's sanctioned interpretation of Islam represents a micropolitics of resistance. To me, it represents resistance on the part of Borneans to accept the regulation of our identity – be it religion, ethnicity, sexuality or gender.

My time online led me to new perspectives and I started to question things. If gender was supposed to emerge so 'naturally' from biology, then why are aliens and robots being coded with a gender? Why are high-heeled boots only reserved for women? Why could I not wear make-up and dresses? There is nothing in my genes that dictates that I shouldn't. Despite these lingering questions, I still held on to biological essentialism – the belief that 'human nature', an individual's personality, or some specific quality such as masculinity or femininity, is an innate and natural 'essence' rather than a product of circumstances, upbringing, and culture. 'Okay, fine, you don't like to wear women's clothes or men's clothes. Fine, but you don't have to create a new gender.' This was still the view I had, even when I had shed the outright hostility towards expressions of *pondan*-ness. Sympathetic as I was to LGBT rights, genders outside the binary still seemed foreign to me. I had grown up in a culture with simple language to describe a simple gender binary. All this talk online about 'genderfluid', 'androgyne', and 'demi-gender' just seemed like an over-complication.

Change for me was slow, but education – thanks to the internet – was quickly being democratised. Videos on YouTube and tweets on Twitter, platforms that academics were starting to frequent, became a common source of learned opinions on many contemporary issues. A YouTuber by the name of ContraPoints particularly influenced me because they made videos about a wide range of topics, with some of them specifically targeting gender. Three videos in particular – *Non-Binary Genders*, *I Am Genderqueer (And What the #@%! That Means)*, and *What is Gender?* – dealt the death blow to my stonewall against queer theory. I was able to see how femininity refers to culturally idealised mannerisms and behaviours of women in a particular time and space; how masculinity and femininity do not have universal meanings above and beyond their historical contexts. Femininity and masculinity are formed by historical circumstances, I reasoned, and therefore, they can also change with historical circumstances. I began to see my race and politics as being inextricably linked to my gender. The label of non-binary identities might be new, but the lived experiences that they correspond to were not. However, with everyone around me categorised as either man or woman on their National Identity Cards, I simply could not reconcile gender identities that did not correspond (at least visibly) to anyone's lived experience in Borneo. That was until I moved.

Moving to Norfolk (UK) in my late teens was an eye opener in some ways because here were people who were unashamedly whatever gender they identified with. Here were people who were openly defiant of the gender binary. In school, there were people who identified in a range of different ways in terms of their genders and sexualities, such as bisexual, homoromantic, asexual, and agender. It was quite overwhelming at first, but the LGBTQ+ society in school was open to anyone who was questioning their gender and/or sexuality. Moreover, I had taken up English Literature while I was in Sixth Form and I was exposed to Feminist Theory and Post-Structuralism for the first time. Learning from my friends and my teachers, I could see how the gay–straight binary was collapsing and how sexuality was often read through the lens of gender, and this allowed me to be less guarded. I started to question more, and to question better. Why were certain attitudes and emotions gendered? Why was empathy seen as a feminine trait? Why was science gendered as a masculine discipline? Why was the public sphere traditionally the exclusive domain of men? And women's domain the domestic sphere? Armed with the ammunition of Critical Theory, I questioned every assumption I had held about gender up until that point. Strength need not be defined in terms of masculinity, and emotions need not be inherently feminine. I started to express myself in a way that felt more authentic to me. Friends in school could notice how much more camp I was becoming. I became more flamboyant with my gestures. At one of the school's fashion shows held for charity, I strutted on that catwalk with full eye make-up. And without anyone policing my gender, I was able to let it out. I could feel the gender that was thrust on to me from birth slowly loosening its grip. I was able to be myself, and I was neither masculine nor feminine. I could finally wear what I felt comfortable in, what I felt powerful in.

I was excited to start university. I knew that this was a time for a radical revamping of my identity. I chose a new name for myself as I introduced myself with my middle name: Vynn. Culturally odourless, and completely gender neutral, Vynn was what everyone would know me as from here on out. I was ready to start experimenting. Clothes, sexuality, pronouns, everything was on the table. What a perfect opportunity presented itself during the Freshers' Week of university. Cabaret Night was a chance for the boys to 'cross-dress' and put on a persona for the night. The boys would go full out in drag, and the girls would have fun helping them doll up. That was the first time I had ever worn a dress. I bought boots to complete the ensemble. And the night went by and we enjoyed it thoroughly. Most of the boys laid their satin skirts and stilettos to rest after that night. But for me, this was only the start of me having fun with my gender expression. Slowly I replaced my parentally approved clothes with garb that was more androgynous. I grew my hair out. I started wearing eyeliner. And yes, it was clumsy at first. But the more I did it, the more comfortable I would feel with all this. Today, my typical outfit would be knee-high boots with a black turtleneck and white skinny jeans. Gone were the childhood stigmas of being called a *pondan*.

The contrast between Borneo and the UK was very significant for me. I was afforded new freedoms and choices, and I could express myself in new ways. Although my experiences in Norfolk were in contrast to my previous ones in Borneo, and I attended a school where there were other visible queer and gender diverse people, I am aware that the sense of freedom of expression that I felt around my gender is not an experience shared by everyone in Norfolk. Moreover, the way that trans and non-binary people are discussed in the media has changed in the last few years, as has the political context. I feel safer in experimenting with my gender in the UK compared with how I did in Borneo; however, the current situation in the UK is still less than ideal for trans and non-binary people.

Looking back now, many of my early attitudes towards gender were very much influenced by not only the religious nature of Bornean society, but also the sociopolitics of Malaysia at that time. It would take years of self-education and self-reflection before I would realise how many of my assumptions about gender were not a given and, therefore, were open to reinterpretation. At the time of writing this, I am still questioning my gender and what it means to me. One thing that *is* certain: gender has always been fluid and every culture ascribes different meanings to it; meaning that is constantly evolving.

BIOGRAPHY

Vynn (they/them) is a native Bornean with Malaysian citizenship who grew up in Sabah, a state in north Borneo. Vynn is currently an undergraduate student at the university of York studying Biomedical Science. They are passionate about the intersection of queer identities and how it is regulated within the emerging discourses of Islam, the Malaysian nation-state, and regional politics.

Email: svc503@york.ac.uk

Twitter: @SurenVynn

Chapter 4

From Skinnies to Skirts and Crop-Top Shirts

Traversing Transfemme Troubles

Ynda Jas

As a transfemme genderqueer/non-binary person who was assigned male at birth, there are many barriers to publicly expressing myself in the ways that feel most authentic. I'm going to talk about my journey towards increased visibility, including reflecting on the issues I've faced, how I've tried dealing with them, where I am today and where I'd like to be. I'll be considering the balancing act between levels of self-expression versus physical and emotional safety and wellbeing. My perspectives and experiences are informed by my non-binary genderqueer identity as well as my general disinterest in being read as a cis woman.

First, a quick overview of my transfemme journey. Until 2017, skinny jeans had been the ceiling of my public femininity for my entire adult life. In July 2017 (about 15 months after coming out as non-binary) a trans, non-binary and intersex conference and a Trans Pride event in Brighton (UK) jumpstarted my journey towards increased public displays of aesthetic femininity. Things have changed a lot since then, but the journey continues: there's still a way to go until I'll feel able to dress in whatever I feel like every day. I've come from wearing skinny jeans all the time to differing degrees of femme presentation based on context. These days out in public – my day-to-day environment being historically working-class but increasingly gentrified parts of East London – I might wear short shorts, leggings and longline/oversized t-shirts and t-shirt dresses. Then in specific spaces, or in the presence of specific company, I might dare to wear other types of dresses (those that are unlikely to be read as loose/long t-shirts), as well as playsuits and skirts. If I do choose to wear the latter more strongly femme-coded styles of clothing, I'll usually either get changed at my destination or cover any skirt, playsuit, or dress with a long coat, so as not to draw attention in more 'general public' spaces.

The barriers I (and many other transfemme people) face include the risk of physical and emotional abuse, lack of understanding, and dealing with standing out and reactions to dramatic change in appearance. Physical abuse is perhaps one of the more obvious barriers to walking the streets in non-conformist ways – in ways that destabilise the mundane and the cisnormative environments we find ourselves in outside of gender-diverse spaces. As I walk down the street or ride the Tube, I'm made aware that my colourful sartorial palette stands out from the crowd, not just by my own observation but also by the feedback given by those around me. I know I'm marked because of the groups of adults (presumably cis and predominantly men) who have directed verbal street harassment at me on a few occasions because of the way I dress. I know I'm marked because of the kids whose understanding of cultural politeness norms have not yet developed and who therefore stare when they see something unexpected – something that disrupts their learning about what certain bodies should look like. I know I'm marked even from positive interactions: the two to three people a day in a visit to New York (mostly, if not all, fairly femme-presenting) who would stop me in the street or in a museum and compliment my outfits. Would they do that if they perceived me as a cis woman? I doubt it. People read me as someone assigned male dressing femme, or at least queer, and react. Sometimes negatively, sometimes positively, sometimes ambivalently. But they react.

As is well reported, trans women and transfemme people are generally subject to higher levels of physical violence and murder than other trans populations (with trans women and transfemmes of colour particularly vulnerable). Being marked, in the case of transfemme individuals, has the potential to turn nasty: to lead to violent repercussions. The knowledge of this threat leaves me scanning every individual body around me as I walk in public when dressed femme: are *you* a threat? Are *you* a threat? Are *you* a threat? I tend to look out for groups of hypermasculine-looking people and the intoxicated. Of course, what we base our evaluation of threat and hypermasculinity on can be problematic, with working-class and Black bodies in particular victim to prejudice in this regard.

So, what makes me personally marked, and by extension physically unsafe? First, my physical features. My height, protruding larynx, deep voice, flat chest and thin, short hair act as markers of maleness for those who don't factor trans people into their understanding of gender and sex. Though my deep voice can be a source of dysphoria, I see it, my flat chest and my short hair, in combination with my more femme-leaning aesthetic choices, as key parts of my genderqueer identity (while recognising that these features are entirely valid for women). Regardless of my actual identity, my physical features make it unlikely for me to be read as female by mainstream society, to whom 'not female' still equals male. Though I don't seek to, my physical features also make it hard for me to be read as a stereotypically cute femme, at least without good make-up skills and vocal training. My physical features and my femme expression combine to mark me as other. Wearing leggings and colourful outfits while being read as male, or assigned male, conveys a certain queerness about my aesthetic and my person. I don't fit neatly within the confines of normative expression for people assigned male – I don't represent an acceptable masculinity. So, on the street when I'm wearing more femme-leaning clothes, most people are likely to read me as a tall man dressing colourfully and effeminately, which can be seen as a violation of society's body-regulating standards. I'm marked both as other and a violator.

Essentially, I'm read as a 'man' in 'women's' clothes. Contemporary 'Western' society, by and large, genders clothes binarily. While dresses, skirts, leggings and tights can fit and look equally good on bodies of any gender, they are all arbitrarily deemed 'women's' clothes. Even where styles can be either 'women's' or 'men's', such as waist-length, standard-fitting cotton t-shirts, there are often subtle differences between what you'll find in 'women's' and 'men's' clothing sections. With t-shirts, to continue the example, you'll tend to find that with 'men's' versions the sleeves will cover at least half the upper arm – likely more – while 'women's' versions will cover only a quarter to half of the upper arm. One obvious reason for this is that everyday sexism dictates that (at least young, slim, able-bodied) women should show more flesh for the (cishet) male gaze. But the very idea that there are such things as 'men's' and 'women's' clothes is one of the main issues at play here, a key ingredient in policing bodies and reinforcing normative understandings of gender and expression. Yes, bodies do transform into slightly different shapes as a result of hormones from the onset of puberty, but variation in bodies is far from limited to two shapes. If we're to acknowledge that binary and non-binary trans people are real, that surgery isn't a prerequisite for trans identification and therefore that physiology does not dictate gender, then we must also recognise that the effects of hormones are not strictly gendered: any individual body can belong to a person of any gender. While it can be helpful to accommodate people with different chest, hip, or genital sizes by providing multiple cuts of a given style, describing any particular cut or style as 'women's' or 'men's' both erases many trans people and reinforces harmful gender norms. The idea that there are clothes that women should wear and clothes that men should wear – as well as erasing my non-binary identity – lays the foundations for me being read as other and a violator.

So, what can make me safer, or at least feel safer, when out in public? Part of what makes me unsafe arguably also contributes to my safety. While my physical features mark me as other, they also have the potential to make me appear less vulnerable than other types of bodies. I'm not of a muscular build, but the confidence I attempt to convey (whether genuine or not) as I stride about the place, the space I take up in various environments, and my height may individually and in combination make me appear to onlookers as less vulnerable and not the easiest of targets. This suggests able-bodied privilege; however, it may also work the other way. Based on being read as able-bodied and (assigned) male, I may rather be considered an acceptable target for attack (I'm assumed capable of defending myself).

I've also begun to stare back in certain contexts (particularly daylight, when other people are not far away, and when the starer doesn't appear to be overly threatening) as if to say, 'I see you, I don't care what you think and I don't fear you.' But again, my able-bodiedness and relatively low levels of anxiety in particular contexts allow me to do this and have a potential impact other than dangerous provocation. In contrast, when I feel more vulnerable and directly threatened, I do the exact opposite: complete lack of acknowledgement. I've had two recent instances of this – the fact it's only been two, and only verbal, I have no doubt is partly down to White privilege, and perhaps my geography (living in a partially gentrified – though somewhat high-crime – area of East London). As a White person it's much easier for me to 'get away with it' and have my femme aesthetics passed off as White, 'hipster' behaviour. One instance of direct threat ironically took place when I was walking to the Tube station with a friend after a gender conference I'd co-organised. Having covered up my dress, I had a lace t-shirt and colourful parrot-print leggings on show. A person amongst a laughing group repeatedly shouted, 'You like dick?!' at us as we walked by. Another instance saw me walking home late at night, this time alone. Wearing a long, pink coat and pink leggings,

I saw a group of four people over the road from me. Given the lack of other people around, I put my phone away and looked straight ahead, walking with conviction. As they drew closer, in the corner of my eye I saw at least one of them slow and look in my direction. One yelled, 'Are you a boy or a girl?' 'No,' I thought to myself while I continued walking, gaze unshifted. 'Batty boy,' they loudly concluded. I came out of both of these incidents physically untouched, but was this because of how I acted, or was I just lucky? Both incidents illustrate how transphobia and homophobia oftentimes are intertwined, both stemming from societal forces that dictate and police what certain types of bodies can be and do.

One obvious way of reducing physical risk is to limit my transfemme expression. I can choose to wear less feminine-coded clothes, reducing the amount of attention drawn to my aesthetic and thereby minimising the risk. But limiting my expression can affect my emotional wellbeing. In order to present in a more masculine or neutral way – though ostensibly neutral clothing tends to be gendered automatically by the cues my body gives to the people around me – I must constrain and suppress a key part of my identity and my inner sense of self. This is an unhealthy practice to keep up over a sustained period of time.

Another solution is wearing safer clothes out in public but packing feminine clothes in my bag (space permitting) to change into when I reach a safer space. Of course, this still means limiting my femme expression, but it does allow for me to express myself fully in at least some spaces. Another option is to wear more normatively acceptable clothes on top of clothes that are more authentic to who I am. This is often referred to as 'covering up'. As Travis Alabanza noted in a June 2018 *Metro* article, this tactic has long been common within trans communities. While I'd much prefer to be showing off my style – as a representation of a part of who I am – it feels better to be wearing something I love under something I don't mind, rather than just wearing something I do mind. However, Travis raises a key issue with this tactic in their article: that it's weather-dependent. Assuming it fits underneath, it's no trouble to wear a long coat over a pretty dress in the winter. Roll on the height of summer and you might find yourself getting sweaty in just one layer: covering up is a sure-fire way to turn up drenched.

In addition to physical safety, there are considerations I make about emotional safety and my mental readiness to deal with certain situations. Much of this relates to being contextually radical. This can be reflected in discussions about, and references to, gender, both by how aware individuals are of contemporary thinking on gender within their society and how open they are to progressive, trans-inclusive ideas (with which they may be unfamiliar). Negative experiences, particularly with regard to openness to progressive ideas, can leave me feeling less able to air my own thoughts on gender and express my gender more fully. I might be left considering how much I should limit expressing both my views and my aesthetic orientation in order to avoid a situation where I might become emotionally overwhelmed at having to argue a case or fight a cause.

I have also found myself limiting my expression in broadly safe contexts in order not to draw too much attention. I generally prefer to test out and transition elements of my expression (aesthetic or otherwise) slowly, drawing less attention and easing people in to new versions of me. I find positive feedback on my aesthetics validating, but I don't generally want to be under the spotlight in everyday contexts. This can result in a lag between gender-diverse queer spaces, where dressing my transfemme self doesn't make me much of an outlier, and spaces where I am contextually radical.

Being viewed as radical has also had an impact in my romantic life: not all partners of trans people are perfect allies, even if they're otherwise good people. I came out as trans and non-binary when in a relationship with a cis gay man. Though he didn't take issue with my identity per se, various comments indicated that there were limits to what he found acceptable. These included indicating a preference for 'manly men', suggesting my own trans identity was inspired by a friend who came out not long before me, and saying it would make him sad to see me in a dress. This put a strain on both the relationship and my mental wellbeing: I felt restrained in how far I could go with my transfemme identity whilst maintaining my relationship, and thus my feeling of connectedness began to fade as I saw the relationship as a barrier to my own development.

These and other issues (such as misgendering) where meaningful support for my transness is lacking can lead to me being emotionally vacant from situations, unable to properly engage with the people around me.

Being viewed as radical (or my perception of this) is also reflected in other contexts such as the workplace and in sport. Earlier this year I was working as an advisor in a careers department where, rightly or wrongly, I perceived a pressure to convey conventional masculinity as a form of 'professionalism'. While I was open about being non-binary before the interview, I still felt pressure (in a body that would be read by service users as male) to conform to the norms of those around me, wearing a shirt on top and trousers or smart-looking jeans below. At first, I would wear colourful shirts in line with how I dressed towards the end of my previous office job, but that was about the extent of my deviation from the situational norms for male-read bodies. However, a short shift one day and a Christmas party on a day when I wasn't working provided opportunities to test the reception of queerer and more femme aesthetics. Positive feedback made me feel more able to experiment when I came back to work in January, and eventually I got to the point of feeling comfortable in t-shirt dresses at work. I took a similar approach to developing my expression when playing tennis in LGBTQ+ groups dominated by cis gay men who, despite me being out as non-binary, questioned my initial reluctance to join a new group for gay men. I gradually incorporated leggings and more colourful tops into my aesthetic, creating looks that were occasionally lightly jested by a friend. Though I'm uneasy about making trans (or indeed cis) people feel marked for expressing themselves in ways that deviate from the conventions of their assigned gender, I knew this friend had a history of progressive, trans-inclusive politics and so I persevered, gradually testing the limits while remaining conscious of not stepping too far at once and drawing (more) unwanted attention to myself and my identity.

A big part of improving my emotional wellbeing and mental readiness to deal with these kinds of situations has been growing my confidence through safer spaces both online and offline. On the online side, Instagram has proven to be an invaluable tool for developing my self-expression and my queer femme aesthetic. Early on, it offered a space of relatively high safety – I initially only really connected with relatively safe-feeling friends (mostly those who were unlikely to offer critique, even if well intentioned). This enabled me to test the reception of progressively queerer and more femme looks and gain validation from an audience without worrying about what other parts of my network(s) might think. As I gained confidence in different types of aesthetics – knowing that I had friends who recognised and appreciated them – I gradually began letting more people in, following them and by extension alerting them to the presence of my profile. Over time the femmeness of my output gradually increased in terms of both quality – how femme I dared go – and quantity – the proportion of my posts that were femme-leaning. Eventually I took a big move by sharing some of these looks, as well as a link to my Instagram profile, on Facebook, where I have close queer friends as well as family, people I went to school with, and pretty much anyone with whom I loosely associate. I relaxed my guard, knowing I had support from the friends who followed me on Instagram at the time. This still meant making myself vulnerable and moving into unknown territory, but I had to take this step in order to move forward, and it paid off.

Instagram and selfie culture are not just about narcissism – though it should be noted that what we often label 'narcissism' is simply having a positive relationship with yourself and your own image, which shouldn't be a shameful thing. Instagram and selfie culture also serve as important tools of validation and solidarity for people whose bodies are non-normative and/or marginalised, whether that's due to being trans or perhaps a particular size or shape, disabled and/or a person of colour.

Also important for me in developing my emotional resilience and mental wellbeing have been queer spaces: specifically, gender-diverse queer spaces – not mainstream (L)G(B)-oriented spaces. Two spaces that combined to jumpstart my journey towards publicly presenting in unambiguously femme-coded clothing were the Annual Brighton Trans, Non-Binary and Intersex Conference, and Trans Pride Brighton in 2017. Enabled by supportive friends – but still very hesitant – each day I tried out integrating a new type of clothing into my aesthetic, from wet-look leggings and longline/oversize t-shirts to a dress for the day of Trans Pride itself. Instagram supplemented these queer spaces both to provide broader validation and, in a way, to come out as transfemme to a wider network. This meant I needn't have so many anxiety-ridden in-person experiences of someone seeing me in a dress for the first time. However, it did mean I was more reluctant to dress in femme-leaning ways in the company of people not on Instagram until I started sharing my femme development on Facebook.

Other queer spaces that have helped me gain confidence have included most prominently Bar Wotever and other Wotever World events, and Non-binary London. Bar Wotever is a progressive and often radical weekly queer cabaret event with non-binary people highly visible on stage, behind the scenes and in the audience. I initially went to Bar Wotever after going to another Wotever World event: Non Binary Cabaret. Since then I've performed poetry and become part of the crew in the DJ booth, and it was there that I found more opportunities and excuses to try out dresses and femme aesthetics that went beyond oversize t-shirts and leggings. Similarly, meetups of Non-binary London – a group I founded on Facebook in 2017, and which now tends to meet at least once a month – have provided opportunities where I know I can wear pretty much whatever I want and be accepted and even appreciated for doing so. It's in these spaces that I've truly begun to feel a part of the idea promoted by Travis Alabanza and many others before them: that trans bodies and people can offer up new forms of expression to wider society, liberated from their fossilised (gendered) conventions.

Physical and emotional risks have presented barriers for me in the development of my transfemme identity and resulted in it taking 18 months to two years since coming out to feel something close to comfort in my everyday aesthetic. I've found ways of making myself safer – or at least feel safer – when outside in non-queer contexts. I've used gender-diverse queer safer spaces to experiment with more radical departures from my old aesthetics and taken a gradual, iterative approach to introducing femme elements into my everyday looks. It's been a balancing act of gender dysphoria and gender euphoria, as well as physical and emotional safety and mental wellbeing through authentic self-expression. Slowly I've been tipping the scales in my favour.

In order to make it easier for other non-binary transfemme people to live their best lives and feel free to express themselves more fully, with pride and celebration, we should start by undoing the ideas that:

- there are 'women's' and 'men's' clothes

- you can tell someone's gender by looking at them

- certain aesthetics and behaviours are acceptable only on and by certain types of bodies

- any violation of the norms that dictate this must be punished, erased or otherwise regulated out of existence.

We're here, we're queer, let us dress how we wish without fear!

BIOGRAPHY

Ynda Jas (they/them) is a queer non-binary transfemme activist, socialist creative, lapsed academic and developing coder. They're the founder of Non-binary London and York LGBTQ+ History month and DJ coordinator at the iconic weekly queer cabaret event Bar Wotever (at the Royal Vauxhall Tavern). They're also a poet, music producer, tennis enthusiast and gamer.

Twitter/Instagram: @yndajas

Chapter 5

Who Needs Gender?

LJ

To me, gender has always felt like a prison. I think the whole thing should be abolished.

I've never felt that I benefited from the concept of gender, apart from the ease of explaining myself in a gendered society. I'm non-binary transmasculine. People can wrap their heads around that. They understand what my body was, and they understand what I'm going for now. They can comprehend me.

But I feel a sense of loss. Within five minutes of meeting someone, I've somehow already been neatly placed in a box. Categorised. Rationalised. Explained away.

When I lived in Ghana, I got approached regularly in the market by strangers, questioning me about my gender. If I was a woman, the usual response was, "Then why aren't you wearing earrings?" My girlfriend bought me a pair—the kind that only gay men wear—and the questioning ceased overnight. We both laughed at how I could appease the curiosity of the general public and flag the gay community at the same time.

In that culture, my earrings spared me a lot of uncomfortable interactions. But I've yet to find a single accessory that is quite as effective in other contexts. My colleague here in the UK tells me I'm too soft-spoken to be a man. But my Canadian family says I'm too outspoken for a woman.

Not man enough. Not woman enough. Not trans enough. What is enough?

I've spent a long time trying to measure up. First, it was as a meek and graceful, proper Christian daughter. I stumbled all over myself. I became the butt of my own jokes. I embraced the label "tomboy." It was a derogatory term, pointing to the ways I constantly failed at femininity. But it was also a comforting term. A label I could pretend to proudly identify with to save me from the terrible truth that I was utterly incapable of performing femininity properly even if I tried.

> Before I knew what trans meant, I knew my mom's opinion on such things. I discovered it the day she ripped the Tony Hawk Pro Skater cartridge out of my Nintendo, never to be seen again. The offending content? An elaborate trick known as the "Sex Change."
>
> The first time I remember hearing the word "transgender" was from my father, raging in the kitchen about Caitlyn Jenner. My initial reaction was, "This person has had no bearing on our lives up to this point. Why all the fuss?"

Due to my sheltered, conservative, religious upbringing, I didn't fully understand what trans meant until well into my twenties. My clinging to my cisness lasted less than six months after that, and it only lasted that long because the more I learned about the road ahead of me if I was really trans, the more I desperately grasped at any other explanation for the feelings I felt. But inevitably, my cisness crumbled, and with it, my belief in the usefulness of gender itself.

As long as everyone stays neatly within their binary box, society continues to function as per usual. As long as people perform within the accepted range of cultural norms, no one has to interrogate themselves or their assumptions.

> While I was growing up, my pastor parents used to quote a Bible verse: "I set before you this day, life and death. Blessing and cursing. Choose life, that you might live."

Is that really a choice? And in a world that punishes gender deviance in tiny, yet consistent and relentless ways, are we even free to consider what we really want?

> "This is a men's fitting room. You'll have to use the women's." I was shocked at the confidence and finality of the attendant's assertion before I had even opened my mouth to speak. "But this is the men's floor. I'm transgender, and I wear men's clothes." "I'm sorry. I'm going to have to speak with the manager if you want an exception."

A certain privilege and power comes with having never felt an incongruence with the role you were assigned at birth. Wherever you go, there's a marker for your gender and a bathroom to match. You have a plethora of models around you to imitate. Even if you are trans, provided you can "pass" as binary, you don't have to educate nearly every person you meet on gender neutral pronouns just to avoid the relentless exhaustion of being constantly misgendered. You don't have to allocate a significant portion of your energy to navigating those challenges on a daily basis.

In my opinion, the very existence of gender allows for discrimination based on gender. You can count on humans to leverage any and every form of difference for their own gain.

I used to think the discrimination was the problem. Now I think it's the boxes themselves.

> As soon as I got on the bus, it began. It started as a low murmur, but soon it turned into a full-fledged argument. My fellow passengers, debating passionately. The subject? My gender. I sat silently in my seat, head down. They didn't realise I could understand the Twi language, and I certainly wasn't going to tell them.

The main limitation I face in a binary society is a constant sense of exhaustion. I think about my gender or lack thereof constantly, and in the rare moments I happen to forget, someone is there to remind me that I don't fit.

> On my graduation day, my mother said, "You're wearing this beautiful dress, now if you could only act like a graceful young lady worthy of it."
>
> My taxi driver asked if I was married, a question that had become a routine part of my daily commute. I responded that I was not, and that I didn't want to be. His response: "Why not? Are you a gay man? Are you a gay woman?"
>
> I was walking down the street in the dark with my takeout pizza. Two strangers approached out of nowhere. "Hey! Can we have some of your pizza?" Startled, I mumbled, "Um...sorry...no." At the sound of my unexpectedly high voice, they screamed, "Ah! It's a girl!" and ran, disappearing into the night.

The point is, no matter what continent I'm on, not a day goes by that I don't have to contemplate my gender and choose my steps wisely. In some ways, I am freer now that I express myself more openly. I don't have a constant underlying sense of discomfort. But instead, I now have a segment of my brain constantly devoted to evaluating the situation, how I am being read, and what behavior is appropriate to keep everyone around me as happy and comfortable as possible. The experience is exhausting, and I often wonder what I could use that part of my brain for if it wasn't perpetually occupied.

And I'm lucky. My experiences mostly fall in the categories of amusing, invalidating, or enraging. But they rarely turn violent. So far (in the summer of 2019), at least 11 black trans women have been murdered this year. My whiteness and my proximity to masculinity afford me a certain privilege that others don't benefit from.

I'm constantly trying to conform to someone else's standard of what I should be. I feel like a magnet, with society constantly pushing and pulling me between two poles. Having successfully broken free from the parts of femininity I don't relate to, I haven't felt free to explore or float or experiment. Instead, I have felt a very strong and immediate pull towards a binary performance of masculinity.

It's this performance that pulls me at the start of every work week to take off my nail polish, lower my tone of voice, and express a far more muted range of emotions than I feel. It drives me to buy men's face wash and socks and other things that have no business being gendered, and confine my love of rainbows, unicorns, and purple florals to my bedroom. Am I man enough yet?

I don't feel dysphoric about every part of my body. I don't feel a need to seek every surgery or treatment available for transmasculine people. But I might do it anyway, simply for the relief that would come from not being constantly visible. The world hasn't yet made space for me as I am.

We can make space, and we are making space.

But in that process, what we cannot do is turn non-binaryness into a third gender of sorts. It can't be just another label or box or standard to be measured up to. I don't believe you can fix the flaws in a binary system by adding a third option.

I already feel not man enough and not woman enough. I don't need society telling me I'm also not non-binary enough.

Non-binary people are allowed to like things that are gendered masculine and things that are gendered feminine, and we don't have to present in a way that seems consistent in order to be valid. Non-binary does not only mean halfway between two genders. It is something different to every person. We conceive of it in varied combinations, leaning masculine or feminine or androgynous, or we might not find common ground with any of those terms. And all of these presentations are valid even if you can't quite wrap your head around them yet.

In my opinion, since I don't think we'll be abolishing gender anytime soon, we should at the very least think about how we think about gender.

We cannot think of gender as a linear concept with masculinity and femininity as opposing poles. Instead, I think we can conceive of gender as a galaxy, with each person determining their own location at any given time. This galaxy is home to planets and comets and shuttles and stations. Some of us will never leave our home planets, some of us will never be home, and some of us will take off and go into orbit for a while and then land again.

Even if you don't feel a need to conceive of your own gender with that level of complexity, for your own sake and for the sake of those of us who do not occupy the more populated planets, I invite you to interrogate how and why you gender certain actions or presentations. Untether your choices from gender and, instead, take pride in tethering them to your own sense of self. Then do the same for others.

One of my favorite parts about being trans is observing people working through their discomfort as they confront their own assumptions. Most days, I find it tedious and nerve-racking to try to explain myself or challenge people head on, but sometimes the situation does so for me. Whether it's my manager struggling to explain the dress code to me or a gay man hitting on me in the bar, the moment when someone realises their preconceived notions are inadequate for the situation at hand is such an opportunity for growth.

I didn't tell the end of the story of the bus, where an old woman in the back seat scolded the whole bus full of nosy commuters, and told them that they should mind their own business. My gender was not an appropriate topic for public debate, even if they didn't think I could understand what they were talking about.

Not every story ends badly. I find that more people rise to the occasion than I ever anticipate, and that gives me hope.

I tried to explain pronouns and non-binary identity to one of my good friends. I explained that it's only society that genders us, our actions, our presentations. But nothing has to be gendered. She was with me for a while, but eventually she sighed, "I hear you, but at the end of the day, I'll only date men who mow the lawn. To me, mowing the lawn is a chore that men should do, and any man who dates me has to do it."

Because of the pressure the patriarchy has put on women, my friend finds it easier to gender a chore than to admit that she only dates people who mow the lawn, because the patriarchy teaches women that they cannot ask for what they want and need without being labeled selfish or nagging. I wonder what else she wants and needs and isn't asking for.

Imagine a world where my friend is free to ask for and receive what she wants from her partner. A world where I can bring all of me to work without jeopardizing my career. A world with presentations and expressions and experiences that don't even exist yet.

We can all benefit from the deconstruction of gender if first we are brave enough to conceive of it.

BIOGRAPHY

LJ (they/them) is a non-binary transmasculine, nonprofit professional based in the UK. Born and raised in Canada and the USA, they spent their early career in Ghana working in anti-child trafficking, before coming to the UK to work for an environmental nonprofit, seek trans healthcare, and pursue further studies. The stories in this chapter span a range of their experiences navigating a non-affirming religious environment in Canada, gradually accepting their queer and trans identities and finding queer community in Ghana, and living as an out queer trans person for the first time in the UK.

Chapter 6

Mediterranean Gender Journeys

*Exploring Gender Identity and Migration
to and from Places to Call Home*

Ludo Tolu and Mina Tolu

INTRODUCTION

We are Mina and Ludo, twins, who were born in Italy, but have grown up in Malta. Mina recently moved back to Malta after three years in Berlin while Ludo lives in London. This chapter shares our journeys to explore and embrace our gender and our journey to and through the spaces in which we [can] belong.

LUDO'S JOURNEY

I've been thinking lately about why I'm in the UK, why I feel comfortable here, and why I don't currently want to move back to Malta. At the moment I'm working out my gender, and it's actually an exhausting exercise! If I moved back, I would then also have to actively work on belonging. Having been away for five years, I am afraid I'd be read as an outsider, so I'd have to work so that my voice in Malta is seen as legitimate. I think I'd find that really tiring. I need space to explore and express my identity – and by that, I mean a mental space rather than a physical one. My mental space would be too crowded in Malta.

Of course, my gender has been policed in both Malta and the UK, in different ways. In 2011 or 2012 I had gone to a counsellor in Malta, where I discussed my desire to get top surgery. She couldn't understand it, and framed it as worrying. She wondered why I would want to perform this 'act of violence' against my own body. I don't think she realised how damaging her words were. But London (in particular) has many resources for trans people, which makes it easier for me to explore gender. There's a trans-specific weekly health clinic called CliniQ, which was set up by trans people. There's also a free counselling service for trans people (provided by Spectra), and therapists who are truly inclusive of trans identities. Having access to health services that are trans-led and trans-inclusive means I don't have to explain myself. I don't need to explain why I find cervical smears particularly invasive, or spend time educating healthcare staff what it means to be non-binary. Explaining myself is exhausting.

The erasure of my identity has happened in the UK as well as in Malta. I was in a relationship for some time after I moved to the UK where my non-binary identity was questioned because my former partner could not understand non-binary identities. So, for many months I'd tone down my queerness to feel accepted. Moreover, in the British media non-binary identities are also frequently ridiculed. We're told we're making this up, and that we don't exist. But where I am now in London there are a lot more people, so there are more queers, and more spaces where I feel comfortable – where I feel like me without judgement.

Being in this space where I comfortably talk about my gender is a recent thing. I'm still working through the years of stigma and shame that accumulated as we were growing up in Malta. Years when I was shamed for not wanting to shave my legs or when I was questioned for the clothes I chose to wear. I felt I was hurting others by choosing to be myself. In particular I felt that I was hurting my mum, who thought things would be easier if I fitted in. So, there were days when I chose to hide myself beneath dresses and blow-dried hair. I never felt comfortable when I was pretending to be female. I felt like I was putting on a face that didn't quite fit. My mum now recognises how happy I am when I'm just being myself, and knows that this matters a lot more than 'fitting in'.

My struggles with expectations around clothes and hair may sound like small things but imagine being stung in the same place over and over again. Eventually it becomes really sore, and maybe you even have an allergic reaction to it! Add on top of that, the recent shame I felt in a relationship in the UK with a partner who would become angry when I'd attend trans events. A partner who would ask me to not talk about the work Mina was doing at Transgender Europe whenever I was around her wider family. Being in London right now, with an interesting job, welcoming colleagues, friends and partners, and with access to queer spaces where I'm not questioned is freeing. This is what I need.

Whenever I think about Malta, I feel guilty. I feel guilty because I know there are things that I could be doing there which could be really valuable. But as I question my gender, I've also started questioning this feeling. Where has it come from? Why do I feel it? Is it right? In 2014, when I was telling people about my plans to move to the UK for a job, there were three people that I distinctly remember reacting in an off-putting way. One was one of the LGBT activists we were working alongside, who said, 'So, that's it? Four years working to improve things here is enough for you? Don't you realise there's more to do?' Of course, there's more to do, but there should be no shame in taking a step back, in taking time to explore other places, and also no shame in taking my energy elsewhere. Don't hate on me for exploring other places!

I've lived in the UK for five years now, and for the most part I feel welcomed, even despite the Brexit vote. My first language is English, so of course that helps a lot. What also helps is that I'm white and middle class. But I also feel more valued in a more meritocratic and less misogynistic culture. I don't think my career would have progressed this much or this quickly in Malta. In the UK I've been promoted based on my skills. In Malta my impression is that you have to rely much more on who you know and that people mistrust those of us who are different. People don't question why I'm here, they don't act like I don't belong. I'm less of an outsider in London than in Malta where I grew up.

Still sometimes I feel unrooted – like I have no place to call home, no place where I belong. I mentioned this to a friend, who said maybe I could view home as a state when I'm at peace, rather than tying it to a physical location.

I feel unfixed in my gender and unfixed in my national belonging. But what does this mean? It means we can find our own queer communities and families, our own spaces of belonging. We can choose them, and we can contribute to them and we can care within them, but we can also open them up wide, make the borders of them flexible. Maybe one day I'll return to Malta but for now I'm working on building my own space to belong. A space where my identity (both in terms of gender, but also in terms of whether I'm Maltese enough) is not questioned; a space where my work is valued and where I can grow. This will give me more strength, and will mean if I do return, I can do so as my whole and my true self.

MINA'S JOURNEY

I have been thinking recently about the ways in which Berlin has helped me to shape my identity as a trans person, and like Ludo, I have also been thinking about Malta.

I feel that Ludo centres themselves and their trans identities in their reasons to remain, for now, away from Malta, so that they can construct their own space of belonging. In this aspect, my gender and trans journey reached a comfort level sooner than Ludo's. Berlin, where I moved to from Malta in 2015, is the place where I finally felt comfortable to come out as trans. Working for the biggest trans organisation in Europe, Transgender Europe, and being around trans people every day, of course helped me to feel supported, seen, and able to make this step without any negative consequences. I have found comfort in being part of a queer and trans bubble; and, especially, in such a big city I have found comfort in being anonymous.

In many ways, I think that the majority of our identities – not just our gender and national identity – are unfixed and non-specific, and extremely dependent on context.

I wrote a poem recently, after a dream I had in which I was walking around a forest in winter. I was alone. I felt at peace.

I wrote:

Dreams.
In a forest
With snow
Down a path.
I ask,
'If a person is alone in a forest
Do they have a gender?'

The comfort I found in being anonymous in this city, away from Malta, is also because I am free to just be myself. In Malta, as an activist, you become known to a certain extent, and parts of your identity are used against you. They're made the only thing that matters, or are completely magnified and constructed into something new.

In 2015 I was the campaign coordinator for a campaign to end the spring hunting of birds in Malta. A national referendum on this issue was being held that April. As the campaign coordinator, my role was both behind the scenes and in the public eye. People who were following politics, involved in green or environmental activism, or following the campaign closely for any reason knew about me.

To provide some context: in Malta, both English and Maltese are official languages. English and Maltese can both be spoken and are widely accepted. However, in political spaces, and on broadcast media like radio and television, it is common for Maltese to be the main language. English is my first language and influences the ways I speak Maltese.

The campaign was highly contested, and we lost by a small margin. It was taking place at the same time as victories in LGBTQI rights, including civil unions for all in 2014 and quick, accessible legal gender recognition based on self-determination in 2015. Campaigns in which I was also active and visible.

In those LGBTQI campaigns and others, I never felt questioned for speaking up. All that mattered was that I was queer. So, I was not prepared for my identities to be picked on and apart during the anti-spring-hunting campaign. I was also not prepared for the validity of what I was saying to be voided by my gender identity, my queer identity, my linguistic identity and my dual-national identity. Suddenly there were many different versions of me floating around. These new versions of me were constructed based simply on context and assumptions.

After my first media interviews about the campaign appeared online in 2015, my identities started to be reinterpreted by others. Parts of things I would have said or done would contribute to new depictions. These could be used against me in ways to invalidate what I was saying.

I can now easily divide these partly constructed depictions into separate groups based on comments and anecdotes from the campaign. For example, *Female-Mina* was sent weekly threats on social media. *Female-Mina* had to 'watch her mouth', or she would be raped. *Female-Mina* had 'to go fuck herself' daily. She had her car-door kicked in and was verbally harassed in a public square. I hadn't been expecting these kind of reactions, and they had a longer-lasting effect than I thought they would.

Internally within our campaign too, I had to fight for my voice. Perhaps my gender, combined with the fact that I was 23 at the time, meant that others felt they could speak down to me, and matters that related to me were decided without me. When I wrote to a potential ambassador, an older man, he called my director to tell him that I was extremely rude to not address him in a formal manner and would not reply to me unless I apologised.

A male campaigner chose to open a case with the police against the man who verbally harassed me, without my consent. After the campaign, when the police couldn't reach me because I had changed my phone number, on being contacted, he told them that they could close the case. Again, without ever asking me what I wanted to do about it.

The second constructed identity stemmed from my sexual orientation. So, *Minority-Mina* also made an appearance: 'Ironic how Ms Tolu was part of a minority group fighting for their rights a few months back but today wants other minority groups' rights abolished.' This might seem puzzling, so I'll explain: hunters tried to position themselves as a minority group during this referendum debate so as to use rights-based messaging in their campaigns.

However, there are also those parts of my identity, which always seemed more fixed to me than my gender or sexual orientation because of where I grew up, that became the most unfixed and contradictory. So, while we have a *Non-Maltese-Mina*, we also have the *English-Speaking-Maltese-Therefore-Elitist-Mina*. Both of these depictions of me by others were used to void anything I had to say about the campaign. 'Where is this so-called Miss Tolu from? With all due respect, what right do I have to go to someone else's country and say what needs to be done?'

I hope that the details in these depictions have an expiry date, for I am some (but not all) of the above. I am no longer female, I am as Maltese as I am non-Maltese, I speak English better than I speak Maltese, but consider them all, along with Italian, to be my mother-tongues. My gender, national and linguistic identities seem to lie outside or between the norms, therefore they will always be to some extent unfixed and challenged.

So, now that I am back in Malta, I continue to be questioned. And, my latest identity, as a person involved in green politics, will also be challenged as it lies outside the norms of Malta's two-party political system. This might sometimes be humorous. People will construct stories about me based on things I say or do. These new depictions might sometimes clash and contradict themselves. They will sometimes be used to try to hurt me too, but if they do, I will take a deep breath, dive under water and know:

When I am alone
in the sea,
I have no gender
And no nation
I am only me.

BIOGRAPHIES

Ludo Tolu (they/theirs/them) lives in London, where they work as an environmental economist at the Department for Environment, Food and Rural Affairs. In 2016 and 2017 they curated an award-winning exhibition on the fight for LGBT rights in Britain, at the People's History Museum in Manchester. And between 2010 and 2014 they led a Maltese LGBTQ youth organisation alongside their twin, Mina. They spend their evenings exploring London's queer venues, and weekends in museums and galleries. They've also recently started to grow vegetables and are busy experimenting with cruelty-free ways to deal with all the slugs that come with it.

Mina Tolu (they/theirs/them) is a trans, queer, feminist, pro-choice, and green activist from Europe. Between 2015 and 2018 Mina lived in Berlin, Germany, where they worked at Transgender Europe. In 2019 they were the first openly non-binary candidate for the European Parliament running for the Green Party in Malta. Mina has over nine years of experience in local and international queer activism and organising, with a focus on communications and campaigning. They have also worked within broader feminist and green movements. To recover from activism Mina writes, plays softball and makes custom rubber stamps.

Twitter: @mina_tolu

Chapter 7

All Gods Are the Same

Kimwei McCarthy

> My friend George talks in stereotypes all the time. 'People like *that*,' he'll complain, 'always do *this*, always say *that*…and If they're not people like *that*, they're people like *this*,' and so on.
>
> 'Wait, George,' I interrupt him during an especially long rant. 'What type of person do you think I am?'
>
> He stops in his tracks, turns and looks at me, as if for the first time and says, 'You know, I have literally no idea!'

My name is Kimwei and I am non-binary. This term can be applied with equal accuracy to my gender, ethnicity, spirituality and sexuality.

My mother is from Penang (Malaysia): the other side of the world from the exotic suburb of Hanwell (West London), where she met and married my father. She had emigrated to Britain to train as a nurse a few years previously; two ends of the earth meeting each other. It was into this place I was born.

As a child, the moment I could understand that I was Malaysian Chinese, I had to understand that I was also British. My father was Christian so I was told that Christ was the only way to heaven, at the same time as learning that for my Buddhist mother this just wasn't true. For her, there was no heaven or hell, but karma and reincarnation.

My parents didn't disagree, they were just different. So, as a child, I learned that these opposing views, instead of conflicting with each other, were like fixing points to attach a string to. Perhaps a huge white canvas is hung from that string and a wide landscape painted on it, depicting everything between those two points.

The points could be 'male and female' or 'eastern and western', 'Christian and Buddhist', but in each case the painting looks different depending on whether you stand back from it, or close so you can't see the edges, or right by one fixing point, or the opposing one. Stand at one end and certain things appear to be true, whilst at the other end, opposite things appear to be true. From a young age, it became obvious to me that things could be true or not true depending on where you were standing – an optical illusion, disguised as opinion.

ALL GODS ARE THE SAME

Ah Huat always wore the same clothes: his white taxi-man shirt, so thin you could see the Mickey Mouse ears on the cartoon vest he always wore underneath, and his faded black trousers. Next to his skin, two strings of temple beads hung from his neck, which if you were a trusted friend, he might bring out to show you. My parents and I were indeed trusted friends and we visited him shortly before he entered the monkhood in Penang.

'What's this sculpture?' asked my mother, pointing to two hands, carved in stone, displayed on the altar in his kitchen. Ah Huat smiled and lifted it from the colourful batik cloth.

'Symbol for All Gods Are the Same,' he replied, inverting it to show us how the ornament was designed so if you turned it upside down, it looked just the same as right side up. 'Today my friend comes to Temple to visit my God. Tomorrow I go to Mosque to visit his God.'

I turned from the window's breeze in the lazy heat. This idea was new to me. 'Ah Huat, what if somebody says all Gods are not the same?'

He looks at me aghast and repeats three or four times, 'Cannot say! Cannot say!'

I came to be untrusting of any truth that claimed *not* to be part of a painting, hung on a string that was fixed to two opposing points. That kind of 'truth' was dangerous, because it was an opinion which *believed* it was truth, because it didn't know that it was just a part of a painting, which only exists because of a string hung between two opposing points, because of our agreement as humans to believe in those points.

Our beliefs and opinions simply form structures for us to momentarily understand who we are. We need that. But who we are is always in movement, so there is a danger in holding on too tightly. To me, being non-binary is about recognising that every binary concept (in other words, every painting) is to be used as a field or spectrum and that we inhabit a wide territory within it, not a single place. This territory is our identity and it has moveable borders. It can change in a moment, as our perception changes; and in those moments, everything is different.

BILLY BECOMES BILLIE

I'm looking at Billie again. She's all flowers today, petal soft. Even the sofa she sits on, holding a cup of tea over crossed legs, is patterned with tiny magnolias. She smiles like she has a secret, or more accurately like her secret is out, running around in the world, whilst she watches.

Today, Billie has an 'i' and 'e'. Yesterday, and all the days before that, she had a 'y'. But today she has an 'ie' and that has made all the difference. She breathes into her new name and I've never seen her so bright. I'm watching the sunlight play on her impossibly blonde hair like it feels privileged to be allowed to and is celebrating with dappled gentleness. Even her face has changed.

'I don't know what my gender is now,' she says. 'The only thing I'm sure of is, just…not male.' She glances from the window.

'And I'm not female,' I say, jolted by the clarity of it. 'That's right. That's all I know too.'

Billie leans forward and looks at me mischievously. 'Well *quite*. Should I call you "chap"?'

'If I can call you "doll".'

We smile at each other then. I can no longer recall her as a man.

'I'm starting to think we should record all of our conversations,' she says. 'So many moments in my history go by, like that one just did.'

'Moments when everything changes?'

'Yes.'

If beliefs and opinions are a way our minds can understand the world, what about our bodies? My experience of gender and sexuality is very much in the body. I've often been asked, 'Why would you want to be a boy?' Anyone LGBTQ+ has probably grappled with this type of question, asked by someone who has fallen into the trap of thinking that difference is a choice. The answer is that gender and sexuality are not things that we *choose*, any more than a heterosexual child looks out across the school playground, at their moment of sexual maturity, and says to themselves, 'You know, it's a tough call, but I think I'll go for people with different genitals to mine.'

It's with that same internal sense, from deep in the pit of my stomach, that I looked across the playground at the boys playing football and I knew I was one too. I didn't know how to play and perhaps didn't want to, but my body felt a kinship to boys and a longing to be included as one of them.

In my school, 'girls' didn't play football. I was grouped in a female changing room for netball, watching its population begin to flower into crop-top experimentation and various octaves of giggling. My body knew that I was *not* one of them and felt it somewhere in the pit of my stomach. I had no idea what they were doing or how to join in.

By this point, you can no doubt imagine me as a kid who was neither one thing nor another in every possible sphere. I couldn't 'pass' as British or Chinese, Christian or Buddhist, or even male or female. Strangely, I was not an outcast but I also didn't integrate. Even now, I am known for 'orbiting' groups: being intensely involved whilst I'm present but not liking to stay for long enough that the group's culture and values become my whole reality. In other words, truth appears to become solid when you stand in one place for long enough; yet since my identity has forced me into the freedom of fluidity, it's a freedom I won't easily give up.

At one level, it may sound as if I am criticising people with a single, set identity and claiming to have superpowers. This is not the case. There is value in both, and successful societies make good use of both.

It has taken me most of my life to find anything useful about my failure to be fully included, as a large portion of this is painful for me. It is those closest to me who have told me how they value my outsider's perspective. Recently, when I was at dinner with a feminist friend, she listened to my thoughts on gender for so long I had to stop and press her for discussion. Finally, she said, 'You know, I am so firmly female that your non-binary perspective is just totally new to me and I don't know what to say. Please keep talking.'

Every society needs designated outsiders. Learning about the hidden gifts of being neither one thing nor another has been key to my happiness. When I am recognised as useful, I have a way of 'belonging' in the world. I've stopped being a round peg trying to find which square hole would be the nearest fit.

DIFFICULTATING

'I've been invited to a discussion festival as a trained "difficultator",' a friend told me.

'What's that?' I asked.

'Oh, it means I ask difficult questions whenever a debate starts to die down, or everyone begins to agree.'

I was thrilled to discover this role being acknowledged and celebrated, because I've always been a difficultator by default. Partly as a result of being non-binary I am the disruptive ingredient whose existence shows that what you thought was solid can be fluid, and what you thought was physical can be transcendent. I challenge what you thought was real.

The gift of being in the less-fluid majority is that of a solid identity which can belong and be used to create stable families and communities.

On these kinds of structures the happiness of individuals and societies can be built. My observation is that those with intersecting differences can provide perspectives when these stable groups become solid and inflexible to their own detriment. In other words, people can become so embedded in a 'painting' that they cannot see its edges, and have perhaps forgotten that it has edges – or even that it is a painting. Oppression describes what happens when these solid systems (such as families and cultures) feel threatened by outside perspectives and defend themselves accordingly.

Identity is a vital component of sanity, so we have a desire to keep the 'story of who we are' solid, to avoid this pain. This applies to whole societies as well as individuals. As someone with a fluid identity, I've developed a tolerance level, or immunity, to fear of identity loss. This allows me to manage constant internal motion without losing myself, but it's also noted that I am stabilised by other factors such as my intelligence and creativity, which have anchored me in the world. It's these qualities which enabled me to stay top of the class at school, and to become a successful teacher on both a pioneering BA and masters in music, as well as a musician/performer. These parts of me, which are easily visible, help me to receive substantial love. I am valued and appreciated for these aspects, about which there is no confusion. I am a musician. I am a teacher. I am a high-achiever. These statements are easy to understand and their nature is not confusing or in dispute.

These dimensions in which I'm easily understood keep me resilient against inaccurate ideas of who I am when they are projected on to me by others, whether positive or negative. Being misunderstood, or experiencing invisibility about aspects of myself, should really be explained as being 'un-loved'. When someone sees me as female (since I'm assigned female at birth, or AFAB), my male aspects are invisible to them and therefore receive no love. This is the pain of being different. If 50% of us is unseen, that 50% is unloved.

It's easy, as someone who is part of a minority, to believe that everyone in the majority group is 100% seen and loved. The reality is, as my friend Billie says, 'There's the narrative of being male, and the narrative of being female, and there are aspects of being human that are left out of both narratives.' In other words, going back to our idea of a landscape, even if most people fit within the conventional 'painting' of binary gender, they are likely to be experiencing parts of themselves as unseen and therefore unloved.

DO YOU SEE ME?: 'NOTHING'S BINARY' (THE SONG)

Being non-binary transgender is something I've always found difficult to explain. It seemed so unfamiliar to anyone, so invisible, so different, something they couldn't relate to. Finally, the only thing to do was write a song, simply called 'Nothing's Binary'.

Fellow non-binary musician Billie Bottle and I recorded it to coincide with Exeter Pride, in May 2016. The tag read: 'It's a song about being non-binary, but also celebrating LGBTQ+ as a whole.' A few thousand views later, we were thrilled that the message had been so deeply received. It turned out, how I feel about being non-binary isn't difficult to relate to at all. I learned that expanding beyond the binary notion of gender is not just relevant to those who identify as transgender, but to everyone, because we are all affected by the expectations of a society that sees gender in binary.

The song resonated with anyone seeking to be seen as who they truly are. We heard from people who feel unseen due to gender, race, disability, or because some other reason leaves them feeling judged and unacknowledged. I learned that when we see and accept each other, we love each other; and when we love each other, we change the world.

In the past, I have fallen into the trap of believing that my unloved-ness was solely due to being non-binary. When I imagine myself with a male body, I'm always better-looking, with a great beard and trim physique and am constantly approached for sex. I never consider the possibility that as a man I might just grow bum-fluff on my chin, or those embarrassing patchy clumps which get caught on the curtains, like Velcro, when wall-flowering at a party.

Back at the playground on a summer's day, watching one boy take his shirt off, sprint across the turf and score a goal, I imagine that the only thing stopping me from being like him is my female body. I fantasise about having a male body, stripping to the waist, tanned and muscular, ruling the field as girls watch and admire. In truth, if at that moment a genie had appeared and granted my wish of becoming a 'real boy', a rub of the lamp would have given me a male version of my *own* body: stumpy, chubby and still totally unable to play football. This is the problem with genies.

Since making a wish is not an option, I find myself again searching for the hidden gifts in being non-binary. The first, as mentioned, is being able to provide alternative viewpoints. The second is that since I am not part of the system which most people are hoping to be included in, I often act as a confessional. I can see people's invisible or unseen aspects. The third gift of being non-binary is that since integration is unlikely for me, I make choices that are independent of any desire to be seen as normal. For the longest time, I had no idea what it was to 'care what people think'. Of course, it mattered to me whether those closest to me loved and accepted me; but when it came to the general public, there was no hope in any case, so no point in trying. This hasn't made my behaviour way out, since I'm not interested in shock value either. However, it does leave me saying 'no' to any decisions that don't suit me.

BOY'S HAIRCUT

I finally got my hair cut short at the age of 12, sneaking off on a Saturday, with saved pocket money and without my parents' knowledge. Up until then, I'd succeeded in looking like a tomboy, but getting that haircut was the final piece in the puzzle. After that, I looked like a boy.

It was a big decision. My child's mind understood two basic principles: 1) I was a girl but I'd rather be a boy; 2) ugly girls are said to look like boys.

So, if I could make myself look ugly, people would think I was a boy – success. But if I was ugly, no one would want to date me. I would never have a girlfriend or boyfriend, and never be loved. In my mind, this was the deal: I had to decide between being myself, and being loved. I chose the former, and cut my hair.

Eventually I found love anyway, but years later it struck me that I made that decision. I wondered where else in my life I'd had to decide between being included and being myself. At that time, I chose the latter. I wonder how many life decisions I've made on the same principle since then.

BIOGRAPHY

Kimwei (he/him) is a singer-songwriter, university lecturer, digital nomad, blogger and lifestyle experimenter, who orbits the city of Exeter where he serves as Bard. During the day, he's likely teaching on Skype, recording, producing or writing. On a summer's evening, if he's not performing, you may find him parked on a hill overlooking the city, the doors of his live-in van thrown open whilst noodles cook on a small gas stove, with Leopard the Bengal cat up a tree nearby. Either that or you'll find him in your driveway, surfing your sofa, or taking care of your house whilst you're away. Kimwei is AFAB, aged 34.

Chapter 8

Latinx Not Latina

Annelyn Janib

Growing up, the only word I could use to describe myself was "tomboy." But that word, like a pair of pants that needs to be tailored, didn't quite fit. I was wrapped in a pink blanket when I was born and that came with a checklist of things I would never fulfil. I never felt like I was a girl, but I wasn't a boy either. I was just floating somewhere in-between. I was just me.

Being a tomboy was especially difficult because I'm Hispanic—vibrant colors, loud music, and strict gender roles. It wasn't until college that I learned more about gender and I finally found a word that defines me—non-binary. The way Latinx culture defines gender, in my experience, means there is no in-between, there is nothing outside of "man" and "womyn." I don't exist. (Just a quick clarification, I didn't spell womyn wrong. I take out the "a" and replace it with a "y" because that's how it's spelt without "man.") Even my beautiful Spanish language betrays me with its lack of neutrality. I'm still trying to figure out where these pieces fit into the puzzle that is me. It is a never-ending balancing act between the different parts of me.

My balancing act began long before I could really understand it. I could never wrap my head around the whole idea of gender. Why were there only two worlds, and why were they so separate? Navigating my way through "boy stuff" and "girl stuff" was so clear and yet so difficult. Even though my birth certificate forced me into the girl realm, I have always lived somewhere in-between. I hated all things pink but loved dolls and dressing-up. But my love of cars, sports, and the outdoors got me labelled a tomboy. I was bullied and alienated by my peers for not fitting into the girl box. My disconnect from the norms surrounding me often led me to question, and at the time, questions always led to God.

Being Hispanic often means that Catholicism is very intertwined with everything. I remember just standing in the hallway one day, wanting to understand why God made me so different. This was probably the most positive part of growing up in a Hispanic culture—I was taught not to question God. This meant I was different for a reason, and I accepted that.

I accepted my logic, and my tomboy label, until college. There I started learning about gender in my sociology classes and in University of Tampa Pride. I had been an active member and president of my high school's Gay–Straight Alliance, and yet I knew nothing about gender. It was a whole new realm for me and I was happy to have stepped into it. For the part of my brain that loved learning, gender was a fascinating topic. I was finding more and more words that I felt I could connect to. I would sit for hours reading and learning about all these new terms and it felt amazing knowing there were words to describe how I felt. So, I began the long process of researching different gender identities until I found a term I most identify with: non-binary. Out of the countless terms, I chose this word to describe me because it best captured how I felt. There were some other identities that had bits and pieces of their definition that matched my feelings. I would get excited reading, thinking, "Yes, that's how I talk about myself." And then as I kept reading, I'd think, "Maybe not." Sadly, I couldn't share the joy of finally finding my word because, unlike my friends, my family only sees two options. Most of my friends are more open to understanding things like gender identities, or like me are queer in some way. My family sees everything in a very binary way. They are far less open to learning about these types of things. Much of it has to do with how they were brought up and because they're not exposed to a diverse set of identities.

Growing up and living with my Hispanic family, as well as other Hispanic people that I have met over the years, means that there is a very strict definition of gender roles and identities and how they are represented. I live every day knowing that despite the unlimited love I have for *carne asada*, *futbol*, *bachata*, and everything about my heritage, there is no space for me. I love a culture that continuously, and without fail, attempts to force me into a box. Anything outside of the binary simply doesn't exist.

In English there is a variety of gender neutral words that people can use when talking about me. In Spanish I find it difficult to think of any words that are not confined by the binary. The word "Latinx" is a word people had to make up because there is no gender neutral way of stating that you're Latin. Almost everything is gendered as masculine (*el parque*) or feminine (*la playa*). This makes it difficult for me to talk about myself in Spanish. Clearly, I exist, but every word spoken is a reminder that I am but a ghost to the world I love. People can choose to invalidate me in English, but in Spanish, can it really be on purpose when our language already does it for them? How can they understand me when I can't find the words for myself? Language is everything. There are no words that exist, so new words have to be made. I found encouragement in this department after watching a video of a young Latina talking about the gender neutral words she made up and uses out of respect for people who don't fall inside the gender binary. She describes how she has to defend her words, because they aren't seen as "real" words in Spanish. But that doesn't mean they can't be, or that people like me don't exist. We come up with new words, and uses for words all the time.

I hold hope that there will come a day when I enter a battle of words, a battle to determine the fact that I am flesh and bones. I will have more than words fabricated from fantasy. I want more gender neutral terms, so that the words people use every day include and validate me. If there are more words, and a better understanding of why these terms and neutral phrases are used, then maybe it'll be easier for people to accept more gender identities.

BIOGRAPHY

Annelyn Janib (they/them) is 22 years old, born and raised in south Florida. They are Nicaraguan and Colombian. They studied psychology and sociology at the University of Tampa. They are currently getting their M.A. in Women, Gender, and Sexuality Studies at Florida Atlantic University. Their thesis will focus on non-binary representation in media. They are the Graduate Assistant for the Women, Gender, and Equity Resource Center.

Email: annelynjmartinez@gmail.com

Chapter 9

Weep and Storm and Swear They Lie

Dang Nguyen

With those who follow a different Way, it is useless to take counsel.

Confucius, *The Analects* (circa 480 BCE)

My grandfather was a Confucian in every sense of the word. I never met him, but I saw him in everything my father said and did, and in the stories my father told us of their family before the war. I don't even know his name – even in conversation, we only ever called him by the honorific title Ong Noi, which signifies Paternal Grandfather. I only knew who and what he was by the shape of the impact he left on my father. But from my father's accounts, from my father's manner and values and virtues and flaws, I could make out the shape of the man, like puzzling out the silhouetted form of a giant against the sky by the stars he blotted out. Ong Noi was a military man. Ong Noi valued integrity and correct conduct. Ong Noi insisted on the proper way of doing things, and respect for elders, and maintaining tradition. Ong Noi studied for his Imperial examinations in order to enter the civil service, and served as a royal guard for the last Emperor of Vietnam, and named each of his children after one of the Four Books and Five Classics of the Confucian canon. My father, Thu, was named for the Classic of Literature, and my name means morning light, a brilliant illumination by which literature can be read. Ong Noi transmitted all these beliefs to my father, who preserved them in his heart amid the chaos and turmoil of the Vietnam War, and carried them away with him like jewels, like heirlooms, from the land of his ancestors to a refugee camp in Malaysia, and then to Australia and to me.

Vietnamese children are not encouraged to know their parents too well. Proper filial piety is always ideally mixed with a little fear in Confucian culture. Respect for parents is a species of awe; all children think of their parents as creatures who are not quite human, but Confucianism institutionalises the phenomenon. I had to learn to perform manhood by observing my father rather than being told that a man must be this or that. I listened as he told stories about his father with obvious reverence, and lived the lessons that his father taught him. From him, I learned that being a man was about going to work every day, and keeping peace in the household, and scrupulously good manners. I learned that being a man was about being firmly grounded in material accomplishment and sensible pursuits. I learned that manliness is to eschew ornamentation and fragrance, to not speak of emotions, to do any work around the house that hurts one's wrists or carries the risk of cuts and bruises, even if there are women far more capable of doing the job. Above all, I learned that manliness meant behaving correctly, from ensuring that there was always a light burning before the household altar to refusing to start dinner until every member of the household was seated.

I hated every moment of it. At times, I thought with the terrifying vertigo of forbidden ideas that I might even hate my father. I hated being told that I must put away my concern for frivolous or beautiful things, and that I must not cry or daydream. Even at three and five and seven years old, I knew that my father was a sort of creature I could never be: tall and stern and angry at the follies and imperfections of the world. Even then I knew I wanted to be Sailor Moon when I grew up, and to marry a boy, and that I wanted a doll's house that I was too afraid to ask my parents for. Even then I carried different jewels in the heart of my heart from the wisdom of Confucius and my ancestors.

As I got bigger, my parents got smaller. An inevitable part of growing up means outgrowing the comforting idea that your parents are huge and all-powerful and all-knowing, and as I learned who I was going to be, I began to see the shape of who my father was and could be. I saw the worry behind every frightening frown, the love in every wearisome lecture, the romantic behind his tired old eyes. I began to realise that these laws of manliness weren't something that came naturally to my father. I wondered if he even liked them. They were something that had been pressed into him long ago, and I saw the marks of Ong Noi's hands and words in the clay, even as I felt him trying to press the same rules and realities into me. I realised, with a sort of slow, weary sadness, that once upon a time, my father had been someone like me – sensitive, romantic, shy, anxious. What kind of man would he have grown to be if he had been allowed to live free of what it meant to be a man?

The difference was that I had other options. I had a wider view of the world in my childhood than my father, and there were other ways to be a man.

White Australian manhood is not without its rules – as severe and terrible as the ones laid down in the Four Books and Five Classics. I learned these rules, too, from observation. Being as I was a rather prissy Asian boy, I was never going to be quite in a position to learn directly from my peers and role models, but I was afforded a rare and dreadful vantage point from which to receive my lessons: I was bullied.

A typical white Australian man will tell you that white Australian masculinity is about toughness, and friendship, and a healthy disrespect for authority. He'll tell you that it's about carefree friendliness and good-natured roistering. And there is some truth to that. But that toughness comes at the cost of toxic repression and lack of emotional intelligence, to the point where the leading cause of death for Australian men between the ages of 15 and 44 is suicide. That vaunted code of mateship applies with strict conditions: that you are part of the in-group; that you buy into the collective larrikinish chillness that depends on general consent; that you ascribe to the clannish loyalty of your social group. That disrespect for authority translates to disrespect and disregard for anybody and anything that tries to exert a moderating influence: girlfriends asking their menfolk to stop shouting, friends telling their peers that their transphobic jokes aren't funny, feminists telling Australian men to examine their behaviours, intellectuals telling them about the world – merciful Ma'at, the anti-intellectualism of Australian men. At least in Vietnam and Japan and Korea and every other Confucian country, intellectuals are respected for their learning – indeed, scholarship and academic accomplishment are part of what makes a man worthy. Here in Australia, there is a distrust and dislike of anybody who purports to know more about something than the average bloke, even if that person happens to be a genuine authority who has gained their knowledge from long study and experience.

And above all, above even the anti-intellectualism and the tribe loyalties and the careful, deliberate disregard for anyone or anything that might tell them that their behaviour is not acceptable, there is the fearfulness of anything different. The quintessential Australian dislike of anything Other. That is what drives their zeal to wear badges of belonging and declare their allegiance to clubs and clans, and makes them despise anybody with the temerity to suggest by their words or actions that they might know or be better. It soaks into every layer and facet of Australia and its men, from the governments that whip up fear about each successive wave of immigrants to schoolboys sensing that their classmate will cry if he is pushed over, that he likes to read and is maybe a little more delicate than them.

And so for all the infractions of being bookish and effeminate and valuing learning, I weathered long years of insults and torments, sometimes snide and sideways and social, and sometimes violent and choleric when the string was stretched too far and the tension had nowhere to go. I suffered for the sake of other boys' masculinity, even as I knew I would never enter that magic circle. I knew without a doubt that their mode of manliness, even though it was the Nirvana to which we were all told to aspire, would never admit me. All their bullying, designed to punish me for my deviation from their norms and reinforce their chummy camaraderie with each other, simply drove me further and further from all the things a man was supposed to be. Before my baptism by fire, all I knew was that I would never be one of them. After passing through it and emerging tempered and bright as new-forged steel, I knew that I hated them, and I hated the reality they inhabited. Strung between a neurotic philosophy of stern uprightness and a psychotic code of aggression, I latched onto anything else I could find that would give me an alternative, any bit of flotsam from the wreck of my life that could keep me afloat.

And I found it in other stories, other lessons I could observe and internalise. These were stories of princesses and witches, of romance and enchantment, lessons meant for little girls, not people like me. Now that I am grown, a critical theorist with a sharp eye for a troubling trope, I know better than to listen to fairy tales for advice, but Belle and Sara Crewe and Fern Arable taught me that it was not only okay to be different and to not fit in, but that it was a rare honour. Being different was a blessing, I learned. Being different meant that I was the main character, and that there was maybe even a handsome prince waiting for me, and that I didn't have to wave swords or kill anything to be brave and strong. And that knowledge protected me against shame and despair and lit my way through everything that was to come, and the stain of self-hatred has never darkened my soul.

I blundered through my adult life, leaving behind the forge-fire of my schooldays a good deal sharper and harder than I had been going in.

But even that didn't provide any escape from questions of manliness and manhood. I had known from the age of six that I wanted to marry a boy when I grew up; morning cartoons had shown me the sleek, snide, top-hatted Tuxedo Mask of Sailor Moon fame and taught me the meaning of love at first sight. The logical culmination of that was turning 18 and entering the world of Grindr, casual sex, and all the rules that gay men use to govern their community. Here, among men whose very lives and existences deny and defy the idea that there is a right way to be a man, I learned that I would be judged by how attractive I was to others, and my good treatment was conditional on my beauty, and that to be a real man – a man worth respecting – meant to be white, to be traditionally masculine in the manner of my schoolfellows, to not be a queen, or fat, or fem, or Asian. I learned that I would never be a real man, and that I would never be welcome because nothing about me was what a man was supposed to be.

That hurt more than anything else, I think; there is a certain narrative that we feed to children in books and television shows about finding your tribe and fitting in. Your *nakama*, your found family, the companions and comrades who will go on adventures with you and see you safely through the world. I had found the people who I had thought would be my tribe. And in a way they were; it was like being an immigrant all over again. Just like being Vietnamese in a white Australian society, being queer in a straight world gave me a shared history with other people that not everyone understood, a rich cultural legacy as an inheritance, an arcane dialect of slang and shibboleths. And just as I was too gay, too Westernised for Vietnam, I found myself too Asian and feminine for gay men. I was twice alienated. I had found a tribe and they had adopted me, only unwillingly. I learned that this was a world where attractiveness meant acceptance, and sex was used as a tool of social bonding, and that sexual rejection meant social rejection. I simply wasn't man enough for them.

And over the years, I came to agree. When I think of a man, the image in my head looks nothing like me. I have never fulfilled the slightest obligation of manhood; I have never been strong in the ways that they told me I must be strong, or hated the things that it was manly to hate, or belonged to the circles that men must aspire to. These impossible standards, intended to scourge the males of the race into correct behaviour and punish them for not attaining the heights of manhood prescribed to them – which chained and leashed my father, and turned my classmates into brutes and savages – excluded me so thoroughly that there was no thought in my mind that wanted anything to do with them. Their terrors designed to make us strive for a place at the top of the totem pole and attain the promised blessings of manliness had made me their enemy. The word *man* is ugly to me now, graceless and unclean, a word full of clumsy anger and careless abuses, and that is not the name I give to the thing I am and want to be. Perhaps there is no word for what I want to be. Not woman, but never again man.

BIOGRAPHY

Dang Nguyen (he/him/his) lives in Melbourne, Australia, and he identifies as a non-binary male. He is Vietnamese-Australian and was born in a refugee camp in Malaysia in 1992. He is currently working on a fantasy novel and has another chapter published in *Growing Up Queer in Australia* by Benjamin Law (2019), and serves as the Oracle of Melbourne, an ancient office dating all the way back to mid-2012. His hobbies include story-rich open-world RPGs, fighting with racists on Grindr and fantasising about being a Heian Japanese princess.

Twitter: @celeste_praline

Instagram: @eleutherios

COMMUNITIES

Chapter 10

Non-Binary Experience in a Liberal Faith Community

Fred Langridge

I've been an active Quaker (or Friend, as we're also known) since my mid-twenties, and took the first tentative steps toward non-binary transition seven or eight years ago, in my early thirties. Quakers (formally called the Religious Society of Friends) in Britain are a socially liberal, religious community who try to live our lives as testimonies to equality, peace, truth, justice and simplicity. There are about 20,000 people regularly participating in Quaker meetings in Britain: it's too big a group for everybody to know everybody else, but small enough that if you don't know someone directly, they're likely to be the friend of a friend of a friend. My Quakerism is central in my life, and has been an essential part of the framework in which I understand my gender. Equally, my exploration and expression of my gender has given me insights that apply more widely in my religious experience and practice.

Equality is a central aspect of Quaker practice. Although this has been enacted in different ways throughout the sect's 350-year history – for instance, in working towards the abolition of slavery and towards equality between women and men – 21st-century British Quakers aim to extend our own diversity and inclusion along multiple axes. Since at least the 1960s, Quakers in Britain have been working towards positive inclusion of lesbian, gay and bisexual people, and in 2009 we made a formal decision to recognise same-sex marriages. This predated legal recognition of same-sex marriage in the UK by four years, although 'separate but equal' same-sex civil partnerships had been recognised since 2005. The experience of trans Quakers is not well documented. I know older Friends who transitioned years ago and prefer not to think about it much now.

More recently, a few trans and/or non-binary Quakers have begun to talk more openly about our experiences, and the Society is becoming more aware of our existence and our needs.

My own story of becoming visibly non-binary among Quakers began with a focus on our testimony of truth, rather than on equality. Truth and integrity are central to Quaker identity: we have traditionally refused to swear oaths in court, on the grounds that our statements should meet the same standard of truth and reliability in any context. The right to affirm the truth of one's words in court, rather than to swear an oath, was called 'the Quaker law' when it was introduced in the late 17th century. Quakers also have a strong tradition of record-keeping, again dating from when we existed outside the usual legal frameworks. Among the records is an annual 'tabular statement' of membership figures, with adult Quakers divided into numbers of men and of women. In early 2015 I had been openly genderqueer for some time and was transitioning in many ways. I felt that I could no longer honestly allow myself to be counted among the women or the men in our records. I wrote to my local membership clerk, explaining that in order for our statement to be accurate, there would need to be another gender option. The local clerk wrote to the national recording clerk, and, by chance, a similar request was being made by another Quaker Meeting at the same time. After a few conversations about practicalities, a third gender category was added to the tabular statement for 2015:

Other: adults who have indicated a gender identity other than man or woman. This might include people who have stated they are agender, neutrois or who have a(nother) non-binary gender identity.

As of 2017, at least seven of the 20,000 Quakers in Britain had asked for their gender to be recorded as something other than 'woman' or 'man'. There was remarkably little comment made about this change, beyond a few people wondering whether we still need to keep gendered records at all.

Within Quaker processes, this change to our documentation was absolutely straightforward: the clerks are obliged to keep accurate records, and the assumption is that Quakers will tell the truth about who they are, so the records needed to make room for that truth.

Cultural change can be more complicated, and, as Quakers make decisions through communal exploration of issues rather than debate and voting, it can seem that change is slow. There hasn't been a national

Quaker statement on trans equality since the consultation around the introduction of the Gender Recognition Act in the early 2000s. However, when I started to talk about my non-binary gender identity in my Quaker meetings, I was delighted at the straightforward acceptance I met.

I was happy to be asked to facilitate discussions and reflections about gender diversity in local and national groups. In those conversations I expected curiosity and maybe challenge. There was some curiosity, but also unexpected fellow feeling and understanding. Quakers are a multi-generational community, and several Friends told me that they wished they'd had the vocabulary to talk about their own gender in these ways before their ninth or tenth decades of life. Some Friends who'd been quietly exploring their own gender have felt able to talk about it more openly, and some links have been made between geographically distant non-binary and trans Friends. Cisgender Friends and older Friends with trans histories left far in the past have become forthright allies to non-binary and genderqueer people. My local and area meetings made a public statement on gender diversity, beginning:

> [We] are aware that our community is a continuing creation in which we seek to know and love one another in all our differences, united at a profound level in our efforts to reach and respond to others in the things that are eternal.

Ultimately, that's why it's important to me to have conversations about gender – about my gender – in a Quaker context. Our spiritual community relies on people bringing their whole selves and trusting that when we really know each other, that will help us find the right ways to live in the world.

Inevitably, in a small religious community on a national scale, the handful of visible trans and/or non-binary people can become the focus of a lot of attention if we express willingness. I am happy to give time and effort to increase understanding, but only because I am so well supported in doing so, and in taking time to stop and recharge my batteries when I need to.

It hasn't all been rosy. Quakers are not separate from the world or the conflicts in it. On a couple of occasions, I've found myself in conversations with Quakers who think that non-binary identity is a delusion, that trans people perpetuate gender stereotypes or that we're intrinsically deceitful. They're a tiny minority, though. A lot of Friends who I already knew, or who I've met since coming out, were mostly unaware of trans and non-binary issues but have worked at examining their own assumptions and making new, more inclusive habits.

Quaker spirituality is experiential: our worship is in mostly silent meetings where we aim to quiet our minds and be aware of 'that of God' in ourselves and in each other. Our theology is of continuing revelation: new spiritual truths can be found through contemplation and through interaction with others. Our decision-making is through communal sharing of observations around a question until the answer becomes clear to the whole group. In this context, I find it hard to imagine a Quaker response to diverse experiences of gender that isn't gently enthusiastic, loving curiosity.

While my Quakerism has influenced my experience as a non-binary trans person, my experience of visible transition has also influenced my experience of my own Quakerism more widely. In my activism and in my religious community, I'm often drawn to administrative rather than demonstrative roles. I'll happily chair committees, write minutes, book meeting venues and draw up rotas, leaving others to create campaign slogans and make emotive public speeches. When I was asked, a decade ago, to speak about my faith at a public event, I felt completely unable to do so. It is important to me to apply my religious principles throughout my life, but this is usually more about actions than words. An unexpected consequence of my need to be truthful about my gender identity is that I now regularly find myself speaking and writing about the effect of my Quakerism across the whole of my life. My religious community's loving welcome of my whole self has encouraged me to express that whole self, including the religious element, more widely.

BIOGRAPHY

Fred Langridge (they/them) has been a Quaker since their late twenties, and has been coming out as genderqueer and trans since their early thirties. They work on diversity and inclusion, particularly on LGBT+ issues and disability, and also work in IT for a charity. Fred's activist roots are in bisexual community, and they've helped several BiCons and related events to happen. For fun and relaxation they walk, cycle and swim, sing, watch birds and films and sometimes find time to write. Fred likes making things, but the thing they're not good at making is time.

Chapter 11

Queer Identity as a Spiritual Calling

Rev Rowan Bombadil

I believe for a number of reasons that the lens of calling is a useful and relevant way to look at gender...it becomes our spiritual responsibility to explore fully the nature that God has given us... It is about authentic selfhood and about service in the world.

Justin Tanis, *Trans-Gender: Theology, Ministry, and Communities of Faith* (2018, p.149)

I couldn't tell you what came first – the aching pull to minister to queer community, or the sensation and realisation of my own genderqueer shapeshifting nature. If the former came first, it must surely have included the longing to minister to my hidden queer self; if the latter, this realisation was most certainly a spiritual experience as much as it was anything else.

What I can tell you is that I'm now an Interfaith Minister in service to the LGBTQ+ and alternative communities, who also happens to run sex-positive events full of queer bodies – and that my longing to curate safer space for queerness, and for my own gender experience, are still inextricably intertwined.

When I reflect on the times when I'm most acutely aware of how my gender is also my ministry, I think of circles. Three particularly spring to mind: the circle of my interfaith seminary class; the opening circles at the events I hold; and the circle of community standing round the recipients of the Rites of Passage for Gender Transition that I facilitate.

During my initial year in that first circle, I stayed relatively quiet. I was already feeling the familiar discrimination of being the youngest out of 51 students, so I kept my head down and got on with my work. In the second year, by which time the group had both shrunk and bonded, we held a session on gender. At this point, tired of being misgendered and stepping out for exercises that asked the room to divide up into men and women, I confess I rather let them have it. As well as re-clarifying my pronouns and other assorted labels, I talked candidly about invisibility, identity and desire, throwing words like 'cock' and 'fuck' around like free candy.

The response I received was unprecedentedly positive in terms of my experience of that group – I was hugged and affirmed by people I'm sure had never spoken to me before that moment. What I found really interesting was the way my sharing in the group transformed a one-to-one peer counselling relationship. Up until that point, my peers had been extremely guarded in their sharing, and I as their counsellor increasingly frustrated. After my outburst, they opened up about a whole chapter of their past – a chapter that was unquestionably queer – and shared how my story, and the language I was using to describe myself, had given them new ways to frame and describe their own experience.

If I had any hesitation about being visibly queer and standing firmly in my sex-positivity as a minister, that moment made it abundantly clear to me that my gender *is* my ministry. It is the embodied truth that creates safer space and holds a bright mirror to the truth embedded in other bodies and spirits, and allows me to be in service to them.

* * *

In the opening circle of the event I've been running for the last four years, an event which combines ritual magic with erotic play space, we always include a pronouns round – an invitation to participants to share both their name and their pronoun with the group. My own pronouns have shifted during that time to 'they/them'. This is absolutely because those pronouns fit with my experience of myself as both genderqueer and multiple. It is also absolutely because, when I add my pronouns into circles I'm holding, I want to make it abundantly clear that this is an event by queers, for queers. I want the queer bodies in the room that are tense with trepidation, taut with that question-mark we carry around our own welcomeness every damn day, to relax a little in the knowledge that they are not just seen, they are wanted. Having a pronouns round has also allowed us to gauge when someone in the room has not been capable of participating in such a diverse space, and gently invite them to reconsider their attendance accordingly.

My queerness is not always visible on first encounter. I have not adopted all of the markers that have been so quick to coalesce into a stereotype of what a genderqueer person looks like, ought to look like. This is partly because, even as I come to know my gender as my ministry, I'm also very clear about the ways in which my gender expression is not for other people. I am clear with myself that my gender is not my wardrobe, and I am cautious about tailoring my look for the sake of fear – fear of being misgendered, or fear of not being 'queer enough' for the queerer-than-thou self-appointed gatekeepers of the community. What I do with my hair or the cut of my shirts is first and foremost a matter of self-consent and personal pleasure; I know that the latter are what I need to spend my energy reclaiming, rather than reaching for approval. But I rely on my 'they/them' pronouns to be a sign-post, building blocks for safer and more welcoming spaces.

* * *

The purpose of ceremony for me is to carve out space and time, to have the recipient stand in the centre of what has been carved out, and give them the gift of being witnessed as they acknowledge 'this is happening'. 'This' could be one of the few remaining life events we still hold ceremony around as a culture – making a love-commitment, for instance – but it can also be one of those thresholds that we are expected to cross quietly and without fuss – such as an ending, or the arrival of the menopause – or a line our culture would rather we didn't cross at all, like gender transition.

I see that purpose writ large in the circles gathered around the recipients of ceremonies I've facilitated for queer community, in the gathering together of their people – who make the time, hold the space, stand as witnesses, and beam their love at the person being celebrated. I believe that witnessing is a fundamental human need. My experience is that being seen by others is a profound and integral step on our journey towards self-actualisation, our journey towards a sense of our own enoughness. Being witnessed in our vulnerability, our brazen truth, and seeing love reflected back at us from the mirrors in the eyes of another – that is an extraordinary affirmation of our innate lovability.

And this is all the more true of our queer selves. Being seen as we feel ourselves to be, and being loved as our shapeshifting, time-travelling, gender-fucking selves, is medicine for our queer hearts, bodies and spirits. The words below from a recipient of a Rite of Passage for Gender Transition are testimony to this:

As I stood in the middle of that circle I felt more love than I have ever felt before. I felt held, seen and respected in ways that I did not know could be possible, and also so grateful for the many wonderful beings that I have in my life. I experienced a sense of belonging and appreciation that will stay with me for many years to come. That will offer me strength in darker times and help me remember that however lonely I may feel, I am never really alone.

I recall with such acute tenderness the first moments when I myself experienced being loved because of, rather than in spite of, my queerness. Those moments set a light under my calling as a counsellor and celebrant, to be a similarly loving mirror to my clients, and to create circular shining mirrors for the recipients of my ceremonies.

* * *

I couldn't tell you what came first, my queerness or my ministry. All I know – and am reminded of by moments such as those described in the three circles of the interfaith seminary, the opening circle at my events, and rites of passage for gender celebration – is that they walk this path with me hand-in-hand, and the experience and mystery of each is enriched and deepened by the other.

BIOGRAPHY

Rev Rowan Bombadil (they/them) is a UK-based queer sex witch, psychosexual coach, and interfaith minister, dedicated to bridging the binaries between sex and spirit. Their work inspires individuals and groups of all genders and orientations towards a more radical, creative, and intersectional vision of conscious intimacy. Through coaching, ceremonies and workshops, Rowan seeks to facilitate personal and planetary transformation through pleasure. They are the author of *Igniting Intimacy: Sex Magic Rituals for Radical Living and Loving*. A nerd as well as a sex geek, Rowan's other passions include books (non-fiction, high fantasy, artists' books and graphic novels), deep ecology, punk rock music, messing about with fire, and practising radical intimacy with the people they love.

You can find Rowan's ceremonial work at reverendrowan.co.uk, and their sex magical work at makinglovewithgod.co.uk

Chapter 12

My Kind of People

Finding Empowerment as a Unicorn

Calvin Hall

I recently sat in a local coffee shop with a friend, my favorite thrifted navy-blue Oxford shirt wet from summer rain. We ordered hot drinks: I, a coffee too large for an 8 pm conversation, and them an exotic-sounding tea. As we discussed our multifaceted selves, both of us surviving, but not thriving, as proud, queer academics of color, I felt a foreign need to open up in a way I previously had not been able to: "I use they/them pronouns, though I do not publicize that fact to all. My passion has been, and always will be, discussing sexual and intimate partner violence advocacy, not academic research. I love the stylings of Woodie Guthrie just as much I do New Edition and Minor Threat. I equally identify as Black, non-binary, and a geek, a fact that is apparent when viewing the smiling ebony faces, multiple 6' by 6' pride flags, and 70+ action figures that line the walls of my tiny room."

Without any hesitation, my friend plainly stated, "Calvin, you are a unicorn." I quietly sat in contemplation. While this was the first time someone had used the term "unicorn" to describe me, I cannot say the thought had never crossed my mind.

Growing up in a rural county in Virginia, I was always the only Black child in my honors courses. By fifth grade, I had come to the realization that outscoring my White counterparts on tests and assignments meant social exclusion at lunch tables, claims that I had painted my skin brown, and hurtful comments from teachers about how "unlike other Black people" I was. As a result, I constantly struggled to figure out where I personally fit in at school and in life.

In stark contrast, at home, I had a unique upbringing. I was fervently taught that to be Black was not constrained by insensitive stereotypes, expectations, or biases. My mother, a hardworking school teacher with a love of R&B singer Teena Marie, engaging biographies, and a ravenous love of learning, taught me that Blackness was inquisition, strength, and mental fortitude. My father, who introduced me to the soulful music of Eric Clapton, ignited my love for science fiction, and still shows love for his family through cuisine, taught me that Blackness was patience, laughter, and kindness. In a lot of ways my parents did not, at least explicitly, subscribe to strict gender roles or expectations. They simply were; living as their true selves with little thought to how they *seemed* to be. It is this overall message that led me to challenge gender stereotypes in my young life.

While my parents were progressive in many ways, they were not perfect, nor could they have been. Whenever discussing this topic, I am transported to a rainy day in middle school, when adolescent angst, confusion about identity, and a need for social belonging filled me. Not unlike any normal school day, I had just finished my hour-and-a-half-long bus ride through the rural county I then called home—my ears still ringing from the cutting guitar riffs of American emo bands: The Used, My Chemical Romance, and Taking Back Sunday. As I walked into my house, desperate for the sanctuary of my room, I was stopped by my parents. "Do you have nail polish on?" they jovially remarked. I remained silent. They asked again, "Do you have nail polish on?" this time with disbelief in their voices, to which I mousily muttered, "Yes."

Shame and a sense of otherness instantly overcame me. I *knew* that boys didn't paint their nails unless they were looking for a beating. I could recall all of the names *they* were called, "gay," "un-godly," "queer," or those who had "too much sugar in their tanks." I wasn't one of them. I couldn't be. I like *girls*.

My parents sat me down, and began an onslaught of endless questions that are familiar and commonly received by many people who skew the lines of gender: "Are you gay?" "Do you think a woman will love you if you paint your nails?" "You don't want to be a girl, do you?" While my parents' questions were very understandable and came from a place of concern, they have forever followed me into my adulthood. However, as is the case for many who wrestle with their identities, I pushed these ideas out of my head, waiting for a time when they could more fully be explored.

In the subsequent years, I worked very hard, which allowed me to take my pick of colleges. Instead of shooting for the stars, as many often urge young students to do, I decided to attend a university a mere 45 minutes from my home town. In hindsight, the reason for this was simple: the school was a safe choice, and I knew that the support of my family would shield me against any personal challenges I might face.

After taking several courses as a freshman, I fell in love with psychology. Discussions of intergroup relations, schemas, and implicit biases were all fascinating and gave me a glimpse into *why* negative attitudes toward marginalized groups were so pervasive. It wasn't long before I decided to pursue a degree in psychology and began to solidify my dream of becoming a university researcher.

During the same time, I discovered a passion for sexual violence advocacy. I soon became president of two anti-violence clubs, developed a love of discussing ways to combat rape culture, and began to challenge the learned violence I had been taught throughout my life. In this personal reflection of who I was and what messages I espoused to the world, I began the process of questioning many parts of myself.

For the first time in my life, I was surrounded by a diverse array of new and exciting people—the most influential being a community advocate I met some years ago. I vividly remember meeting her in passing at a local advocacy event: a tall, statuesque Black woman in her early thirties, who exuded both grace and power in her movements, speech, and being. Her elegant, yet casual floral dress flowed, despite a lack of any wind. From afar, she seemed to be the kind of person who could command a room, while up close she warmly greeted me with a smile and genuinely asked, "How are you doing?" Her personality, blackness, and transness culminated in the existence of a type of beauty that one encounters rarely in life.

Upon the fading of my disbelief, I asked myself, "Why can't I look like her?," a thought I quickly discarded as comical, unacceptable, and ludicrous. "I am a Black *man*. I am supposed to like sports, fixing cars, action movies, and woodworking. Femininity, for me, is nothing more than a death sentence." I forced the idea of wanting to be feminine out my head as best I could.

As school progressed, I continued to suppress these thoughts, afraid that any disruption in my personal life would hinder my career goals. After four years of working with survivors of sexual and intimate partner violence, being invited to the White House in 2014 to discuss these issues with the then Vice President Joe Biden, and working with a number of local and state organizations on violence prevention efforts, I was given an opportunity to serve as a community-based sexual assault advocate full time. While there, I relished in the experience to provide legal, interpersonal, and systems support to survivors of sexual violence. This hands-on experience helped me see the negative health consequences of biases on sexual assault survivors and helped me solidify my belief that in order to effectively address complicated issues, such as biases and social injustice, interventions must be informed by research. Despite a love for my work, I struggled as the only Black advocate at an organization that mainly served Black people. As a result, I decided to pursue graduate-level study, in the hope that I would be able to make more lasting change for those like me.

For my doctoral training, I decided to return to my undergraduate university, in order to continue my study of stereotyping, implicit biases, and attitudes. I had a successful first year: I gave a research talk to my department, proposed my Master's thesis, completed a great deal of my coursework with little difficulty, and presented at a national conference. Whilst demanding of my time, graduate school turned out to be engaging, manageable, and rewarding.

My second year was not so easy. While many students focused on their first major contributions to their disciplines, I was suffering from a number of program-related challenges, the inherent racism in academia, a long-term, quickly dying romantic relationship, and a chasm-sized emptiness that no amount of academic publications could ever fill. In short, I was lost. A type of lost that this naturally pessimistic, often depressed, then 24-year-old had never experienced.

In the Christianity-rich region of the American South, many older Black people speak of so-called "come to Jesus moments." These can be defined as grand epiphanies that influence one's life to accept Jesus as lord and savior. I am not at all religious, but it is this colloquialism that I feel best describes the magnitude of the realization I had after the academic and personal challenges I faced in my second year. I realized that I needed to make a change, but more importantly, I needed to stop suppressing the person I had always been: a strong, inherently loving, extremely pro-Black, non-binary individual.

At 24, I began the continual process of coming out, not because I wanted to, but because if I did not, I knew that I would be living a lie. I changed my pronouns in my academic email signature, explained changes that may occur to my long-time friends, and shed the people that were holding me back from myself. In doing so, I learned that being non-binary, at least to me, meant being neither male nor female, but inhabiting the space of both. It meant not being constrained by expectations of gender and/or race, since Black and Brown bodies are inherently gendered. It meant accepting and loving myself for who I truly am and, unbeknownst to my parents, the way I was raised. While I am not currently out to them, I will one day explain that they raised me so skillfully that I have been able to nurture and explore this part of my identity. I will be able to thank them for teaching me how to be the *person* I have become. I will be able to tell them, with great certainty, I am okay. I am genuinely happy, and it is all because of them.

While I am, for the first time, comfortable in my own body, my life is not without challenges. To be both Black and non-binary in academia is a double-edged sword. I often cannot tell at which identity my classmates' and colleagues' disapproving glances are directed. I fear the consequences my identities may have on my future career. It is no secret that faculty members of color are few, but queer faculty members of color are even rarer. More importantly, I fear for my life if I were to wear a skirt, lavender nail polish, or even a light-colored shirt in public. The reality is that many Black femmes die every day, with little news coverage. The truth is, too many Black people die every day for no more than standing outside their homes, walking down the street, or living. When you are Black in America, you must carefully plan your leisurely walks in predominately White neighborhoods, overly enunciate your words when speaking with law enforcement, and constantly justify your right to live to a country that was built on the back of the enslavement of Black and Brown bodies.

Those like me do not have the luxury of *simply living*. We are forced to conform and crumple under the weight of transphobia, homophobia, and racism. We cannot *be*. We form ourselves into something palatable for academic, White, cis-heteronormative consumption in fear of being labeled "too Black," "too queer," or "a problem." Even in some social justice activism spaces, non-binary people are viewed as illegitimate, those who cannot make up their minds about their gender(s), and a product of confusion. In college-adjacent queer spaces, non-binary identities are legitimate, but often only if they are attached to non-Black, non-Brown bodies. Many have sneered that I am the only non-binary Black person they have ever met, as if my identity is not valid. Further, to many Black people, non-binary identities represent Whiteness, are synonymous with homosexuality, and simply are not " natural." Despite disapproval from the communities I hold so dear, I know I am not alone.

For that reason, when my friend plainly stated, "Calvin, you are a unicorn," I asserted, "I am not the only one." There are many femme-leaning Black enbies in the world who would rather wear Sally Hansen's "Punk-ish Purple" nail polish than a tie. There are too many queer academics, striving to change the world through their groundbreaking research. There are so many bluegrass-loving geeks who are looking for a place to belong in the world. There are far too many people like me to mean my efforts toward changing the status quo will stop. I fight through my academic work and activism because my people are valid, strong, and we aren't going anywhere.

BIOGRAPHY

Calvin Hall, MS, (they/them) is a fourth-year graduate student in Health Psychology at Virginia Commonwealth University (VCU) and a passionate social activist. They will receive their doctorate in 2021. As a scholar, Hall examines the effects of social biases on decision-making processes and their effects on health, with a focus on queer individuals of color. As an activist, Hall has eight years of experience working with survivors and advocates of sexual and intimate partners on a local, state, and national level. They currently act as a trainer, organizer, and volunteer at multiple community organizations.

Email: hallcj4@vcu.edu

Chapter 13

Out in the Establishment

The Gender Journey of an Outside Insider

Edward Lord, OBE, JP

INTRODUCTION

I have never felt totally comfortable in the spaces or boxes into which being assigned male at birth (AMAB) automatically put me. I pretty much always knew I was queer, but didn't find any particular connection with gay men. I went to an all boys' school, but didn't really fit in. I look very masculine but don't feel it. I shudder at the inevitable association that my physical embodiment creates with toxic masculinity. People see me and make assumptions about the person that I am. That is made more complex by being what I often refer to as an 'outside insider', a queer radical who lives their life at the very heart of the British establishment with all the inevitable privilege that comes with it. I bet there are very few non-binary people who have found themselves over the years deep inside two of Britain's main political parties, the Freemasons, the Judiciary, the City of London, faith communities, London private members clubs, major charities, the board of a FTSE listed plc, and some of the UK's top sporting bodies. This is my story.

SCHOOLING IN MASCULINITY

My old school sits in the heart of a rather dreary Lancashire industrial town ten miles north of Manchester. It was the centre of my world for 14 years, from arriving in kindergarten aged 4 to being spat out aged 18. Like so many of those types of independent grammar schools, it was intensely gendered. From the age of 7 upwards, I was part of the boys' school, separated by a street (which might as well have been an ocean) from the girls who had been my kindergarten classmates. I was taught by an almost exclusively male staff (the few women teachers were addressed as 'sir'!) in a very male-dominated environment where sport and the cadet force were the principal extra-curricular occupations. Those of us who were more attracted to drama, music, politics and debating were definitely in the minority.

It was in this environment that I discovered my sexuality, or certainly that aspect of it that was attracted to masculinity. It was also clear that this attraction was to softer masculinity, whilst at the same time feeling alienated by the robust laddish nature of the more mainstream cohort in the school. Reflecting back on it now, I was hugely put off by the primal instincts of the other boys, often egged on by the schoolmasters – the need to win, to be the best, to be strong, to not show emotion, to never admit to being a victim. This was my initial exposure to what I now know of as toxic masculinity, and I didn't like it. But, counter to those schoolmasters' aspirations, their toxic masculinity never made a man of me; being able to be an authority figure with kindness gave birth to the person I am.

I found my sense of self by becoming a somewhat larger-than-life character at the centre of school activities: writing for the school magazine, taking leading roles in school plays, acting as scorer for the 1st XI cricket team, being the often knock-about star attraction in the debating society. During my final year at school, as a prefect, I set out to protect those boys who were picked on for being outside the mainstream: those of minority faiths and ethnicities, the players of chess or Dungeons and Dragons, and the boys who were probably queer even if they didn't know it yet. Life at school was tough, but it did help me to become the person I am today, engraining in me some of the values that have found a voice in more recent years. It was also the start of the journey that led me into public service, of which more later.

STUDENT LIFE AND THE GAY STRAIGHT-JACKET

Arriving at the University of Essex in October 1990 was liberation. Not only was it some considerable distance from home but it also enabled me to explore my self-assumed sexuality as a gay man. My only sexual experiences up until that point had been with other boys at school, and only then secretly in hidden corners of the campus. So, on my second night, I found myself at a Freshers' disco in the Union in the arms of a beautiful guy, the first time I had been able to kiss a man in public, and it was electric. Coming out as gay was liberation but it also became, ironically, a straight-jacket.

Being in a co-ed space for the first time also exposed me to the 'opposite' sex and that became a revelation. I was not only attracted to men. Indeed, thanks to the determined pursuit of a fellow student who re-took my virginity, I discovered that I also very much enjoyed exploring a woman's body. What was also clear, though, was that my taste was for those women who were less conventional, especially if presenting as more masculine of centre. Unfortunately, however, the political dynamic in queer communities at the time was very binary – you were gay, or you were straight. Bisexuality was not an option, nor were they particularly welcoming spaces to trans people, not that there was much trans visibility back in the early 1990s.

This became even more apparent when, on graduating in 1994, I was elected to the national executive of the National Union of Students (NUS) and attended my first LGB campaign conference. In fact, it was the first-ever LGB conference. Up until that point the NUS campaign had been steadfastly Lesbian & Gay, and it was clear that bi people remained unwelcome – there was vituperative talk of 'breeders' and the women's caucus had morphed into a lesbian-only space. Suffice it to say that any mention of trans people was greeted in an even more unfriendly manner. In such an environment it became clear that I should keep very quiet about my growing sense of attraction to some women and certainly never entertain any questioning of my gender identity.

PRIDE AND PREJUDICE

Life immediately after NUS remained focused on queer community. Early in 1996, I joined the board of the Pride Trust, the then organisers of the London Pride march and festival, which had just become LGBT Pride rather than Lesbian & Gay. The change of name was, however, superficial, and hostility remained towards both bi and trans people – Pride's women's advisory group, for instance, resolved that trans women were not welcome in the women's tent at the festival. And yet, despite their refusal to include both bi and trans folk, it was some of these lesbians that I found myself drawn to emotionally and physically.

The soft masculinity and humanity of many butch lesbians drew me in at the same time as I felt increasingly distant from gay male culture. I think a substantial part of this attraction came from the more collaborative and collective behaviours and politics of many lesbians, which contrasted harshly with the individualistic and rather self-centred and self-absorbed nature of quite a lot of gay men, as well as the misogyny which so many gay men did (and still do) exhibit. I remember an article in the *Pink Paper* by a lesbian activist expressing anger at the absence of reciprocity from gay men to back issues facing lesbians despite all the efforts that lesbians had put into, for example, the campaign to support those living with HIV/AIDS and the fight to equalise the age of consent for men who have sex with men. That truth really hit me, and made me feel desperately awkward about being, because of my body, identified with such a selfish gay male world. I so deeply wished that I hadn't been born male.

A very personal experience of the difference between gay male and lesbian realities came when I was dumped by my then boyfriend in the centre of Soho late in 1996, leaving me heartbroken and frightened. Not one of my gay male friends was available or seemingly interested in being there for me in my moment of need. But one of my closest lesbian friends, Rachel, and her partner, Jo, dropped everything to take care of me that night. I felt so incredibly lucky to have such supportive people in my life. Rachel and Jo remain two of my closest friends to this day.

THE GENDER QUESTION AND COMING OUT AS BI

My experience of the disparity in approach between queers of different genders was so stark, it made me begin to question whether I was being constrained by the physical body I inhabited. I certainly felt much more like the lesbians I was close to than many of the gay men I knew. And that was often remarked on by friends, who said that I seemed like a fellow lesbian trapped in a gay man's body. Well perhaps I was? I started to wonder whether my attraction to a butch aesthetic was actually more that I might be one of them rather than simply wanting to 'be with' them. Certainly, in my mind's eye, I allowed myself to fantasise about being a soft butch with short floppy hair who was loved and protected by stronger masculine-presenting women. My female persona even had a name: Alex.

At the time, though, in the mid-to-late nineties, there was very limited information or support for people who were contemplating their gender, and the possibility of someone male assigned at birth transitioning to be anything other than a hyper-feminised woman was impossible under the strictures of the UK Gender Identity Clinics at the time. In any case, I don't think I was anywhere near wanting to take such life-changing steps, especially given the very clear negativity that I had already experienced in lesbian and gay circles about trans women. The idea of transitioning only to be rejected by those I wanted to feel loved by remains too horrible to contemplate.

What also made it difficult was that my career was starting to move forward, and whilst being out as a gay man was just about acceptable, announcing to the world that I was bi, or that I had some 'wacky' idea about my gender, was really not going to cut it, either at work or with my lesbian and gay friends. Indeed, I did not come out as bi until I was in my early thirties, after I fell in love with my first girlfriend, herself someone who, as a Stonewall staffer, had adopted a lesbian identity due to the hostility towards bi people in that workplace. That was not easy, and indeed some of my friends, both lesbian and gay, rejected my new bi identity, with one in particular cutting me out of their life.

OUT IN THE ESTABLISHMENT

As my career developed, and I became more engaged with various aspects of the British establishment, it became harder to confront what remained an ongoing question in my own mind about my gender. More and more I was antagonised by toxic masculinity – both gay and straight – in the worlds of work and my voluntary and community activity, but more and more I felt like I didn't know how to respond.

In 2001, I was elected as a Common Councilman of the City of London, an ancient and highly gendered title which is essentially a local councillor. The toxicity of the place was palpable. At 29 I was the youngest elected member of the Council and I was clearly unwelcome. The average age of my colleagues was over 70, and the vast majority were male and often boarding school-educated. Privilege was everywhere, as was prejudice. Jokes about 'queers', 'blacks' and women were still the order of the day for some councillors. Bigotry was built into the culture of the place, with members being instructed that they must only bring guests of the 'opposite sex' to Council functions. The arrival of a young outwardly gay man with progressive ideas was a red rag to a very large bull.

Over the 18 years that I have served as a City councillor, the officially sanctioned prejudice has decreased and many younger City councillors have been elected, advocating for change and determined to see it happen. I am now quietly hopeful, but recognise that some of the behaviours remain toxic; an undercurrent of bullying and backhanded comments still exists, which when challenged often attracts a 'man-up' style response, such that it took me until the middle of 2018 to begin coming out about being non-binary.

But change is slow. Only recently, I was told by a senior colleague that I displayed too much emotion and shouldn't take things so personally. Another man also 'advised' me to drop any public reference to being non-binary and that he certainly wouldn't refer to me using 'they' pronouns.

Despite this, there has been progress both personally and institutionally. For example, in 2017 we finally succeeded in getting the rainbow flag hoisted at Guildhall for Pride week. As of 2018, I chair the workforce committee and lead on diversity and inclusion, including heading up a policy review on gender identity and trans inclusion, although that led me to be publicly outed as non-binary in the *Sunday Times*.

Elsewhere in my career, I have been at the forefront of tackling discrimination. Perhaps most visibly was in 2014 as a member of the Football Association's (FA) inclusion advisory board, where I was the only member willing to speak out publicly when football's most powerful administrator was caught sending incredibly sexist emails to colleagues. It seemed remarkable to me that the FA refused to take action against a man so clearly in breach of the game's anti-discrimination rules, dismissing it as either 'a personal matter' or 'just banter'. Of course, in the culture of football, had the email content been racist, he would have been out of his job the next day, but somehow sexism was acceptable. This was toxic masculinity at its worst, and I challenged it, and in return I was sacked, for speaking truth to power. Whilst football may not have liked what I said, a letter published in the *Daily Telegraph* supporting my stance was signed by 28 leading equality campaigners, politicians and sport officials.

Perhaps the oddest aspect of my activism has been in Freemasonry. The obvious question is why would someone as passionate as me about diversity become a Freemason? Well, the answer is because I made a promise to my dying step-grandfather. But then why stick with an organisation which is so institutionally sexist? First, I think that, despite its sexism, it actually does some good. The values espoused by Freemasonry chime with my own: integrity, kindness, honesty and fairness. Equally, the Masonic obligation to charity through education, healthcare and care for older people mirrors my own commitment to public service. Also, other than gender, its membership is actually remarkably diverse – certainly based on race, religion, sexual orientation, disability and even class – regularly bringing together people from differing backgrounds who might otherwise never meet.

That said, it is an institution which clearly needs to change, and I have tried to use my position as a high-profile member to encourage that change from the inside. In my valedictory address on standing down as chair of one of Freemasonry's national committees in 2017, I demanded wholesale cultural change. I said that the male Grand Lodge of England should formally acknowledge that many thousands of women are Freemasons and recognise the lodges they belong to. I called for a change in male Freemasonry's misogynistic language and anachronistic approach to gender roles in society. I said that the overly hierarchical structure that can lead to bullying must end and that Freemasonry should more openly acknowledge that it has many members who are gay and bisexual. It has taken a while since that speech, but some of those changes are now happening.

FINDING MYSELF

After so many years of fighting the inner demons of toxic masculinity and campaigning to change the culture in several major institutions, it has only been in the last few years that I have really begun to readdress the issue of my gender. And that was significantly influenced by being with my partner as I supported them through their own gender journey. Had I not been with MJ, learning alongside them, the concept of being non-binary may not have felt like an identity that I could adopt, and I am enormously grateful to them for being my guide and my mentor, and for the love we have shared.

Even with that support, I still fear that my presentation is too masculine, not queer enough, not genderqueer enough to be accepted and 'pass' as non-binary. By way of example, at a recent Stonewall conference session on non-binary gender, the highly feminised appearance of the two AMAB enby presenters made me feel particularly dysphoric.

I have to keep on reminding myself that my gender is what is in my head and not measured by the way I (or others) appear. Despite still feeling very much like the soft butch of my earlier dreams, I no longer want to change my body. In fact, since growing a beard and accepting my presentation as a big queer bear, I have been a lot happier with the body I inhabit, and grateful that it is often recognised as genderqueer. Indeed, what has also been wonderfully affirming is the number of close trans and non-binary friends who proactively say that they 'see me', with one saying that he knew from the moment that we met that I wasn't a cis guy but rather a fellow trans person, another who calls me their butch, and another their dykey-bear.

Nonetheless, the intellectual concept of my gender remains a challenge, not least because I know that to most people I do still appear as a man. And I recognise fully that I have grown up with and still receive male privilege, which I try to check constantly. I'm also very aware that it is substantially because of this male appearance, and the male privilege that comes with it, that I was granted access to the establishment which has allowed me to be the diversity advocate that I am.

But, at heart, I know that I am neither exclusively male nor female, but somewhere in-between; a soft butch, presenting as a queer bear. Hopefully, eventually, the rest of the world may one day recognise that – even in the establishment.

BIOGRAPHY

Ed Lord (they/them) has been at the heart of LGBT communities for many years and is a trustee of LGBT Foundation and the Bishopsgate Institute, and a Stonewall role model. They are a senior elected member of the City of London Corporation, currently chairing the workforce and inclusion committee; as well as being a Justice of the Peace in central London, a trustee of Trust for London and City Bridge Trust, and a director of the British Basketball League and Middlesex County Cricket Club. Ed received a UK national honour in 2011 when they were appointed as an OBE for their public service in promoting equality and social inclusion.

Twitter: @edwardlord

Chapter 14

All Gender's a Stage

Eli Effinger-Weintraub

UNIT LLT: *I do not possess primary or secondary sex characteristics. I am 'the woman' only because the Primary User assigned me a traditionally female name and gave me these clothes. I am no more 'woman' than you are.*

SARAH: *I'm a woman because that's how I was born. I do possess female primary and secondary sex characteristics.*

UNIT LLT: *You possess primary and secondary sex characteristics. Someone told you they are female. Then someone told you that these characteristics required you to adhere to particular standards of behaviour. My data indicates no biological basis for these divisions. They are arbitrarily created by society, and differ among cultures. If a society can create them, could it not also destroy them?*

Unit LLT, by Eli Effinger-Weintraub

A lot of artists create art that grapples with questions and issues at the center of their lives at the time of creation, which makes sense. I've never liked my life to make sense, I guess, so I work backward: my art is often the first signal flare from my deep self that my subconscious is wrestling with something that will become conscious in the not-distant future—usually within 3 to 12 months.

At the age of 37, I wrote *Unit LLT*. It's a one-act play about a late-19th-century robot who, despite having no intrinsic gender, is assigned a female name and clothes and then has to navigate the restrictions society places on those it perceives as female. So, I shouldn't have been surprised when, four months later I came to understand myself as agender. It still managed to catch me out.

But while this new understanding radically altered my sense of self, little of my outward life changed. I started using 'they/them' pronouns in certain trusted circles and checking different gender boxes on surveys. And that was pretty much it. I didn't even change my wardrobe (I have a whole rant about clothes and the presentation of non-binary gender, but that's not the chapter I promised the editors of this collection). I foolishly (and a bit smugly) allowed myself to believe that my new understanding of my gender would change little about my external life.

Then the organizer of my playwrights' group posted a link to the group list, with the header "Submission opportunity for women playwrights!"— one of a dozen similar links that folks have posted to the list over the years. Excited, I moved to click on the link.

And then I froze.

Each year, the Lilly Awards are awarded to honor significant contributions by women in American theater, both individually and organizationally. In 2015, the Lilly Awards issued the first report on The Count, an analysis of theater productions in the USA, broken down by gender. The numbers in that report were staggering. Nationwide, only *22 percent* of plays produced were written by women. Broken down, the statistics paint an even grimmer picture: 14 percent by white American women; a heartbreaking 3.4 percent by American women of color; the remaining 4 percent by women playwrights from outside the USA (see http://thelillyawards.org/initiatives/the-count for more information on The Count).

These numbers are awful, and they *have been* awful for decades, for centuries, and they don't seem to be improving with any speed. Many women theater professionals try to balance that disparity by creating women-centred and women-only spaces: play festivals, script collaborations, and theater companies dedicated to centering women as playwrights, directors, performers, designers, and technicians.

This has *not* happened (as I have heard certain cis male playwrights oh-so-condescendingly claim) because women "can't compete" with men. It has happened because the mainstream theater establishment in the USA has shown time and again that it doesn't value women's stories and talents (as it also doesn't value the stories and talents of people of color and indigenous folks, queer folks, people with disabilities and neurodiversity… You get my drift). It has happened because, given the choice between constantly battering at the gate of mainstream theater to demand the crumbs it offers or creating a banquet for themselves and their kin, many women, unsurprisingly, choose the banquet.

A lot of resources available for folks newly coming out as non-binary—at least that I've found—are geared toward people in their teens and early 20s. And that's *great*; those folks frequently need more support and resources than us older folks. But it does mean that those of us who are shifting our gender journey later in life can't always find resources relevant to our situations. How do we navigate our changing terrain if we already have partners, and/or kids, and/or careers? Or, when we've made something of a name for ourselves in realms specifically associated with a gender that we no longer perceive ourselves as being part of?

I'm a three-time participant and one-time semi-finalist in Little Black Dress, Ink's Female Playwrights Onstage festival. I've written for the 24:00:00 XTREME THEATRE SMACKDOWN, an annual 24-hour theater event for local feminist theater company Theatre Unbound (TU), a staggering 12 times, and collaborated on TU's 2015 production *Title IX*, about women's sports in the USA. I've submitted to, and been accepted for, multiple women's theater festivals around the USA—and submitted to, and been rejected by, many others. I'm no Christina Ham or Sarah Ruhl, but if you've spent enough time around the women's theater community in the USA, you may have come across my name.

Like most playwrights, I *love* seeing my work produced onstage. But it's equally important to me that the theaters I submit my work to stand for something I agree with. That's been more likely to happen with women's theater companies, dedicated to presenting lesser-told stories, than it has with more "mainstream" companies, dedicated to working their way through the safe Western dramatic canon of plays by dead cishet white dudes (and a few closeted gay ones), thinking that "being modern" equals putting on a few plays by *living* cishet white dudes. In a way, submitting to women's theater companies has been as much a political act as an artistic one. (Obviously, my gold standard is submitting to LGBTQ+ theater companies, but those are surprisingly small in number.)

Then, too, there's the community aspect. Many of us who participate in the TU Smackdown have been working together for *years*. I've formed so many friendships, both in-person and online, with the playwrights, performers, directors, and technicians I've met through women's theater. We've built community out of our shared commitment to bringing women's stories to the stage.

But suddenly there I was, finger hovering over the mouse button, wondering if I was part of that community anymore. It *hurt*: the thought that, by being honest about my gender, I may have banished myself from a community that's become very important to me.

I had the brief, terrible thought that if only I hadn't come out, I could keep being part of that community and no one would have to know. But even as I was thinking it, I knew it wasn't true. I'm not out at work, and I chafe at people there calling me "Miss" and "she," at someone saying, "Hey, ladies!" to a group of co-workers that includes me. Even if no one else were to know that I'm agender, *I* know, and I couldn't have gone long without starting to feel like I was cheating. While there are definitely still situations where I need to be closeted about my gender, I never want to feel like a sneak in communities I respect.

In preparation for writing this chapter, I emailed folks from several women's theater companies I've been involved with, or at least submitted to. This wasn't a journalistic or academic inquiry by any means; just a small group of questions to gauge what a small group of women theater-makers feel about the situation. All the soul-searching in the world does me no good, after all, if women's theater companies and festivals won't *accept* submissions from non-binary playwrights.

It wasn't a lengthy survey, just four questions. I invited the respondents to answer as many or as few as they chose:

- Have you ever produced a work of any length by a non-binary playwright?

- Do you accept submissions from non-binary AFAB [assigned female at birth] playwrights?

- Do you feel that non-binary AFAB playwrights have a place in women's theater?

- Anything else you'd like to say about the topic?

If I had it to do over, I might leave out the "AFAB" modifier, to gauge the companies' attitudes towards non-binary people as a whole. For now, baby steps.

I sent the email in early April 2018, and within two weeks, I had five replies in my inbox. And there they sat, unread, for almost a month, because I couldn't bring myself to read them. What would they contain? A harsh rejection of non-binary playwrights in women's theater? That would hurt almost unbearably. A more open approach, leaving it to the individual artist's discretion as to whether they feel they "belong" in the community? That would turn it back on me, forcing me to be a damned grown-up and know my own heart and mind.

I hate being a damned grown-up.

Finally, in the last week of May, with the deadline for this chapter winging toward me at an alarming speed, I took a deep breath, cuddled my cat closer than she would've preferred, and read the emails.

I'm relieved to report that the women who sent responses seemed as confused as I am. Replies ranged from "we've never worked with non-binary playwrights, and we don't have a policy on this," full stop, to "we don't know if we've ever worked with a non-binary playwright, and we don't have a policy on this, and maybe we should," to my personal favorite: "I started the company because I saw female-identifying artists being excluded based on their gender, so as my understanding of gender evolves, it makes sense that we would expand our mission to include anyone marginalized due to their gender. To that end, I am trying to find a way to express that that doesn't just say 'everyone but cis-gendered [sic] men.'"

Where does all of that leave me? Gentle reader, *damned if I know*. The thought of leaving the women's theater communities I'm already part of makes me want to cry. But at the same time, the thought of submitting to *new* women's theater opportunities makes me feel disingenuous and, well…*twitchy*, especially if I don't know where the producing company stands on inclusion of gender-expansive folks. Can I examine each new opportunity as it arises and "grandparent" myself, so to speak, into continuing to contribute to the ones I've always been part of? Do I need to contact every theater company that puts out calls for "submissions by women" to determine its stance on AFAB non-binary playwrights? Or is the onus on them to determine where they stand as a company and to make that clear to would-be submitters? Or is it, perhaps, time for me to step away from the shore of women's theater and see what's out there in the rest of the ocean? (And why do I have to be agender *and* have anxiety, which leads me to obsess over this question far more than can *possibly* be healthy?)

When I submitted the abstract for this chapter, I warned the editors that it would be more questions than answers. While non-binary folks have existed for longer than human society has been trying to shove people into binary genders, public awareness of us as anything but "really rare, really weird, and somewhere else" is growing slowly. Those of us— people and institutions alike—who were particularly connected to the binary gender model in some, or many, ways now find ourselves in the exciting (*and completely terrifying*) position of rethinking, oh, basically everything we thought we were. Not knowing where we're going, or even having a map for how to get there, can be so nerve-wracking.

But the whole reason people built "women's theater" in the first place is that men built this institution they called "theater" and built a moat around it to keep out women (and people of color, queer folks, people with disabilities, etc.). It seems right that, as women's theater moves forward into the relatively uncharted waters of non-binary inclusion, we do so together, with *everyone* in the boat. Even if no one knows which way we're rowing and the danged robot's run off with the life-jackets.

BIOGRAPHY

Eli Effinger-Weintraub (they/them) is a playwright and prosaist living in the Upper Mississippi River Valley region of the USA. Their stage work has been presented by Gadfly Theatre Productions, Theatre Unbound, Little Lifeboats Theatre, Little Black Dress, Ink, and others. They are an agender anxieteur, an Earth-focused witch in the Reclaiming Tradition, and a promoter of honest conversations about end-of-life decisions, especially in minoritized communities. Eli lives with their spouse, visual artist Leora Effinger-Weintraub, and two water buffalo disguised as cats.

Twitter: @tangleroot_eli

Website: https://tanglerooteli.wordpress.com

Chapter 15

From Gender Essentialist to Genderqueer

Al Head

I was a second wave feminist. In many ways I still am. I'm also a part of the third wave: I have always maintained that everyone has the right to be their own kind of feminist and I understand and support intersectionality. My daughter tells me that fourth wave feminism is 'third wave feminism with social media', and so I am part of that too. But in many ways our beliefs are rooted in our first 'awakening', and my feminism is rooted in the second wave.

I was born in 1961. My upbringing was full of awareness of anti-racism and alternative education, but feminism took longer to reach me. I first became aware of it in the mid-to-late 1970s, first in the form of Feminist Theology and then at college and university, where I gradually discovered more about sexism and the patriarchy. Apart from a few loved, but not consciously understood icons, such as David Bowie, I had no role-models of gender fluidity, or awareness that anything apart from the binary gender structure could, or did, exist.

Looking back, I think I, and maybe Western society as a whole, couldn't get to a point of understanding gender diversity until we had taken enough steps along the path of undermining the gender roles that were so rigidly around us: roles that told us what to wear, how to behave, what we were allowed to study in school, what jobs we were allowed to do, what relationships we were allowed to have, and much more. The culture for young people in the UK is different now, with many of these conventions broken, and with so many possibilities of gender and sexuality to find a place in. Queer community, now, is a place of freedom for many, and seeks to be open to everyone who wants it: but the only use of 'queer' when I was growing up was as an insult for gay men. Sexuality-wise we had only 'lesbian and gay' until the 1980s, when 'bisexual' was added, in certain places and amidst much controversy, to the mix. Nowadays the term 'bisexual' seems all too binary to many of us: but in those days it was the cutting edge of sexual, and to a smaller extent gender, fluidity. The early 'bi movement' was itself heavily influenced by feminism; and it was a key part of my own, and others', journey of awareness.

As a child I thought that 'boys had all the fun'. I had short hair, wore shorts, climbed trees and was happy when I was mistaken for a boy. Feminism taught me that girls can do anything that boys can do, and for a while I thought that that was the answer to my gender diversity. It took me many years to realise that the answer was more complex than this; and my journey took me along many different paths, of which claiming the power of being 'woman' was one of the most important. This may seem an anomaly to some, but it does make a certain sense. Finding the strength in being a 'woman' saved my life, and that of many others. Feminism taught me to question, and to work to change, my early gender conditioning. My awareness was opened to the daily sexism that I had been experiencing and I realised that my feelings of being a victim, of being weak, of being second-rate, were not my fault. My first copy of *The Women's Room* by Marilyn French had 'this book changes lives' on the cover. And my life was being changed!

Feminism was about breaking down the patriarchy, in the system and in our individual lives. Our cry was 'the personal is political' and our practice was 'consciousness-raising', a collective way of working that has influenced alternative movements ever since. Feminism helped us to reclaim our bodies, learning to celebrate them as beautiful and claim our autonomy over them: over our fertility, our sexuality, our health. Menstruation, for example, that we had been taught to think of as a 'curse' and to hide away, became a time for many of self-reflection, creativity and power.

My feminism came of age in the early 1980s at Greenham Common. Greenham Common was a women's peace camp, or rather a circle of interlinked peace camps, around the edges of a US nuclear missile base in the UK. It's hard for me to remember that I have to explain this, because at the time everybody knew what it was; whether because they were part of it, because they supported it, or because they denigrated and attacked it. Greenham Common politicised a whole generation of women. Even today I meet people and know that they are 'Greenham Women'; and in some ways, although I now have a different gender identity, I, too, will always be a Greenham Woman. I visited several times and took part in large-scale actions, such as 'Embrace the Base' when 30,000 women made a circle around the nine-mile perimeter fence.

The ethos of Greenham Common was feminism, anti-militarism and spirituality. The women there reclaimed the word 'witch', and combined a practical pagan magic with direct action. Being a woman was essential to the message: we felt that it was men who had got us into this mess and that it was women who would get us out of it. This was partly practical politics: the image of women standing up against the 'men's wars' and the 'boy's toys' was a strong one and drew many in, having a considerable influence in many parts of the world. Fighting for change together as an oppressed group also empowered many women and brought them into political and direct action for the first time.

But there was more to 'the women's peace movement' than this. The Greenham Common women, along with women from earth-centred religions in many other parts of the world, were building a new kind of spirituality that came to be known as the 'Goddess Movement'. The Goddess Movement was a feminist movement, in that it was reclaiming spirituality from the patriarchy: replacing God with Goddess and celebrating the potent, unique power of women. It popularised the growing research into pre-patriarchal societies, much of which had been suppressed or misinterpreted by male historians: evidence of a world where 'The Goddess' was worshipped and women were equal to men, if not actively in charge.

But this movement went further. Its spirituality was based on the identity, as well as on the bodies and minds, of women. It connected the land with the essence of womanhood, calling the earth 'our mother' and equating the rape of women with the rape of the earth. This gender essentialism was also inherent in the political and spiritual beliefs of much of the feminism of the time.

I think this is a big part of where the attitude of many feminists towards trans and other gender diverse people in the 1980s and 1990s came from. If we were reclaiming women's power, setting an 'us' up against the 'them' of the men who had so oppressed us, then how could we understand the concept that gender was not such an essential thing after all? If our female identities were part of a spiritual belief system, how could we embrace a world-view that saw those identities as permeable and liable to change? If women could be born in 'men's' bodies, or if men could 'become' women, what would that do to our sacred view of the feminine? If 'women' were 'becoming men', was it not because they had been so damaged by the patriarchy that they were denying the very femaleness that we were seeking to reclaim? And if binary gender did not, ultimately, exist, then how could we know who the women whose rights we were fighting for actually were?!

There was a book that was being passed around in the early 1990s in the circles I was in called *The Transsexual Empire* by Janice Raymond. I don't have it anymore, as I, and many others, later threw it out, so I can't quote from it. But I do remember it saying that the 'medical empire' of gender reassignment was a plot of the patriarchy, and that transwomen (though the book did not refer to them in this way) were 'invading women's spaces', as 'men' have always tried to do. Looking back, I wonder how many of us at the time were convinced by these arguments. Did we really think that 'men' would go that far to invade our spaces? Could we not see the incredible bravery it took for a transwoman to face the hostility of the 'born women' and enter 'our space'? At the time I, along with most of the women I socialised with, got everything we understood/knew about trans people and gender non-conformity from the papers or from our reading of feminist books. Maybe, given the climate at the time, it made sense to us that the patriarchy, which had invaded every other area of our lives, would take this ultimate step. Maybe we had felt the need to fight for our spaces so much that defending them had become a default position. Maybe we were so buoyed up with our new-found power that we were unable to think clearly. Or maybe we just took it with a massive pinch of salt!

Second wave feminism, as some of first wave feminism, did often take things to extremes. For example, there was the *SCUM Manifesto* (the Society for Cutting Up Men), and there was also the idea that men were in fact a mutation: that originally there had been only women, who reproduced only girl-children by parthenogenesis, and that eventually, if we refused to have anything to do with them, men would die out. I am not sure now how seriously this was either taken or meant. Some of it was deliberate provocation, but the sheer audacity of it held its own power. My view on it then, which I still to some extent believe, was that society had tipped so far in the direction of male power that it would take an equal pressure on the other side of the scales to start to redress the balance, and that these extreme ideas were a part of the tipping.

Separatism was an important tool of second wave feminism. Making women's spaces, women's communities, even women's lands, was central to the process of reclaiming power and moving towards a more equal society. In women's spaces we could breathe freely, away from the sexism that filled our lives. We could get away from the patterns of behaviour that men and women fall into when they are around each other. Today, most men still talk more than most women (or trans and genderqueer people) in mixed spaces. We didn't have the term 'mansplaining' then, but we definitely knew what it meant! We realised we were conditioned to boost men's confidence, to give way in opinion and will to men. Mixed groups easily fall into stereotypical, gender-based jobs and roles. All these were things we needed to get away from. We had to find ourselves and what was important to us so that we could stand up to men in the rest of the world. Some of us, including myself for about ten years, spent most or all of our time in women's spaces. Many of us 'gave up' sexual relationships with men because we felt that sexism could not be taken out of these relationships, however hard we all tried.

Women's spaces were integral to an era of identity politics: where people who had a common identity came together and gained strength from fighting their shared oppression. I think there is still a place for identity groups to meet separately, to build solidarity and hear others' voices reflecting their own reality. This process created Black Power, feminism and early Gay Liberation, and is now reflected in trans, genderqueer and non-binary spaces.

I, along with many other transmen, genderqueer, and non-binary people who earlier identified as women and/or lesbians, now have a complicated relationship to 'women's spaces'. Many of us, before we were able to follow our onward paths, found a home and a haven in women's spaces and often specifically in lesbian communities. Some of us still feel connected to these communities; but others do not, and the feelings of betrayal can go both ways: lesbians can feel that we have betrayed them by becoming 'the enemy' (and by making them, retrospectively, feel they have had sex with genders they didn't choose to) and we can feel that our communities have rejected us. For me, now identifying as genderqueer, it is perhaps even more disturbing to be told that I am still welcome, but in a way that seems to deny my current gender. There is still much confusion, and much communication is needed before we can all feel safe with each other again.

My own understanding of trans, non-binary and genderqueer identities didn't properly start until I discovered the word and the concept of Queer. Again, this was in a spiritual context, that of Queer Pagan Camp.

This was the first time I really got to know people who did not hold cis binary genders and I was challenged in my assumptions on many things, including the gendered nature of the land. This was the first time, since I was a child, that I started to question my own gender identity. I began to feel what I started to call 'gender-morphic', first in 'magical' space and then more generally. I grew over the next ten years or so to feel that my essence, along with the essence of energy itself, was at its roots non-gendered, and that all the infinite possibilities of gender were but different manifestations of that energy.

At Queer Pagan Camp I found people who were reclaiming the worship of queer, trans and gender-morphic deities. It was a process I recognised even if the details were new. In some ways it felt like a continuation for me of the process of rejecting the patriarchal religions that I had begun at Greenham Common. Once again, I was with people who allowed me to 'raise my consciousness' at my own pace, who did not tell me what I should think, and therefore let my thinking develop along its own lines. Eventually my journey led to my current identity of genderqueer. The communities I feel most comfortable in now are queer, genderfluid and non-binary, and many of my connections, friends, loves and lovers now are part of these communities, just as in the 1990s most of them were part of 'women's spaces'.

I still define myself as a feminist. As an old slogan says, 'I'll be a post-feminist in post-patriarchy', and we are still a long way from that! In the past I would have identified as a radical feminist, and for this reason, as for many others discussed here, I feel sad when I hear the term 'TERF' (Trans Exclusionary Radical Feminist), whichever 'side' is using it. I feel sad that we are in this place of having 'sides'. I feel sad as well as angry that some people, in the name of feminism, which is still so important to me, are excluding, denigrating and abusing trans people. I understand how painful it is to be excluded. And I know that in the past, consciously or unconsciously, I too have excluded trans people from events and spaces.

And I feel sad because some members of my trans/genderqueer/non-binary communities are, out of a completely understandable reaction to attack, now attacking 'feminists', my long-loved people. Sometimes it seems that the 'TERF' phenomenon can feel worse to us than the exclusion and abuse dealt out by the rest of patriarchal society. Perhaps it is understandable that we would feel more betrayed when we are excluded by feminists, either because we were a part of the women's movement and now feel excluded from it, or because we were excluded from the beginning.

But I also wonder if some of the attacks on feminists are part of the backlash that has been going on ever since there was a feminism to lash back against. And I wonder if the internalised oppression of those of us who identify, or who have identified in the past, as women leads us to attack other women more, or to expect more from them than we do from men?

I find myself repeating, over and over: not all feminists are 'TERFs' just as not all feminists are lesbians; not all lesbians are feminists; and not all feminists are women. There is a complex history here, and I have only been able to touch on a part of it.

I now believe that not only sexism but binary gender itself was created by the patriarchy and that breaking down the patriarchy will involve freeing us all from the constraints not only of gender conformity but also of binary gender. Some feminist discourses have developed from breaking down gender roles to seeing gender as performative, and the logical next step that is being taken by many feminists is the breaking down of the notion of gender itself. But not everyone has reached this place. Whilst I would never condone the attacks and the exclusion, I would like to make a distinction between those who are actively abusing others, and those who are tentatively, and often clumsily, trying to understand something that is a long way from their previous mind-set. Many people, to my great gratitude, were gentle with me when I was beginning to explore these issues, and this gentleness allowed me to find my own path. Sometimes the people who protest the most against a new way of thinking are the people who are close to the point of change. Recently I have heard some beautiful stories of dialogue between these different world-views, and I am hopeful that we can find spaces for more of these, and for continued learning and growing and changing, in spaces that are safe and respectful to all of us.

BIOGRAPHY

Al Head (que) is a Queer, genderqueer human. Que has had articles published in magazines such as *Beyond Sexuality* and *From the Flames* and in 2016 published que's first book, *Queer Deity, Sacred Slut*. Que is a performer and teacher in physical theatre, aerial theatre and Fooling, a musician and song-writer and a workshop leader in sacred sexuality. Que is an environmental, disability and LGBTQ activist and has been working to build community for LGBTQ people for over

30 years. Que is a parent and a grandparent, a pagan, and was born and lives in the UK.

Websites: www.alhead.co.uk, www.thequeerfool.co.uk and www.movingenergy.me.uk

Chapter 16

The Chicken Soup of Identity

*Talking from the Intersectional Prism of Judaism,
Gender, Sexuality, Health and Disability*

Chai-Yoel Korn

כל העולם כלו
גשר צר מאד
והעקר לא לפחד כלל

*The whole world
Is a very narrow bridge
and the main thing is to have no fear at all.*

'Ges her Tzar Me'od', Rabbi Nachman, Bratslav (1776–1810)

When I think about being genderqueer (non-binary), I think about the visible and the invisible intersectional prism this self-presentation takes. In this chapter, I will begin by looking at how my Jewish faith, genderqueer identity and sexuality intersect. I am a third-generation Holocaust survivor, so I have a good understanding of the impact of intergenerational trauma. My grandfather chose to keep to the Jewish tradition and faith, and so I also feel a responsibility to find spaces and ways where my Jewish faith, gender and sexuality can come together and be celebrated. I feel it is important to say that I am not an expert in my faith, and that there are also many parts of my identity that do and do not intersect. I will explore the parts of my identity that may not intersect, or only intersect in parts of the communities that I belong to. Through case examples, I will then lead the reader through the transcultural and LGBTQ+ affirmative psychotherapeutic work I do in my therapy room.

My grandfather (top left) and his family. This photo was taken just before his brother asked him for support with his tailor business in France. As the Nazis entered France, he and his brother jumped on a boat to the UK. They were the only two surviving family members. The rest were killed by Nazis in their hometown, Sambir, Poland (since the Second World War, Sambir has been located in Ukraine).

The Jewish Masorti community I choose to belong to is perceived as more liberal than that of my family. However, I always feel a sense of guilt when I hear about someone speaking negatively about trans or genderqueer people at my family's Shabbat table. I feel I have the responsibility of making them aware that their child, who is now an adult, is queer. I know that my family love me for who I am today and I feel that they deserve respect from their peers. I also know that the people at their community tables may not know someone from the LGBTQ+ community. Whilst they would not condone an anti-Semitic remark, they do condone LGBTQ+ phobia and discriminatory remarks. I know that my parents may not always challenge these comments, as they fear being the subject of gossip in their local Jewish community and possible rejection from it due to my being 'open and out there' about my own identity. I hope that their peers have more interesting things to gossip about.

Moreover, I have accepted that it should not be my parents' or family members' responsibility to speak up in their own community. Throughout my Jewish education, there was a belief that 'each Jew is responsible for every Jew'. The Rabbis taught us that our good deeds (in Hebrew, a Mitzvah) shape our relations with our fellow Jews and with humanity in general.

I grew up in a traditional United Synagogue, modern orthodox, within a very conservative Jewish community and family. I lived in the Jewish community and went to a Jewish school. I was unable to escape the bullies at school, as some of them attended the synagogue my family belonged to. At school, my sports teacher dealt with bullying by allowing me to get dressed in the accessible toilet. The bullying from the age of 8 to 16, along with the legal challenges such as Section 28 and the Age of Consent, prevented me from developing a strong and confident sense of gender or sexuality.

My favourite Hebrew song, 'Gesher Tzar Me'od' (quoted above), was released by the Israeli pop artist Ofra Haza on her album *Li-Yeladim (Songs for Children)* in 1982. The words are from a collection of thoughts originally written by Rabbi Nachman of Bratslav (1776–1810). A large part of my childhood was spent attending meetings of a Jewish youth movement where this song was one of many that we learnt and sang. Perhaps it was being 1980s pop music that queered it up or, in retrospect, perhaps the lyrics provided me with an important message about the homophobic bullying and anti-Semitism I experienced growing up. It was not until recently that I learnt that Ofra Haza died on February 23rd 2000, at the age of 42, of AIDS related pneumonia. While the fact that she was HIV positive is now generally known, the decision at the time by the Israeli newspaper Haaretz to report it shortly after her death was controversial in Israel. Just as me sharing my HIV status in this paper will be to my family and the Jewish community.

In 1994 aged 16, after finishing my GCSEs, like hundreds of my Jewish peers I went on a tour to experience Israel with the Association of Jewish Six Formers (AJ6). That was the first time I had met new friends away from school and my Jewish community. I remember fulfilling my younger dream of climbing Mount Masada in the early hours of the morning and getting to the top with the sun rising, looking out over the land and realising the bullying I had faced was over. AJ6 was one of the only Jewish youth organisations that I had contact with at 16 who were willing to have conversations about my faith, gender and sexuality. I did not come out to myself until I was 17 years old.

Within the Jewish communities, there are many ways of being Jewish, and within my family we represent the spectrum from atheist to ultra-orthodox. Hebrew and the Torah are binary in language, using male and female pronouns, and so this makes it a challenge to be genderqueer, as there is no language for us within the texts. Had we even had the genderqueer label back then, I wonder if my life would have taken a completely different path.

When I initially came out as gay, my mother was worried about my father finding out through seeing me at Pride on ITV news. Therefore, to make me less recognizable, she lent me her cocktail dress, and another good friend lent an Eliza Doolittle hat, and with these, I went on my first Pride with the Jewish Gay and Lesbian Group in London. To my mother's surprise, when my father discovered the truth, he went out of his way to find a synagogue that was inclusive of LGBTQ+ people. That synagogue, the Beit Klal Yisrael in West Kensington, remains to this day. He also found a grassroots group called Chofetz Chaim, a Jewish LGBTQ+ Friday Night dinner that received strong disapproval at the time from the *Jewish Chronicle*, which attempted to out those attending. Today the *Jewish Chronicle* is much fairer in how they report LGBTQ+ issues.

When choosing the synagogue I wanted to be a member of, my Rabbi's thoughts and understanding of gender and sexuality issues were important. I now identify as a Masorti Jew, a practice that adheres to the traditional synagogue service I am accustomed to. Masorti Rabbis continue to develop a more comprehensive understanding of gender and sexuality and attempt to move towards a culture of inclusivity and the creation of a safer space for LGBTQ+ Jews. I feel that one main issue still arises: whilst modern and more liberal Rabbis will take different understandings of the texts, we cannot change what was written thousands of years ago. We can, of course, look at the texts through the modern and queer eyes of today. But through some of my family's eyes and Orthodox Rabbis' eyes, the laws are written in black and white and are specific to a time and place in our culture. Traditional Rabbis may argue that these laws do not alter in respect to our modern and societal understanding of gender and sexuality. However, my Masorti synagogue would be more compassionate to our LGBTQ+ community. Long before this movement to create a more inclusive environment for the LGBTQ+ Jew, the Masorti movement was trying to re-address the role of women within the synagogue service. I am grateful that my Rabbi, Jeremy Gordon, has been supportive when my family has struggled with issues such as my new genderqueer identity, when I was going through Hepatitis C treatment four years ago, and when I struggled with being HIV positive.

When I was 21, I left the North London Jewish community, with the desire to live anywhere but in my own faith community. I no longer wanted to worry about being 'found out' and the possible repercussions for my family. I was also tired of needing to leave my gayness outside the front door. At one time, the LGBTQ+ community was hidden in the UK Jewish community; this has begun to shift in the last ten years. The seminal work of Peggy Sherwood (OBE) and the management team from the Jewish Lesbian and Gay Group laid the ground for new blood and energy to come and create change within the Jewish community.

Under Liberal Judaism, the creative and dedicated Shaan Knan founded and managed landmark oral history projects – from Rainbow Jews, Twilight People and Ritual Reconstructed to Rainbow Pilgrims. Ritual Reconstructed had a commited steering group which included Margaret Greenfields (Professor of Social Policy and Community Engagement and founder Director of the Institute for Diversity Research) and Searle Kochberg (filmmaker and lecturer); it was also wonderful to be involved with Tess Joseph, a close friend and ally. I became actively involved in these projects, which healed my internal wounds of sometimes needing to park my gender and sexuality outside my family home or synagogue door, so I can feel strength in knowing I belong in my own faith community.

My first partner died of AIDS. His mother was fiercely homophobic, and she never shared any photos of him with me so that I could remember him. Now, living with HIV, I want to be remembered for the work I have done to support change within the Jewish community and broader society. KeshetUK is an LGBTQ+ organisation, formed following a case in a Jewish school where a teacher showed a clip from Yonah, a Jewish Conversion Therapy Centre. The secondary school where this video clip was shown was the secondary school I attended; at the time of this happening I wrote to the head teacher about my experience of being bullied. The head did write back to me and assured me how the school has changed. The lack of insight around showing the Yonah video showed that they still had much more work to do. Keshet's hard work has created allies across the Jewish community, and in 2018 the Chief Rabbi published guidance for Jewish Orthodox schools on how to address LGBTQ+ issues within the curriculum.

Six years ago, I returned to North London whilst these organisations were developing projects looking at LGBTQ+ and faith. I realised I could not expect full acceptance from my family unless I lived in closer proximity to them. Today, the changes to my community, self and society enable me and my family to talk more about these issues. Only recently, my sister felt able to tell my nephews and my niece that I was gay. I know it will take my family longer to get used to my genderqueer identity. It is a new challenge for all of us. I feel that without the changes that have occurred within the community these conversations would not have happened within my own family.

I am fortunate that my parents are sensitive to all the family's individual and unique wants and needs. My siblings and I have very unique individual identities, we are fortunate that our parents have instilled within us the idea that we are all valued, this has shaped our world view to be inclusive and made us closer and to those around us. We enjoy coming together for Shabbat, festivals, holidays and family occasions. For many years I have had times where I have felt uncomfortable in my own skin. Today I identify as genderqueer, after 20 years of identifying as a gay man. Some gay men have responded to this by suggesting that I am giving up on my community or giving up the work I have done in the community. My response is that I no longer see gender or sexuality as a cycle, or linear or a spectrum. I believe we are born as a baby, develop into a child and we may develop a better understanding of our gender and sexuality as we age. When I came out aged 16, as a gay boy my sexuality was not legal (the age of consent in the UK at the time was 18 for gay men and 16 for heterosexual couples). I dived into a hedonistic gay scene that provided the validation I needed. If I had had access to labels like genderqueer back then, I wonder how different life would be today. I came out towards the end of the AIDS epidemic and lost many friends, including my first partner. I just tried to fuck and dance the pain away. There would have been no time to process how I was feeling in my body. It would not have felt right whilst those beautiful, creative minds were still dying around me. I was too busy saying goodbye to friends and lovers to think about myself.

Now, on the journey of recovery, I realise that I was using drugs to self-medicate how I felt in my body. Genderqueer was an epiphany; it gave me a new language to feel comfortable in my skin. Some friends have questioned my choice of re-coming out as genderqueer whilst I was in recovery. This demonstrated to me that there were unwritten rules of who I could be in those friendships and I am sure there may be more losses to come. I see that this will make more room for the right people to come into my life: someone who will be more embracing and accepting of who I am today, not who I became for them.

As a Jewish genderqueer person, some LGBTQ+ community members project their own experience of their faith background onto me, or immediately ask where I sit with Israeli politics, something that I am not prepared to discuss. I do not want to decide between supporting those I love in Israel and my LGBTQ+ community here. Just like some of the decisions the UK makes, I do not condone all of Israel's actions. Israel winning or hosting Eurovision in 2019, stars like Dana International, and the camp nature of Eurovision have supported my being able to integrate my faith, gender and sexuality. When situations happened in Israel, or when we voted out of Europe, people asked if I was going home. However, my family, on my maternal Grandma's side, have lived in the UK since the 1800s, so this is very much my home.

The invisible parts of my intersectionality are living with two disabilities: chronic pain and HIV. Fifteen years ago, when I learnt about my HIV diagnosis, I went to the then Jewish AIDS Trust. Similar to the experiences reported by Black, Asian and minority ethnic groups, it was hard to find confidential spaces to get help and support about living with HIV within the Jewish community, my ethnic group. I felt I could only talk about my HIV status outside of the Jewish LGBTQ+ community. The first counsellor I was offered was a sister of my parents' best friend; they not only shared the same faith as me, but I would say today I see their family as part of my extended family. I was able to gain the support I needed outside my own community, yet I felt I had to explain much to my therapist around what being Jewish meant, and this got in the way of my doing the work. Now, I have spoken in Jewish synagogues and schools about living with HIV and received a warm and non-judgemental response.

Some of my family still do not know I live with HIV and they may learn about it through reading my blogs or this chapter. I didn't want that part of my family to treat me differently. I made this decision with myself when at one family gathering a member of my distant family asked me if I wore gloves and a mask when doing my work with people living with HIV. I know that my immediate family will find it difficult that I am being so public as to write in this book about my living with HIV. My belief is that we can only change stigma and educate others by leading the conversation about HIV that still carries stigma. I never thought I would say that I am proud of being HIV positive, and 15 years on from my initial diagnosis it is amazing to see the medical advances being made with HIV. To know I am unlikely to die from HIV itself is life-changing. However, at difficult times I am only human and do worry about what the future holds.

I'm living with chronic pain and walking with a stick, yet people do not understand that my pain is not as simple as taking a tablet and the pain goes away. People do see the stick and treat me differently, and I have been rejected when dating because of the stick. In the workplace, organisations have found it hard to accommodate my physical support needs. I have taken this challenge personally when these organisations are supposed to be there to support those with health and wellbeing support needs. The Jewish community is still not brilliant in being fully inclusive around those living with a disability or learning support needs. Some of the community is still very focused on academically and professionally doing well and treat those that may not succeed differently.

After ten years of being a counsellor, and 20 years working and volunteering in the LGBTQ+ community, I was on placement with CliniQ, Facilitate Heart and Soul Therapy Group with them and now a Director on the Management Board. CliniQ is the only holistic sexual health and well-being service in the UK led and ran by trans and non-binary folk. CliniQ caters for the transgender and genderqueer community, as well as their friends and allies. Being in a trans and genderqueer affirmative space has been incredibly valuable and instrumental in my journey of my acceptance of who I am today.

I have always attracted clients where we have shared a similar narrative, or where there is what I call a 'meeting of minds' in the therapy room. Whilst I am careful with self-disclosure, I feel we are doing a disservice to our clients if we do not disclose aspects of ourselves that are relevant to clinical work. Also, there can be healing and good therapeutic work through our disclosures. I do this in a safe and measured way, with supportive supervision in place.

I will now outline some questions that I have reflected upon, when thinking about the relevance of intersectionality in my client work. Rather than going into great detail about the client work, which might breach the confidentiality of the cases I am going to present, I have opted for a question and answer format.

How have you developed your understanding of intergenerational trauma in the therapy room?

Early in my therapeutic work one of my first private clients came to my home from week to week. Part of their story was that they had a family member involved in the Hitler Youth Movement. I had not spoken to them about being Jewish as I felt this would move away from their focus in therapy. We were saying goodbye just before the Christmas break. They turned around and saw religious objects illustrating my faith background in my home. They apologised for not noticing that I was Jewish and never returned for therapy. What healing could have occurred for perpetrator and victim guilt in the room, had they returned. This instance clearly showed how necessary disclosure can be, and how non-disclosure can fragment the therapeutic relationship.

Have you ever worked with clients from different faith groups?

When working with a Muslim trans client, they brought their anxiety and experience of 'coming out' as trans, and their subsequent experience of the lack of familial support. I felt compelled to share my own lived experience. I checked in with them about how they would feel about my own personal disclosure, and whether it felt appropriate for them, and they said they were happy for me to share something about myself. I said I felt that I was facing similar issues in my Jewish family. This enabled a significant discussion around faith, gender and sexuality. Indeed, as I said towards the end of the session, it felt like we had a meeting of faiths coming together in this session, and if only more of these conversations could happen between our communities. The client was able to vocalise that their previous therapist did not acknowledge their cultural heritage and were not trans affirmative. The client was able to build their confidence in the therapeutic process, and although the focus kept changing, they felt seen and heard in therapy. My hope is that this prepared them should they decide to move into long-term work with another therapist.

Have you ever worked with clients that identified as non-binary? If so, how did that affect the therapeutic relationship?

I remember working with a non-binary client just after I had started to self-identify in the same way. Their feedback was: 'The most important intersection of our identities, for me at the moment, is gender. As you know, I've had some frustrating experiences with cisgender therapists in the past, who have struggled to use my pronouns or have asked me to explain what non-binary means when the feelings are still too raw for me to explain. You not being cisgender makes me feel much more secure in our relationship and I think it means we have a shortcut to a better understanding as we share a vocabulary around gender identity and certain aspects of our queer lived experience. I've never felt doubt or confusion from you when I've talked about the way I feel about my gender identity, and this makes it easier for me to trust you and to bring up deeper, more difficult issues that may have remained buried with another therapist. It feels very non-threatening to work therapeutically with another genderqueer person and I think that improves our working relationship immeasurably.' In this therapeutic relationship, I sometimes came out of the session asking myself, 'Am I genderqueer enough to be working with this client?' I realise this may be countertransference. In my work with my clients there are two of us steering the boat together, hoping to get to the safe shores. For myself, therapy is about what is going on in the work now, with the destination in sight.

Have you ever got frustrated when a client misgendered you?

On one occasion, I worked with a female bisexual client who came presenting with delayed grief. We had a conversation about her being left with her stepdad, after her parents had both died young. I asked how she had developed a positive female identity when the man she was left with had what the client described as 'toxic masculinity'. Interestingly, I had assumed she knew I was genderqueer. The client described her previous experiences of seeing a male and female therapist. She looked at me and said, 'I can work with you, as you are not a threat as a male.' At that moment I felt stirred as the client overlooked my non-binary gender. I asked whether there were any other questions. The client asked why I used a walking stick. I said sometimes we do not have permission in society to ask someone what their disability is. I asked whether this caused concern in the client that the stick presented the probability that something was wrong. I did not want to cause further anxiety to a client dealing with delayed grief and internally checked whether it was helpful or ethical. We talked about this openly and frankly, and I gave the client permission to come back with any concerns.

When I asked about gender, she responded, 'I have always preferred counselling with a male, or male-presenting counsellor, as I find their manner is more direct and they're unafraid of asking questions and guiding the conversation in a way that I have found female therapists more reluctant to do. I hadn't been aware that Joel identified as non-binary until we discussed the intersectional elements of our relationship and I had assumed him to identify as male, but with a clear LGBTQ+ identity and disability. As someone who has had difficulty with a stepfather who displays very typical "toxic masculine" behaviours, I find it important to have a counsellor who is aware of how damaging this behaviour is and of itself can be, and recognises the pervasive, destructive, silencing and undermining force of patriarchy and misogynistic behaviour. I would struggle with a counsellor who either identified with, or displayed, similarly "toxic masculine" behaviours and failed to understand how damaging years of conflict with a very heavy-handed patriarchal figure have been for me as a young woman.' Afterwards (and within this session with the client), as I had for 38 years of my life identified as a gay man, I felt angry for what the body I am born into activated in another. I could feel the shame in the transference and frustration about the privileges men have in our society. I used supervision to separate these out as to what was my anger and what was the client's.

What is the relevance of gender in the therapy room and supervision?

When I had a discussion with one of my supervisees about the intersectionality in the room, it allowed them to feed back that they were not coming to supervision to discuss our relationship. I recall them saying, 'Why am I interested in your gender? I do not see or feel gender in the room.' This felt like someone erasing my non-binary gender, proof that what happens in the therapy room is a microcosm of the world. As non-binary folk, we are often overlooked, and our identities are seen as 'just a phase'. This supervision relationship ended abruptly.

These examples show a glimpse of how important I believe our identities are in therapeutic practice, both those that are visible to others and those that are waiting to be seen. I will continue to bring my intersections into my work as I believe they can be powerful vehicles for healing.

*** *

Over the last ten years I am fortunate to have worked with a diverse client group that has been open about talking about the differences between us in the therapy room. I have had to take great care around opening up these conversations in this situation. A wise supervisor once said to me that unless we look at our past, we do not move forward in life. I see this also with the adversity and challenges that my Jewish faith, genderqueer identity, sexuality, disability and health have provided. If I had not looked deep into, and understood, myself, how could I be there for my clients? I have detailed how I bring myself into the therapeutic work I do: the fact that I do not feel it is possible to leave these parts of ourselves at the door, and the intimacy and healing that can indeed come from sharing these parts of myself with those who come to me.

When I was aged 16, I stood outside the Houses of Parliament with my first boyfriend as the age of consent was lowered to 18. I walked away knowing the relationship I wanted was illegal and feeling numb. My first partner died of AIDS not that long after. I only told my family about my first partner in my early thirties, as at my school the counsellor told me to keep my gayness a secret as it would be dangerous to share with the world outside. I felt it was my shameful secret. I have grown up in a time where we had Section 28, and the mental health system and society thought you were mad, bad or sad for being LGBTQ+. Thankfully we have progressed and moved on in many areas.

My faith has some catching up to do around how faith, gender and sexuality come together. Fortunately, there are allies and organisations within the Jewish community, such as the UK Chief Rabbi Ephraim Mirvis speaking out, Masorti, Liberal and Reform Judaism and KeshetUK, doing amazing work. Maybe not in my generation, but certainly for the next, it will get there. We have to have patience. I will end how I started, with my favourite Hebrew song. 'Gesher Tzar Me'od' says, 'The world is a bridge, a very narrow bridge (Haza 1982).' On a more personal note, by the time I finished writing this I found a more gender-neutral name; my family and friends are still getting used to it, all be it slowly, there is no rush. I have come realise by my faith not having the words or language for us that this allows for more creativity how liberating!

BIOGRAPHY

Chai-Yoel Korn (they, them, or just Chai) is an Integrative Body and Trauma psychotherapist and supervisor, Chai-Yoel funs Joel Korn psychotherapy, they have a decade of experience offering counselling services to individuals and groups. Chai-Yoel's specialisms include relational body psychotherapy, sex and relationship support for those that live with learning support needs or disability, as well as gender, sexuality and sexual expression, trauma and youth counselling for those aged 13+. Joel describes themselves as an LGBTQ+ and HIV activist and ally, a passionate expert, motivational speaker and trainer. They also have experience of writing around themes of wellbeing and other specialisms for journals and magazines.

THE LIFE COURSE

Non-binary children exist.

Non-binary parents exist.

Non-binary elders exist.

Chapter 17

Triremes and Battered Pineapple Rings

Karen Pollock

When I was seven, my life plan was clearly set out before me. I was going to marry my best friend, Michelle, and we would run her parents' fish and chip shop. If I am completely honest, I think a large part of the attraction was the idea of an unlimited supply of battered pineapple rings. Look, this was the 1970s and healthy eating meant salad on Sundays with sliced corned beef and Heinz salad cream. It was a good plan, and I had never heard of same sex marriage, being gay, lesbian, or even bisexual. I just knew that one day we would walk down the aisle together in matching wedding gowns. It even had the advantage of consent, since Michelle agreed marriage would be a good idea, and her only demand was that she got to use the chip-making machine. Surprisingly, even the nuns at my convent school did not object as we walked hand in hand and announced our plans. Was this my first moment of realisation of otherness, or simply two small children trying to navigate their ideas of adulthood? I do not know the answer, but I do know that we were using the language we had available. It's that idea of the availability and accessibility of language that I want to explore in this chapter, as it is a theme which has run through my life.

First though, let's fast forward quite a few years and, sadly, pineapple rings, battered or otherwise, are denied to me. I developed a severe allergy to pineapple ten years ago and even touching it causes my hands to swell. This was even more ironic because I spent nine years living on a tropical island where buying a bag of freshly chopped pineapple from a farmer who had driven into the city was the perfect end to a work day... Spearing sweet chunks chopped with a machete in the back of a pickup truck as the heat of a summer's evening enveloped me… Now I am even further in time and space and experiences from that small child growing up in the west end of Newcastle. The space between then and now has been filled with so many different experiences of myself, and is full of my attempts to grasp the right words to describe these different experiences. Is this who I am? Is this who I was? The process of trying to name myself recurs again and again.

You might wonder about the relevance of a child's innocent wedding plans and a hymn to pineapple in a chapter on sexuality and non-binary identities. Yet, for me they speak to a central feature of my own inner life, and one that as a therapist I rarely talk about, even if it is at the core of my journey to becoming who I am today. We grow up with the idea of being fixed entities, from 'born this way' to the binary idea of always knowing we are either XX or XY, male or female, gay or straight. Yet the reality, for everyone, regardless of their gender or sexuality, is that being alive is a process of constant change. My reality is that I cannot think about gender and sexuality, and how they intersect, without thinking about that process of change.

There is a very old problem from Greek philosophy which has been presented to generations of undergraduates. Consider a trireme (an ancient Greek ship, powered by oarsmen). Over a period of seven years, each part of it is replaced as it wears out, even down to the smallest nail. Is it the same ship as when it began? Or has it been replaced by a new ship? I can feel a connection to the seven-year-old who dreamed of marrying her best friend, but when even my pronouns are not the same, when my much desired pineapple now poisons me, am I the same person? If I am not the same, what about all the people in-between? Did I change from one to the other in noticeable moments, or was the process unseen? If how I describe myself has changed in some fundamental ways, how do I connect to all those previous versions of myself? Are they still there, or have they been replaced?

For me these are some of the central questions of identity. I sometimes joke that I am the ideal gender, sexuality and relationship diversity (GSRD) therapist because I have been lesbian, straight, bi, cis, non-binary and queer so far in my life. Just as there was never a promise that I would always be able to indulge in pineapple, there was no guarantee that my sexuality, gender or relationship style would never change, could never change. However, from early childhood we behave as if this rule exists. Or perhaps to be more accurate, we behave as if the words might change, but the identity remains fixed, and I am not so sure that this is the case.

Perhaps those two smiling children walking hand in hand and declaring their intention to be married would have met more opposition had they announced polyamory? The looming straits of Scylla and Charybdis which overshadow us growing up not only include gender and sexuality but very fixed ideas and language around acceptable relationships. The phrase 'the straight and narrow' comes to mind as the perfect description of how we are meant to blindfold ourselves to the wealth of possibilities that exist.

A marriage based on an inexhaustible supply of pineapple rings might sound like a poor decision, but we form relationships based on the promise to ourselves and to others that we remain unchanged. We make vows with the idea that 'the now' is in fact 'the forever'. Once, my body embraced pineapple, relishing the sharp sweetness, the scent, the juice filling my mouth and throat. Now, because of a change in that seemingly most concrete of things, my physical body (specifically my immune system), I can no longer enjoy those sensations. If something as simple as an allergic response can change our bodies, then how much more possibility is there for change around complex ideas such as our gender or sexuality?

There seems to be a yearning for fixed identities and clear binaries which permeates British culture and society at present. Some call it 'black and white thinking', the split into light and shade, as if twilight never exists. In this binary world not only is sexuality fixed, but it is known, clearly, and without confusion. Every model of coming out fits this black and white world view. Little Johnny, or Jessica, realises they are different, they discover the name for their difference, claim the name, and come out, once, to a parade of rainbow ticker tape and kittens riding unicorns. The ship never changes, because why would you replace any part of it, why would you even contemplate change? The ship is perfect as it is – even as sails rip and nails buckle, even as the sea air rots the timbers.

Into the narrative of fixed identities and clear-cut binaries comes the idea that we were somehow wrong about any previous beliefs we had about our gender and/or sexuality. We were 'born in the wrong body' or 'in the closet'. We would always be able to eat pineapple with relish (I may be labouring the pineapple analogy, but I really miss pineapple). What if, though, each of those previous identities were as valid as our current one? What if I was as much a cis lesbian as I am a queer non-binary person?

It almost feels like heresy to write that last sentence. The ship must be unchanging, and every inch of it declared perfect. Even as boards warp and no longer fit, and bilge water pools below decks.

Except...

Except I know how much change there has been, from minor repairs to dry dock refits. It feels that the world expects me to be ashamed of, or apologetic about, those repairs, to explain why I was wrong before and to assert with 100% confidence that now I will never change again. Perhaps it reassures the wider world that we are born this way, that change is an impossibility, but it means that only those designated others have to worry about finding the right words to express their otherness. Saying that our identities can change, and that through choices we make and/or labels we embrace or reject we can change our identities, can be a challenge to the norm of fixed identities. Perhaps the greatest resistance comes because it implies that even *you* could change from seeing yourself as cis, or straight, or a man, or a woman.

One of the engines of change for me has been words. This is no surprise. As a bookish child, words were my escape; as for so many other working-class kids who never quite fitted in, words were my freedom. However, finding the right words was not as simple as the 'usual' coming out narrative assumes. This is an issue because words matter; when you are trying to navigate how and why you belong to the box that is simply marked 'other', they matter a lot. There is no Santa Claus of words, no tooth fairy who leaves the queer lexicon beneath your pillow as you sleep. My identity as a non-cishet person did not begin with a lightbulb moment of claiming the words that applied to me, because the words were yet unknown. Instead, it was a negative reaction, a response against, rather than a claiming of space. I knew what I was not, not what I was.

Could it be that in the process of discovering the right words, of replacing the worn-out parts of that ancient Greek ship, I was making it more fit to sail the metaphorical oceans of life? Perhaps the terms 'lesbian' and 'bi' never quite felt right because other words like 'woman' never quite felt right. However, in the perpetual now that makes up my past, they were the only words I had to explain the box marked 'other'.

When we are discussing how identities are intersections, perhaps it's better to say, when I consider the intersections which make up me, that class and age are used against me in the oddest of ways. I am told to 'go back to Tumblr', that 'when I grow up' I will understand why singular 'they' can't be a pronoun or why non-binary is a made-up term. My identity as a middle-aged working-class person is erased because the words I have found that replaced the words which never quite fit are apparently unsuitable for me.

The process of discovering the right words, of replacing the mast and the hull of the ship, has convinced me that any exploration of my own self can be nothing more than a snapshot. It is a snapshot where I attempt to stand out with myself and consider how I might be perceived by others. Yet, the snapshot people seem to want to see, and the actuality, the living breathing person, pineapple allergy and all, arouses ire and rage that I am not a teenager who can be dismissed.

What are those words which attempt to say who I am? Or rather what words have I found to cut my way through the forest undergrowth merely marked on the map as 'other'? I am white, assigned female at birth, non-binary, raised working class, educated in, but not from, London, queer, a kinkster, identifying under the bi umbrella, dyspraxic, a parent.

Are these words worse than 'cis person', 'lesbian', or 'queer woman'? The answer to that question comes from how those words were worse for me. I do not feel that who I am has changed. To answer the philosopher's question: I am the same person I was when I was seven and wanted to marry my best friend, or when I was 17 and wearing Doc Martens and a tweed jacket.

Being the same person does not mean being unchanging, however. I still remember that first moment of 'this is a better fit' when I discovered the word 'bisexual'. I was not, as I feared, the world's worst lesbian; instead there was a thing, an identity, which called out to me.

By going to bed a teenage lesbian and waking up a teenage bisexual, in the eyes of many I replaced some pretty important parts on our metaphorical ship. For me, however, it was simply a process of finding the words to say who I was. Who I was and who I am are impacted by all the other things I am. The child growing up with an outside toilet and tin bath did not know the word 'bisexual' and they barely knew the word 'lesbian', but they did know they were other.

The child liked battered pineapple rings, and the adult looks longingly at pineapple in the supermarket.

The ship is the same ship, even if every thread of the sail has been resewn, every board refitted, every nail prised out and then replaced.

Sometimes, though, the very process of replacing how we refer to ourselves, of finding the better words, is prompted by a knowledge that how we are now does not quite fit. Again, this challenges the preferred idea that we as queer people know from the moment of birth exactly which shade of the rainbow fits us. What if we don't know though? What if we simply wear the available label, until something which feels more apt comes along?

And, as if a cartoon lightbulb has appeared above my head, I realise there has been another false binary in my thinking. It is not being the same person, or being someone different. It is not about being the same ship or a completely new one. Instead, as the understanding changes, as individual parts are replaced, a chain is forged between past, present and future, and it is the links of the chain which make me who I am.

BIOGRAPHY

Karen (Kaz) Pollock (they/them) is a queer, non-binary person who returned to the north east of England after many years of wandering the globe. In their time they have been a teacher, dishwasher, podium dancer, stay-at-home parent and poet. They are now a therapist, cat wrangler, writer who is passionate about empowering those whose voices are rarely heard, and promoting better mental health for all. When not working they can be found wasting far too much time on Twitter.

Twitter: @counsellingkaz

Chapter 18

I Am Three

Age and Non-Binary

Igi Moon

I was re-assigned in the sense that there was a body. Rather than it being assigned as simply a body, it was assigned a sex at birth – female – without any negotiation. After all, it wasn't my choice. Immediately, those cis-normative lads (Maslow, Freud, Erikson and the rest) were allowed to have their theories squat on my fragile flesh and fit me out as 'a female'. It would take years of grooming, but with childhood stages so neatly scribed then it was really all a matter of time. Early developmental patterns showed a wonkiness that needed cissing. My mum bought me a beautiful baby doll. I tattooed her fat plastic face with its fake smile using a sharp biro. I stole her pram and made a go-kart. Fuck that baby doll. It hadn't gone unnoticed. My favourite toy was a car, my favourite game was playing pirates, and I loved putting bricks in the boot of my tricycle. It was so simple. And easy. Okay, so occasionally I had to wear clothes such as dresses and skirts that I didn't like because I couldn't move in the same way as I did when I had on shorts. But once these were scuffed and full of mud, then it was back to shorts and T-shirts. Fortunately, I was only young. I had no idea these actions were in the least bit 'boyish'. They were just me-ish. It's fortunate that my mum and dad came from working-class, poor backgrounds. Survival was Darwinian. My mum was one of 12. A child is a child. Meanwhile, their girl-child could do what she wanted. I was three.

Lucky me. I was mistaken for a boy most of my younger life. The woman in the newsagent's where I bought Mars Bars thought I was a boy until I was seven and turned up in a school dress. I had a binary 'male/female' name (a name that both boys and girls were assigned) so I was a boy-girl. I was doing 'boy' without actually having that *knowing*, and nobody was there to stop me. I just never recognised the phenomenology of femaleness. I had it all planned. I was going to do technical drawing, play football and sports, climb, fight, wear brown jeans. Take up space.

But class and status anxiety free-floated. As the wealth of battered continents bathed the post-war population, the UK had greedily entered the era of 'Mad [cis] Men' – Eden, Macmillan, Wilson and their mates. Alongside a newly ensconced monarch, they yanked the working class into believing they could leave poverty and deprivation behind if only they worked harder to consume a new way of life. Men needed to make the country proud while women would bake us to happiness. Their emotionality was tied into a coarse political ordering – men needed to be tough and women would weep, and together they could procreate their way to middle-class wealth. My parents worked to hold onto this post-war ethic. They believed in the core traits of working-class people: honesty, integrity, hard work. But it hurt them. They did good and followed their orders. Education, something my parents had been forced to relinquish at 14 years old so the country could get back on its trench-foot feet, now became central to a new order for the children of the working class. I was taken out of my mixed school where I was literally fighting to be me, and sent to an all-girls school, specifically chosen because 'it made girls into ladies'. I could no longer see myself in the mirror. Who the fuck was that person? Uniformed up. As I see it now, I realise how dissociated I became from my 'self'. Looking back, I realise how school was a fucking nightmare from the start. No one really understood how I wanted to dress or 'be' and I wasn't considered very bright at all. 'You could be a nurse or work with children when you grow up.' Vomit. There was no one who understood this tiny world I lived in. No one spoke my language or seemed to be the same. I hated being forced to like things I simply could not go near like 'Scottish Dancing' and sewing. Just not my thing. I was force-fed gender. No wonder food became such a problem.

Puberty. A time of personal and social menstruation. The blood was the tears (or tears) of my non-binary self. Until that moment I had managed to feel as though there was a chance. As my body changed, so did everyone's way of reacting to me. Actually, I had never thought of it (the body) as 'female'. To me it was a body transitioning into something else. I had never connected how this would mean everyone would now think of me as 'becoming a young woman'. Or that I would need to 'do female' – no chance of doing my own body. I had to undergo femininity 'treatment'.

It was gang mentality as school, friends, family, all worked to shape my hormonal body to be female and feminine. In those days there was male/masculine and female/feminine. Girls wore this and boys wore that. I wasn't either, I realise now. But there was simply no language, no way to experience a body in the way I wanted. I remember playing football and realising these 'things' were getting in the way and lying in bed at night thinking about how to remove these breasts or stop them from growing. I hoped with all my life they would stay small. Invisible lumps. I was bulimic by the age of 14 years old. Sicking out all that curviness, all that 'puppy-fat' into the porcelain bowl. Thinner and broad shouldered. Hips like my bro'. I wore his underpants because I couldn't stand the frillies. It wasn't going to be a phase. Femininity was a tough disease.

As I write this, it saddens me. So much time has passed and yet those days marked who I would become. I wish they'd seen it. Someone. Life at home was hard for lots of reasons, not just for gender. But realising how my gender was so lost, so unrewarded, so uncelebrated is pretty tough. As we grow up, we hope parents or siblings look beyond male and female, boy and girl, and try to see that this child in front of them may not be either or it could be both. Adults have to ask what they are doing with bodies that are so easy to manipulate, to groom into cis-ness. My parents did what they were told. They did what they could for the society they were told that they should contribute to without question. Cisgendering was their fundamental contribution to a 'good society'.

Age and crossing from one terrain of a decade into another is a strange phenomenon. I remember so desperately wanting to stop being a teenager. There was no such thing as non-binary in 1970s England. There were the 'funny people'. Men who liked men and women who liked women. But it was all hush hush, giggle giggle, sad fuckers, kick the shit out of them. I quite liked crushing on other women. But that was it. I still looked like a boy and I liked it. I tried to fancy boys but I didn't like their smell. Even their words smelled 'off'. Boys were dangerous. Because boys were sex. And sex was dangerous. Sex was only hetero-sex. It was like they had a right to do what they wanted simply because they were 'a boy': 'I'll touch your leg just here. Come on, take off your top and let me see your tits.' But who do you think will win the FA Cup?

It would be easier to say I wanted to 'be' a boy. But I didn't. I wanted what they had. I was watching my brother and I wanted to have his boyness. Politically, and socially, and emotionally, boys had been given far more, while socialisation as a girl seemed unfair and mindless to me because it was so unequal. Feminist tropes were useful in engaging with notions of inequality, and I could focus on women and femaleness and try to understand the way it was being shaped and how that was aimed at me. More grooming. I wanted what my brother had. I wanted boy clothes, boy power, boy easiness in the world, boy casualness at not doing anything domestic whatsoever, their God-given right to playing 'out there' in space.

I see now that gender was so central to it all. I was locked into a phenomenology that could not be shared or experienced fully because there was no recognition of its existence. We were still in male/female. At the height of the 1970s and 80s we were doused with second wave feminism. What the fuck was going on? Politics and the fight for equality became real. Feminism had this therapeutic 'affect' – I fully understood the inequalities faced by women because I had to exist as a woman. I felt the anger of being refused a job because I was 'a woman', the frustration of being refused access to certain sports because I was 'a woman', the sheer burden of being expected to 'care' for my family or my society because I was 'a woman'. It was shit being 'a woman'. *The Female Eunuch* was freedom. There was a trope that made sense from a woman who wasn't wanted by women or men. Germaine Greer. Queer?

But I wasn't the type of 'woman' that feminists had in mind. I had come out as a lesbian in the early 80s because I could be more me. But not a lesbian feminist. There were quite a few of us who simply didn't obey the new rules of lesbian feminism. We wore leather jackets, listened to music by male bands and vocalists, set up magazines and marches, wore make-up, enjoyed penetrative sex, got pissed, took drugs, set up S/M clubs. The opening night of Chain Reaction (a club for leather-wearing lesbians) brought out a dozen dungaree-wearing lesbian feminists carrying pieces of drain-pipe to attack us on the way into the club as they hailed us as 'men-loving dykes'. So, I look back to the 1980s and early 90s and that lesbian feminist entourage as represented by a rather hard core of self-righteous 'wimmin' who spent most of their time denouncing leather-clad lesbians and claiming the right to exclude us from housing and 'wimmins' space' because we weren't 'real women' who 'hated' men. I see the very same crew attacking trans women today and denouncing them as 'not real women'. It's tragic really.

I don't think I thought about my gender in my twenties. I was at the edge most of the time. Any second I could drop to my death with drugs or drink. It had to end. I needed to find a profession. Not easy in the time of Section 28 when most of us worked in the voluntary/public sector and lived in shared housing because of low wages. We were hated. The media wanted us dead. Politicians and police backed their call. We were AIDS carriers, filth, shit, scum. Bleach us. On Pride day 1988 it was a choice between my cousin's wedding with *all* the family, or Pride. They didn't speak to me for two years. Somebody help!! I decided to have therapy and then train as a therapist (it was the 90s!) – ending up working in alcohol and drugs. Well, with all that personal experience!! And then I started a PhD in my thirties. I qualified, worked, studied and met someone fab, and that was it. We had a cat. Somehow you think you have grown up in these later decades. But there was so much more to happen.

My mid-forties were marked by two major changes. The first was the death of my brother. I miss his masculinity. He was cisgendered, a cis man, a 'real' man. Shaping that little boy body into man-ness so it couldn't feel sadness. Find a 'man career'. In the RAF and a Flight Lieutenant. I learned a lot about maleness from him and the way he also found cisgender masculinity demanding and excruciating and had nowhere to talk about it – 'just keep it in bro''. Those expectations and all that space. He got lost in space. I realise now how his gentleness had been torn away. Boys don't cry. They die.

The second major change was my gender. I was based at Warwick University doing research when I met Ruth Pearce, then a student (now a very smart researcher) and a very proud and out trans woman. I finally found my genderqueer self because of Ruth. She listened to me, and not like a therapist but like a person who just offered gentle understanding. I began to realise that I could put phenomenology and physiology together and become me. Not sure about where to go next, I found my new name, Igi. I began to explore binders and wore what I wanted. I told work about the name change and that I was genderqueer. I was loving it. I tiptoed into the idea of hormones and asked myself if I wanted to find out more with this old body. It made me think about blood and cells and gels. Cyborg. I got my hair cut at Open Barbers and went along to trans meetings. I felt like that three-year-old was back. I felt me. I was edging into my fifties. It was a new beginning.

And then I got ill. With rheumatoid arthritis. It has its own name, Ra-Ra. It made me transition. But not the way I wanted. It's a fucker. My hands didn't work. I couldn't walk. I couldn't even clean my teeth. The idea of gender fell away. I just wanted to stay alive. Stay in there with my partner who helped me through those shit days. Thing was, gender also gave me the strength. Fuck that fat plastic baby doll. Fuck it. I am going to be genderqueer and wear what I want. I'm genderqueer and I'm not going anywhere.

And so, four years and a hell of a journey later, I'm still here and genderqueer! I do research into trans and non-binary areas, have been involved with the sexual health clinic, CliniQ and the fabulous young people's service (ages 8–30!) Gendered Intelligence, have met wonderful and beautiful trans and non-binary people and am thankful to all my trans and non-binary friends and clients. I am old, but I am young. I feel me.

I am three.

BIOGRAPHY

Igi Moon (they/them) is a researcher, lecturer and clinical practitioner. They have written on therapy, sexuality and gender in *Feeling Queer: Queer Feelings: Radical Approaches to Counselling Sex, Sexuality and Gender* and are editor of *Counselling Ideologies: Queer Challenges to Heteronormativity*. They are currently working on developing a trans-therapeutic approach to working with trans and non-binary people. They enjoy their life despite its ups and downs and have finally found where they want to be – at home with their partner and cat!

Chapter 19

Non-Binary Intersections and Gender Euphoria

Meg-John Barker

Throughout my life, being non-binary in my gender has intersected with many other aspects of my identity where I've been between, both, or beyond binaries. All of these have been inextricably woven together with each other, and with my mental health. In this chapter I want to say a little about those interconnected non-binary experiences. Then I want to say rather more – because it's a lot more fun to write – about my recent experiences of gender euphoria. This challenges the overwhelming historical emphasis (in the West) of understanding gender difference in psychopathological terms, often reducing us down to negative experiences of gender dysphoria. We are so much more than this.

MIXED-CLASS, NORTH/SOUTH, HARD-OF-HEARING, BISEXUAL, NON-BINARY

The experience of being between, both, or beyond binaries has similarities whichever aspect of identity is concerned. For me, growing up, a particular kind of invisibility, difference, and alienation echoed through my experiences of class, location, disability, sexuality, and gender, with each element compounding the others.

My parents came from very different class backgrounds. My dad's parents were working class: my granddad a carpenter, my gran working in a factory and very involved in the miners' strike when I was a kid. My mum's parents were upper-middle class. They belonged to a family of mill-owners. Thus, much of my childhood was spent visiting one set of grandparents in a bungalow, with occasional trips to the other set in a mansion house. Two very different kinds of food eaten, media consumed, and topics of conversation. Always feeling like I didn't quite fit in either world.

What my grandparents did have in common was that all of them were from the South. When I went to middle school in the North of England, I was bullied as much for my 'posh' accent as for the sense that I was something other than the rest of the working-class kids there. The wrongness about me was scattered in all directions: my voice, interests, and passion for studies marked me out as snobby, swotty, and getting 'above' myself, yet my charity shop clothes and the fact that I wore the same outfit all week marked me out as lesser or dirty.

The concept of being mixed class is barely acknowledged or studied even now, so it certainly wasn't something I was aware of back then. I remember watching the news on TV and hearing the loathing reserved for the 'scabs' who broke strike and went down the pit. Neither one side nor the other, between the miners and the police, these men were the worst of the worst: suspicious, treacherous, greedy, betrayers. Somehow I associated these things with the similar words I heard hurled at me. Interesting how such comparable characteristics are associated with those of us who fall between or beyond the binaries usually associated with sexuality (e.g. bisexuality) and gender (e.g. non-binary).

And, of course, non-binary was not a thing either. I remember being lined up as girls and boys and realising that I could never be with the people I had the most in common with: the geeky guys who were into games, computers, and dinosaurs like me. Looking at 'my' line, I had nothing in common with anyone. The occasional girl known to me was allowed to do some kind of tomboy masculinity, but they were always physically brave, outdoorsy, and sporty: three things I most certainly was not. Over those years I was also equally drawn to people from both lines, yearning romantically after boys and forming intense, equally romantic – although that was not named – 'friendships' with girls. More invisible otherness.

The final alienation came from being hard-of-hearing. One doctor estimated I was hearing about one word in three and filling in the rest. Not significant enough to be regarded as a disability or even really to be known as a thing about me at that time. But it was bad enough that it left me struggling as much to understand the words of those around me as they struggled with the wrongness in the ways I shaped my words. The set-apart sense of being unable to hear completely always feels to me very much like the alienation of depression: just under the surface of the water with everything slightly distorted, unable to quite contact anybody else.

My childhood left me with depression for the majority of my life. The further binary between home and school was the clincher. For many reasons it wasn't possible to speak at home about the bullying I was experiencing, just as it wasn't acceptable in the school context to be the home-person I was. I became disliked in both places as I struggled. I disappeared more into myself.

And there's another (non-)binary around the depression itself. Like many people, I got caught between the either/or of whether I was 'really' depressed, meaning: whether there was something wrong with me that was fixed, unchangeable, and out of my control; or whether I wasn't 'really' depressed, because whatever had happened to me was not bad enough to warrant it, and I was therefore blameworthy for my struggles and responsible for sorting myself out. Never quite able to position myself in one place or the other, the in-between place only resulted in more confusion, alienation, and self-blame. Like so many binaries, I now know that it's a false one built on so many faulty cultural assumptions.

The sense of being unacceptable at home and in school meant my leaving behind important parts of myself in those years: soft, geeky masculinity, the cocky funny rebel I might've become if my confidence hadn't been erased, and any sense of being strong or powerful as the views and opinions of others – and the wider world – eventually broke me. By my mid-teens I was learning to perform a clunky femininity, and had developed a strong inner critic who would ensure that I shapeshifted into whatever form it thought would be pleasing to others – and crash into self-destruction whenever I couldn't manage it.

GENDER EUPHORIA

Several trans writers have played with the idea of 'gender euphoria' as a kind of opposite to 'gender dysphoria'. On his guest appearance on *Oh Joy Sex Toy*, Evan Clamours defines gender euphoria as 'a state of happiness and contentment with one's own gender and/or body', using the example of gender affirming moments such as being called your name for the first time, something I definitely relate to.

For me, gender euphoria has particularly occurred in moments when I have viscerally reclaimed some of those lost – or disowned – selves which I mostly left behind in my childhood and teenage years. I say 'mostly' because it's more complicated than that. Now that I look back, I do see flickers of them emerging over the years in the relationships I've formed or the projects I've pursued, but by and large they were hidden, and those moments often felt confusing or dangerous for that reason.

The erotic has been a major element in all of this – and what could be more euphoric than the erotic? All of these selves – once disowned – found their ways into my fantasies. I've always had a rich fantasy life, and it took a long while to realise that the masculine characters in them – the vulnerable boy, the cocky trickster, and even the strong, steady Bond-alike – were parts of me, not (just) characters I was attracted to. This is why I love Audre Lorde's concept of 'the erotic': the sense that this can be a spiritual and/or therapeutic path to greater fulfilment and being our potential in the world.

The potential of the erotic is also why I would question the common psychiatric assumption that eroticising ourselves means not being 'properly' trans. Denying ourselves the possibility of connecting with differently gendered parts of ourselves erotically is at best limiting. At worst it's a violence to our self as it denies us the potential to reclaim those disowned selves where much of our joy, creativity, courage, and other wonderful qualities may lie.

Let me share with you three key moments of gender euphoria. All are – in one way – quite classic moments on a trans journey. In other ways they deviate far from anything like the conventional trans narrative.

Diagnosis and vulnerable masculinity

It's taken me five years to decide to go for top surgery. The first step is to get a diagnosis and a referral to the surgeon. As I walk the streets of London to the clinic, fear courses through me. What if I'm deemed not trans enough? What if, having finally found the courage, I can't get this bodily change that feels so important to me? Should I rehearse a crafted story of my past that'll be most likely to get me what I want?

I'm incredibly lucky though to have my appointment with the wise and wonderful Stuart Lorimer, who I already know a bit. I take the risk and decide just to be completely open with him: to expand instead of contract. It's something I've been practising.

I come out of the appointment with a smile, a diagnosis (Gender Identity Disorder Unspecified), and a referral. Completely critical as I am of psychiatric diagnosis, I'm staggered by the impact this exchange has on me. I stand in the sunshine in a London park and I feel a feeling I have never felt before. The only way I can describe it is cradling. I am cradling myself. Is this what people mean when they talk of loving themselves? It is the opposite of the self-criticism, self-monitoring, and self-loathing that I'm much more familiar with. In the weeks and months that follow I feel it more and more, and I'm increasingly able to embody that vulnerable masculine side that I left behind so long ago. He is part of me now. I feel him there. I cradle him.

T and cocky masculinity

I think I've discovered my self: this soft, gentle, vulnerable masculinity. I think that this is who I am, or who I want to be. I see it echoed in other transmasculine people and I feel at home with them.

But then I begin to experience a completely different energy flickering up, and taking over quite greedily whenever he gets the chance. He is an arched eyebrow, a lop-sided grin, a wink in the mirror. He is the comedian in me and surprises me every time he comes out with the witty comeback before I've even had time to think about it. I know that I love this energy and also that it scares me: what if that sharpness could be cruel? What if that confidence flipped over into non-consent?

A couple of years after the top surgery I decide to give low-dose T a go. If the changes I've already been through can bring me so far out of depression, self-criticism, and people-pleasing, then I have to check out whether travelling a little further along this path might bring me even more joy. I can't quite imagine what that would feel like but I decide to try and see.

Again, I'm not prepared for the impact. The first months on T are all about this guy: I feel increasingly confident, joyful, and hot. Such an unfamiliar feeling: this hotness that isn't about making myself desirable for others but seems to bubble up from within. The energy fizzes inside me. I laugh more, I sing more, I write an entire freaking erotic novel about this guy to explore him more. I pursue new love – loving being the pursuer for once – and there I embody this side of me more and more and more.

The gym and steady masculinity

So, I'm getting it now. These selves are all a part of me. I've known them all my life from my fantasies, and now they are here. I can drop right into them in kink play, and I can embody them more and more in everyday life too. I know a few of the others already: selves that I associate more with femininity and queerness. But is there another masculinity in there? There's certainly one more that I've fantasised about over the years: dominant, strong, steady, containing, calm. Could it be that one day I might circle around to him? I kind of love the idea, although I can hardly imagine it.

I feel flickers through play, but the first time I experience him for a longer period I'm in the gym. I never, ever thought I would go to a gym. After an osteopath insisted, I was surprised to find that parts of me loved it. This part especially can emerge there as I feel the strength through my arms and shoulders, see my sweaty body in the mirror, experience my stamina on the treadmill.

He shows up to give me – or other sides of me – a talking to: all steady certainty in the face of my fears about the leaps I'm now taking towards new imaginings of what my future might be. He contains me through that week, and then I can bring him out with my new love in a way that surprises and delights us both. Another point on this human roulette wheel that I'm becoming. And I'm so grateful for him.

WHAT ABOUT YOU?

What to conclude from all of this? Obviously, this isn't everyone's trans experience or non-binary journey. There are probably people within the binary (cis and trans) who will resonate with these experiences, and trans and non-binary people who really won't.

By sharing this, I want to invite you to reflect on whether some of these ideas and practices might be useful to you. If any of them have the capacity to bring the kind of joy they've brought me, then I want you to have that possibility too.

So please do think about whether your gender background echoes with any other aspects of your identity in ways that compound or exacerbate struggles you've had. I'd invite you also to reflect on non-binary experience beyond gender and sexuality: even if you're entirely binary in those areas, might you be non-binary around other intersections? If so, might you experience the same kinds of erasure, invisibility, mis-identification, double-damnation, and alienation that many bi, non-binary, and queer people experience? What impact has that had on you, if so?

Do think, too, about the ways your gender intersects with your mental health. Might it be that unravelling, or shifting, one of these things will help you to understand, and find more comfortable, consensual places to be with the other one?

Consider the selves that you disowned as you learnt how the world wanted you to be. Might they be reclaimed, whether or not that is in ways that specifically relate to your gender or to your body?

Could the erotic be a helpful path on this journey for you too? Reflecting on your fantasy figures – whether in internal fantasies or external porn or other media – can be a great way to tap into unexpressed sides of yourself. Kink play and other erotic encounters can be an awesome place to experience them in an embodied way, which can help you to learn them better and – if you want to – bring them out more in your everyday life.

I – and all of my selves – wish you as much gender euphoria as you can possibly handle.

MORE ON THIS STUFF

- The Evan Clamours edition of *Oh Joy Sex Toy* can be found here: ohjoysextoy.com/gender-euphoria

- Audre Lorde's chapter on the erotic is here: uk.sagepub.com/sites/default/files/upm-binaries/11881_Chapter_5.pdf

- You can find my zine about plural selves here: rewriting-the-rules.com/zines. There's also writing about shapeshifting and binary ideas of mental health on my blog here: rewriting-the-rules.com/blog.

- I've written more about my gender experiences in my book with Alex Iantaffi, *How to Understand Your Gender*, published by Jessica Kingsley Publishers in 2017.

- I've written more about the erotic in my zine with Justin Hancock, which you can find here: megjohnandjustin.com/publications

BIOGRAPHY

Meg-John Barker (they/them) is the author of a number of popular books on sex, gender and relationships, including *Queer: A Graphic History*, *How To Understand Your Gender*, *Life Isn't Binary*, *Enjoy Sex (How, When, and IF You Want To)*, *Rewriting the Rules*, and *The Psychology of Sex*. They've also written a number of books for scholars and counsellors on these topics, drawing on their own research and therapeutic practice. In their spare time they love – er – doing more writing, and drawing comics, and taking long walks with friends.

Websites: rewriting-the-rules.com, megjohnandjustin.com

Twitter: @megjohnbarker

Chapter 20

Genderation

Am I Allowed to Be Non-Binary Too?

Lucy/Luc Nicholas

ME

Am I allowed to be non-binary too? I feel like my age, political background and appearance impact on my 'right' to identify as, or with, non-binary or genderqueer, and I constantly feel disingenuous, embarrassed and inauthentic doing so.

For my whole adult life I have been read as, and 'passed' as, a queer woman. However I felt, which was not exactly like a woman, I did not challenge this reading. I had long-term relationships with men where my status as queer within my queer community felt implicitly in question, let alone my gender. Even now, many in my peer group of queer feminist women value the identity of lesbian and of woman, and some choose strategically to identify with the category 'woman' and attempt to reshape its meaning. As a feminist, I respect and understand this. But it doesn't work for me.

When I first heard about gender neutral pronouns, it blew my mind, and my career-long deconstruction of binaries meant that the discovery of non-binary was a big deal. The choice that I have finally embraced to identify beyond the binary feels freeing, but I also feel guilty, like I am both betraying my feminist sisters and appropriating an identity that is not for me. Yes, I find it freeing and enabling, but I never felt 'wrong' in my body or particularly bothered to be identified as a woman, and I still use my given name (whilst foraying towards 'Luc'). There is part of me that still associates the identity with a certain presentation and also psychological disposition, like it is an identity for people who have struggled to 'become' what they want to be, a *trans* identity. Every time I put a skirt on, I feel like

I am going to get caught being gender normative and that I need to display an ambiguous presentation at all times. Compounding this, at work people don't understand the difference between expression and identity and so belittle or ignore my chosen pronouns. However, despite all of these reservations, the spirit of non-binary or genderqueer as something that is not solely about presentation but can be a way of understanding yourself, and as something that can transcend gender, and the people who get that, make me feel amazing. And it is the younger, millennial folk around me (at whom some of my peers roll their eyes) who inspire me the most. I like 'genderqueer' most because I was so influenced by academic queer theory as an early scholar and understand queer not as an identity or umbrella term but a non-normative position. I see more potential in it for fluidity, challenge, transcendence.

I was born in 1981. I was 16 in 1997 and living in a small, slightly run-down, working-class English town, pre-widespread internet. We didn't have Tumblr, YouTube or Instagram, and I felt a tension between being a straight punk girl *or* a lesbian. There are a lot more boys to date in the punk scene and when I was with one of them, I was read as straight. Most women I dated were not from the punk scene, so I felt detached from it. I veered between these two until very recently; first, by finding the less rigid way of describing my sexuality as queer, and then, when it became a concept that actually reached me, by realising my gender could be queer too.

However, this doesn't feel like an identity, in terms of 'I am *a* non-binary person or *a* genderqueer person', and I always cringe at the idea of 'coming out' as genderqueer or non-binary. It just feels like a better way to understand myself. It also certainly doesn't feel like a 'trans' identity to me. In terms of a (somewhat dated) topology, sociologists Kessler and McKenna (2000) suggested the prefix 'trans' can be understood in three ways: (1) trans as 'change, as in the word "transform"'; (2) 'across as in the word "transcontinental"'; and (3) 'beyond or through'. The third best describes how I feel, but those trans categories can't hold me, can't be imposed on me, and I balk at the idea of claiming a trans identity for myself. In essence, I feel far from 'entitled' to claim a genderqueer identity. I think this is down to a few things, including my generation, my class background, and my political beliefs.

'REAL' TRANS

One of my biggest hesitations is around making a big 'thing' of it when I haven't struggled with my body and when it doesn't exactly crush me to be called a woman. I worry that people will think I am a faker because I don't quite fit the presentation mould of masc assigned female at birth (AFAB) or femme assigned male at birth (AMAB) that many non-binary/genderqueer celebs present. I never felt a deep burning sense of being in the wrong body or wanted to change the parts that society deems 'woman'.

Having said this, it was much easier to present and be read as androgynous when I was skinny. Now I have boobs and a big ass, I have those 'woman signifiers' and I am kind of enjoying them. This lends me 'passing privilege' for sure, especially when I dress feminine. As my partner is more masculine presenting, this means we can often be easily read, when travelling for example, as a straight couple or a soft butch lesbian couple. This can be helpful but it can also be frustrating when it happens in our own communities and people try to read us in a 'butch/femme' paradigm we don't fit into. However, it also means that I am read as unproblematically 'woman', and I feel outright stupid to tell people I prefer 'they' pronouns and feel more genderqueer. I am embarrassed. I feel inauthentic. I don't want to cause a stir or make it 'a thing'.

Most of all, I worry – and this is personal and political – that my academic work and my identity is insulting to those who identify firmly as transgender, in the binary physical transition sense above. This makes me feel guilty for being understood alongside trans people for whom daily (mis)recognition is an issue, who have struggled with their bodies. It makes me think I am not trans. I don't feel like I am *trans*itioning, I feel like I always have *trans*cended. My personal belief is that the categories are so prone to exclusion and boundary-making and maintenance that they need to be challenged themselves. However, one of my biggest struggles with this (sometimes secret, not anymore) contention is that, for so many people including cis women and trans folk, there is a real sense of commitment to these categories, as those who feel they are in the wrong body demonstrate. And who the hell am I to know their realities?

Adding to this, I learned lately that there is a term, 'transtrender', employed for (often young) people who believe that non-binary isn't 'real' and think it is a way for people to get attention. Thus, this sense of being an imposter and a navel-gazing attention-seeker is compounded by the discourse from some people who call themselves feminists and from some transgender/transsexual people too. First, I will address opposition to non-binary/genderqueer from some trans people, and then I will go on to explore the feminist generational strain I feel. I only recently discovered the phenomenon of self-identified transsexual folk who are vehemently opposed to non-binary as a concept as they feel it undermines the realness of their own identities. The vitriol they express is nearly as bad as the right-wing opponents of 'gender ideology' who are freaking out about the end of gender and gender roles. An example of a major set-back for me that demonstrates this real/fake strain, and some generational issues, is when I had an unpleasant run-in at a conference.

The conference was called 'Beyond the Binary'. I was so excited for the potential of a conference about this, and it was one of the first times I asked other people to use non-gendered pronouns for me. However, it was a poorly organised and uninformed event run by a group of cishet people with no background in trans scholarship or community. The organisers consistently misgendered a bunch of participants and responded defensively to feedback. They invited a speaker who had founded a transsexual organisation, and this speaker spent half of her talk discussing how queer theory, non-binary and gender deconstruction was the biggest enemy to transsexual rights.

As an aside, it took me years of being in academia to become one of those people who speaks up and asks questions. For my undergraduate and Master's degrees I went to low-ranking polytechnic universities and then was suddenly thrown in to an elite uni for my PhD. I did not flourish there and kept to myself. It has taken me years of practice to become outspoken (if not performatively arrogant) in these kinds of intimidating environments, and at this point I was five years into my first full-time academic job.

So, picture this: half of the audience has walked out in protest, and I am at the end of a row of millennial and mostly non-binary PhD students, in whom I have taken solace and who are the only voice of reason at this crazy event. They all nudge down to me, 'SAY SOMETHING,' and I feel like a sham, like I am not 'really' trans and the presenter is. Who am I to speak up? But I say something like, 'It's a shame you think of queer genders as mutually exclusive from trans rights, and I don't think it has to be this way.' Then, tongue in cheek, attempting to disarm her with my charms, 'Can't we all just love each other?' She replies with an aggressively toned question: 'Can I ask you something? Are you cissexual?' I go red, I feel caught out, revealed. I just say, 'No, you may not ask,' and walk out. I cried for so long after that interaction.

GENERATION

I don't see as many younger people feeling so much hesitation around claiming these identities as I do, and the people who respond best to my request for non-gendered pronouns are my millennial-aged students of all genders and sexualities. For them, it is a no-brainer, not shocking or confusing, it is 100% an option. They take no time to adapt to gender neutral pronouns and don't question my presentation.

And so it pains me to see millennials described as 'entitled', 'navel-gazing' and 'snowflakes', who think they are all special, because above all what I experience in my time with millennials is a mutual respect. Confidence in themselves, yes (and what is so wrong with that?), but also respect for one another. I know older gay men, for example, who are hostile to younger queers (and especially young genderqueers) because they believe that life is so easy for them, and who feel that their proliferating of gender and sexual identities is the trivial nonsense that is the privilege of those without real struggle. Shouldn't we be happy for younger people growing up in a time with more possibilities? That their lives and politics become less about opposition and more about positive self-creation? I certainly do experience the younger people in my life as much more assertive and confident in claiming their non-binary or genderqueer identities, and I still really struggle to do so. Writing this I was plagued constantly with the feeling that it is trivial.

I have never been settled on my gender presentation, and perhaps over-compensated with extremes because I did not feel like I had choices that put a positive frame around having a messy, unreadable, undefinable gender. The kinds of discourses younger people have now, and the extent of the respect they afford one another in terms of self-identification is incredible, and has been liberating for me. I find such great joy in *purposely* messing around with my presentation now. The very messiness, the changeability, the contradictions, are a *thing*. Don't feel like a woman, AFAB, have woman signifiers, sometimes dress femme, but feel genderqueer? Fine! More than fine, affirmative. Pronoun and name in class intros for all students? Not a problem. Pronoun in name-arounds in work meetings? Don't even bother!

GENERATION AND FEMINISM

Finally, then, it may sound silly that as a gender scholar I had never thought of this, but last year two of my good queer academic friends told me they feel like it is more radical to be a woman and present non-traditionally than to identify as non-binary or genderqueer. And I was stumped. Am I betraying other women, taking the 'easy' route, by challenging the existence of the category rather than transforming it?

Being a butch woman does seem to challenge and upset people more than being a masculine presenting non-binary person. So is it inherently more subversive? I think one of the issues is the perception that all the masc presenting people are 'going' non-binary. In my observations this is occurring to some extent, but I know just as many non-binary folx who are femme or fluid presenting. Like me! In which case, *all* the categories get expanded. Woman isn't being abandoned.

This isn't only a *political* decision; it is also deeply personal. I don't make all identity and presentation decisions for political reasons – it's exhausting. So, in this world of limited choices, I am making a new choice, expanding the choices.

CONCLUSION: LIVING CONTRADICTIONS

Questions I am often asked:

'If you think gender is so bad, why do you go on about it so much?'

'If you want to end gender, why do you use the term "feminist", not "humanist"?'

'If you want to get rid of gender, why do you support trans people?'

BECAUSE GENDER EXISTS. It is what I would teach my students that Durkheim (old, dead, white, cis, male sociologist) calls a 'social fact': gender is something that humyns (Just a quick clarification, I didn't spell humyn wrong. I take out the 'a' and replace it with a 'y' because that's how it's spelt without 'man'.) made but is now bigger than individuals, has its own existence and impacts on individuals. And as long as it exists, then people need ways to navigate it that are as enabling and positive as possible.

I am feminist and non-binary. I'll go on the women's march and Trans Pride. I'll go to the lesbian bar. 'Cause there is the world that is and the world I want. The identities I am given and the ones that I make. I can relate to feminism, not just because the identity of woman has been imposed on me all my life and therefore shaped my existence and opportunities, often in a restrictive way, but because gender does this, full stop. I don't have to be an essentialist to strategically invoke woman or lesbian when needed. Many of my younger friends and the communities they hang out in have no problem being both non-binary and feminist.

Until we can get to a utopian place where sex/gender markers lose their sexed/gendered meanings and anyone can present as they want to present without worrying too much about the identity attached to it, I am going with more choice, not less.

BIOGRAPHY

Lucy/Luc Nicholas (they/them) is a 38-year-old (born 1981), white Anglo-British sociology academic who considers themself genderqueer. They grew up in various crappy little towns in the UK before moving to Australia for work and sun. They are first-generation middle class and first-generation university-educated, trying to keep it real while being an academic. Luc was into the punk scene and anarchist politics when they were younger, an interest that has spilled over into their ideas about gender. They are interested academically in backlashes, the legacies of colonialism and getting beyond gender; and personally in reality TV, drag, eating, sleeping too much, and bio and queer family.

Email: drlucynicholas@hotmail.co.uk

Twitter: @drloocy

Chapter 21

Blood Deal

mud howard

I wanted to write a story about my blood family. In queer community, we get to decide who is in our chosen family. We choose whom we let into the sacred circle, whose house we wake up in, who we want to see and whom we feel seen by. We surround ourselves with the ones who resonate, the ones who believe us and nurse our abusive break-ups with cups of lemon-honey-ginger tea, tarot readings and mugwort to cure the night-shakes. In this way, our chosen family becomes a pack of wolves, backs up against the world. But with our blood families, we don't get to choose. We just take the deal. We don't select who is best fit to give birth to us. We don't control whose DNA braids together inside our arms. I wanted to write a story about the deals we make with our blood families as trans and gender non-conforming folks.

Three years ago, I came out as trans to my parents at their blue kitchen table in the dead of winter. This story is not about bravery. This is not about grief or trauma or linear transformation. This isn't a story about being born in the wrong body (my body). This story is about death and humility and compulsory selfishness. This story does not begin with me and will not end here. This story, this gender swirling inside of me, traces back, deep down the rabbit hole of my lineage. This story is made from the sticky premonitions of my ancestors, each one waking up in the middle of the night like bolts of lightning in warm pools of sweat. This story is for my parents, for their arcs of pain and arrows of love. This story is also for every trans or non-binary person who has carried the weight of their gender on their back. For every gender non-conforming person who has become themselves despite the disappointment and discomfort of others. For every person who wanted to give up in the face of this burden...

but didn't. This story is also for the ones that did give up. You are here too. We carry you with us.

My mom is a nurse. She was born a stone's throw away from the Atlantic Ocean. She spent her summers growing up in a sleepy beach town with candlestick bowling and saltwater taffy. She has a dad who told her that the best way for her to help him with a project was to stay out of his way. I think of her as an East Coast girl who got seduced by the desert (via my clown of a father) and never went back. My dad was born in 1947 in a corn field in Nebraska—at least that's how I imagine it. I see my dad at 14, standing on his lanky legs, leaning up against the wooden fence under a denim blue sky. I see him awake at night, staring at the watermarks in the ceiling, counting down the days until he's big enough to grab his father by the shoulders and throw his whiskey breath straight across the room, as far away from his mother as possible. My dad survived his dad and created his own way to be a father to me.

I always had a special connection with my dad. He coached me in soccer when I was a kid, kicking a pale blue ball into a neon orange goal, my tiny hands eclipsed in his. He would wear a backwards hat and lift me up on his shoulders where I could play his head like a drum in the whirl of a rushing crowd. We would play horsey in the living room, both of us in matching purple pajama pants. I would grip fistfuls of his worn red t-shirt while he bucked like the clumsiest bronco you've ever seen, until I flew off into a palace of pillows, laughing until I cried hot tears of joy.

I think my dad took my transition extra hard. He spent upwards of 70 years communicating with the limited set of tools that we give every young masculine person who is told they should be a man. I try to tell him this now. I tell him that it's okay to be sad about the fact that he lost his daughter. He lost a special kind of gendered relationship: one that the world recognizes and nourishes and makes rituals for and dances about—one that is emotionally legible and easily written about. I tell him that the world doesn't have words for what our relationship is now—the relationship between a dad and a non-binary trans kid—but he denies it. He says that he was too busy watching me grow up into the dynamic person I am today, to worry about any of that gender stuff. I know he is bluffing, but I let him.

When I told my parents that I was trans, everything in the kitchen turned to ice. I was slipping and fumbling for words, a green Heineken beer melting in my hands, while big cracks opened up in the tiled floor and water rushed in. Everything felt like it was breaking. My mom panicked and yelled and asked me if this meant I was going to get a sex change. My dad wouldn't stop playing Sudoku. During the entire conversation he didn't take his eyes off that puzzle once. He kept trying to fit those tiny black numbers back into their boxes—in a grid that made sense or some sequences that fit together. He was desperate for any type of order that could keep things making sense while my words slowly ate away at his reality. When I asked him if he wanted to put down the newspaper and talk to me, he said, "What am I supposed to say? You've been my daughter since I can remember and to me, that's who you'll always be."

It took years for me to get over that.

I decided to start taking hormones. I didn't have a plan. I didn't want to look like a man or anything. I didn't want to grow a beard or get giant muscles or get called "boss" every time I went to the grocery store. I just knew that I wasn't a woman and I was sick of being the only person who knew that. I had just traveled to Australia for the first time and met a trans person with a voice made of honey and twinkling green eyes that looked like glass spit out by the sea. I was fully obsessed. I couldn't stop thinking about them. I couldn't tell if I wanted to fuck them or become them. Potentially, I wanted to do both in that exact order. I couldn't get them off of my mind. I would spend late nights scrolling deep into the archive of their Instagram and witnessing their transformation over and over again. When I got back to the States, I made an appointment with my doctor. Two weeks later, I was snatching a brown paper bag out of the hands of a wide-eyed nurse at the Kaiser clinic with six tiny vials of amber oil clinking around inside.

I didn't tell my parents. I couldn't handle any of their sadness clouding my direction. My mom came to visit me one weekend and we drove off to the Oregon coast. I snuck off one night down to the pier to give myself a shot under the yellow, sticky light of the street-lamps. There was a huge storm brewing purple clouds in the sky above me. I sat below it, my feet dangling off the dark edge of the universe, and watched as the tie-dye clouds expanded and contracted all around me. I felt my body slowly changing and morphing under the heavy rain drops and the weight of this new synthetic liquid coursing beneath my skin. I waited until my voice dropped a couple of octaves too low to be explained away as a scratchy throat. I told people when I was ready.

There was always something off about me ever since I was a kid. Even from a young age, I had this energy that no one could really place. I didn't want to be different, I just was. When I was five years old, I told my friend Andy Gray that he was a wizard and made him give me a penis. When I was 14, I created multiple Myspace profiles of hot teenage skater boys and made all the friends of my best friends fall in love with me. I came out as bisexual to my parents at a poetry slam with my girlfriend when I was 18 years old. The gayness was easier for my parents to take than the trans stuff. My parents just tried to imagine that I had told them I was a vegetarian, except instead of giving up meat, I was giving up men. The trans thing was way scarier. I told them I was trans in that pre-Caitlyn Jenner, post-Laverne Cox moment, where most people were still unsure if trans people actually existed or if we were just a fluke. My parents didn't know anything about trans people. I was definitely the only queer person they knew. My mom had a threesome with a male dentist and a lesbian named Irene back in New Mexico, and my dad's brother's best friend in high school was a lesbian. But besides that, the only gay people they actually knew were my drama partner Tim Peck's adoptive lesbian moms, who owned two old pugs with respiratory issues.

It's hard to rewire your brain to unlearn something as sticky and stubborn as gender. Gender gets on everything, and requires a large amount of skill to un-stick. I had spent years slowly stretching my brain and my body wide enough to fit around the loose constellation of gender. I knew that gender was a matrix deeply sewn into the terrain of our lives, but I think I underestimated the time it takes people to un-gender things. I was so deeply hurt by the fact that the people who brought me into this world could not see me. I didn't know why it mattered to me so much, but, for some reason, it did. They kept saying they loved me, but their love was causing me so much pain. I didn't understand how you could love someone and cause them so much pain at the same time.

I couldn't deal. I reduced all contact with my parents down to a few, loaded novel-size emails every few months. They kept calling. Every time my parents left me a voicemail with my dead name, I would break down crying hot, fast tears wherever I was—in public, on the night bus, in the soft throws of bed. I had one friend that year: a witness to the daily pain and pleasure of transition. A gemstone of a person who was both my mirror and my rock. I hibernated all spring.

I didn't totally realize the head start I had on my parents. I had spent the past four years dipping in and out of Gender Theory classes at my West Coast liberal arts university and making out in the dorms. I had a lot of trans friends in the poetry scene. I already had the chance to read and misinterpret and preach and slowly become critical of the entire canon of Judith Butler. Before I finally worked up the courage to tell my parents, I had spent the past six months wading through the anxious swamp of my own gender identity, crying in sliding-scale therapy sessions, and forcing all my friends to call me by my name. By the time I told my parents I was trans, I was already standing on my own two feet in this brand new me. My parents were in their mid-to-late sixties, sitting at that same kitchen table, coming face-to-face with the first trans person they ever knowingly met in their life: their own child.

I didn't have the capacity at that time to understand what my parents were going through. I was too busy protecting myself to empathize. Last winter, on the 45-minute drive to the airport through a 5 am purple fog, my dad told me I was selfish. He said I never even gave him the chance to understand me. By the time I told him I was trans, I had already made up my mind that he wouldn't get it. He said that I wrote him off, shut him out, and did my own thing. He felt the pendulum of his own identity, his masculinity, his age, and his whiteness swing back towards him and deny him something for the first time in his life. That something was me. I was hurt and hurting and knew that we were already miles, decades, universes away from soccer practice and that palace of pillows and those big hands holding me steady. I was so angry. I couldn't stop shaking for the whole plane ride. But it was true. I was selfish. As a trans person, I had to be selfish to survive. I had spent my whole life compromising myself and shapeshifting for everyone else. I was so scared of inconveniencing anyone, of upsetting people, or of making people feel uncomfortable. This was the first time I was putting myself first. If I didn't do that, I wouldn't have made it. But my dad's inability to grasp what I was going through didn't stem from a lack of love or stubborn pride or even from his identity. He didn't get what I was going through because I never told him. The conversation never made it past my deadname.

It hasn't been easy, but love never is. No one gives you a guidebook on this. I ignored my parents for the first year after I came out as trans. Then, they started correcting themselves on the phone when they got it wrong. My mom would spiral in guilt when she got my name wrong, and I would remind her that I was the person hurt in this situation and that the more she apologized, the more I felt like *I* needed to take care of *her*. Now, my mom tells off women in her book club for using my old name. My dad still calls me "darling" on the phone, but I let him. My dad wrote me a letter and I cried on the hardwood floors of my house reading it. He said that he never cared about me getting married or walking me down the aisle or what gender I would end up as. He asked me to be patient. He said he loved me more than I will ever be able to understand.

My mom still gets nervous and tells horrific stories about my genitals at dinner parties with new people, yet somehow consistently manages to use "they" and "them" to refer to our cat. She gets drunk off one glass of wine and somehow manages to say "sing it sister!" to me, but I just touch her leg now and we laugh together. Sometimes I can't tell if my dad is referring to multiple people, or absolutely nailing gender-neutral pronouns. My mom tells me that she sees trans people all the time in public, and I lecture her on how those trans people might not want her to be seeing them as trans. My dad gets excited and somehow moved from "you go girlfriend" to "you go boyfriend" to "you go they-friend" in a matter of milliseconds. My friends and I make lists of all the horribly awkward and hilarious phrases that our parents use to talk about gender. My parents both showed up at the women's march, in their hot pink knitted "pussy hats," waving a giant trans flag above their heads that you couldn't miss from miles away.

I think it's okay to hold both of these truths at the same time. To me, that's what being non-binary and trans is all about—holding two seemingly contradictory feelings so close together that they shatter and burst and melt into one cohesive thing. We are working on it. My mom told me recently that she's always understood, on some level, that I wasn't a boy or a girl. She says I'm a blend. And that's what it always is, isn't it? A blend.

BIOGRAPHY

mud howard (they/them) is a non-binary trans poet from the USA. They write about queer intimacy, interior worlds and the cosmic joke of the gender binary. Their work has been published in *THEM* journal, *The Lifted Brow*, and *Cleaver Magazine*, from which their poem was selected for 'The Best of the Net 2017.'

You can find more of their work at www.mudhoward.com

Chapter 22

The 'Outsider's' Journey to Parenthood

Eli

'You're a mother now!' the doctors on the maternity ward informed me as I held my baby in my arms. Only a few hours after my child was born, motherhood became a new label that was suddenly assumed to describe me. The celebratory atmosphere following the achievement of giving birth to a beautiful child was short-lived and the sudden weight of the label of motherhood fell upon me. I did not see a place for myself in the narrow possibilities and expectations of what it means to be a mother. Pregnancy, birth and mothering are all seen as essentially and often unquestioningly womanly. While in my experience 'female' is a restrictive category, motherhood is an even narrower label with lots of societal projections, pressures and responsibilities. If children embody society's hopes for the future, mothers are revered as precious instruments in the construction of the child and also conversely to blame for all that is wrong with kids today.

In Western society we do not yet have a shared language to speak of pregnancy and parenthood without attaching it to gender. While I was surprised at how soon the doctors placed me into the unyielding category of 'mother', I did not expect the medical professionals visiting me in the maternity ward to use gender-neutral terms for me. The very desire to have a child is considered to belong to 'women' who are 'maternal'; there is no male equivalent. Men who desire to have children might be called broody but this is a changing emotion, whereas being 'maternal' is seen as a permanent state, like being shy or extroverted. There is no gender-neutral term for 'maternal'. Many of my female friends describe themselves as not being 'maternal'; they battle sexist assumptions that one of their main goals or missions in life should be to become a 'mother'.

They are seen as somehow failures if they do not achieve the social status of a reproducer or family maker. People warn them that it might be too late one day, almost guilting women into motherhood as a necessity, as a societal labour, as something unquestionably desirable.

In the context of this patriarchal pressure on women to have children, and the gendered ideals surrounding pregnancy and parenthood, my longstanding strong desire to be pregnant caused me to re-examine my gender identity. I asked myself: does wanting to have a child challenge my gender identity? Does it make me more female? Am I bending to the pressure to meet a social milestone? Do I seek some form of societal validation as a black queer disabled person so often viewed as a non-(re)productive burden on society? Was I prepared for the transformation that pregnancy would bring to my body? I wrestled with these questions and many others. In many ways this self-examination helped me to be more confident in my identity, while at the same time I became more comfortable with not knowing. I could not predict exactly how pregnancy and parenthood would impact me but I was prepared to take a leap of faith and discover the effect of this transformation on my life.

There are times when my intersectional identities make me feel like a mythical creature, something like a centaur, a biological impossibility. Because there are few places that I see my multiple identities reflected back at me, I am left feeling as though multiple marginalised identities are not meant to exist in one being. I can be a black parent, I can be a queer parent, but a queer, black, Muslim, disabled parent is almost a theoretical identity rather than one that is considered real, or it is considered so rare that it cannot be thought about as fully real. On the one hand, this sometimes leaves me feeling excluded, in a state of never finding community of others with my exact experiences; I'm almost always an 'outsider'. On the other hand, I find that being an outsider gives me the freedom to define myself. I can never fit into society's expectations; it's not easy to stereotype me, and people's projections and speculations about who I am based on how I look are so frequently wrong that I find there is little point in correcting them. Most important to my experience is my ability to define myself for myself, and it is with this power to define myself that I have found a way to sustain myself through this unpredictable and transformative process of becoming a parent.

My gender identity probably falls somewhere between gender neutral and gender fluid. I reject the ways the world is divided so deeply by gender, with men and women seen as so intrinsically different. I find myself expressing my gender in fluid ways, partly because I've never felt like I belong to a male or female category and partly because I don't like the idea that things belong within gender categories at all. I have never felt that my desire to be pregnant was connected to a female identity. While I do not feel 'female' and my body does not align with my gender identity, I've always been fascinated with my body's reproductive potential. I knew that choosing to be a parent would challenge my experience of my gender, both in my social contexts and in my relationship to my body, but I could not have predicted the impact. Pregnancy was a transition in many ways. My body changed and the way people saw me also transformed. As I began the journey, I had no concept of how one could be pregnant and not transition into a 'mother'. There are no genderqueer parenting transition blueprints to follow. Who I would transform into was something I would have to figure out for myself.

From the moment I knew I was pregnant, my body started to change dramatically, becoming more feminised. Before being pregnant I desired a more gender-neutral body. I wanted a flatter chest and a more masculine body shape. I saw my body as an expression of my identity, and with that I saw the clothes I could wear on my body as a tangible way of expressing my gender identity. Being pregnant felt like the reverse of my desired gender transition: hormones and body modification, a new wardrobe, my chest got bigger, my hips wider. Much of maternity wear is highly feminised: frills, flowers and body-hugging clothes. I resisted them until it became so uncomfortable to keep trying to continue to wear my old clothes.

There was something about having knowingly chosen the path I was on that helped me to change my relationship with my body. While I still tried to choose maternity wear that reflected my identity, my relationship to my clothing changed. I felt that for this short period of time my clothes needed to function as items I placed on my body for comfort and coverage. My connection to my body as an expression of my identity also changed; the function of my body as biology became more important. My body intrigued me as it morphed and expanded into a home for my growing baby. The process was miraculous, my body providing sustenance for another human being grown from tiny cells into a kicking baby. My body as something that could be read as indicating my gender, physical ability and identity became secondary in importance; it became valuable rather than a thing I judged as failing to express the gender I felt inside.

The transition was not easy. Being pregnant, I felt less able to be comfortable in my gender expression and it took a much greater effort to reject the notion that certain ways of being, or expressing myself, had to fit into a gendered box. My body transformed and societal ideas about me transformed. I became unquestioningly female and probably heterosexual to many people. 'Oh congratulations,' people said. 'You and your husband must be so happy.' Or, 'Oh, how are you feeling about becoming a mother?' These interactions made me conscious of how outside of the normative model of family I felt. I rarely corrected people partly because I was not really concerned about what people who were not close to me thought about what my pregnancy meant about my gender and sexuality. It was also partly out of a desire to not have to continuously come out as a 'centaur' – as an identity conundrum in a social context in which my intersecting identities are rarely understood.

I also became more acutely aware of the issues that society has with gender: from the ways people constantly assume my gender, to the way that people really wanted to gender my unborn child. It was amazing to me just how many times while I was pregnant I was asked what gender the baby was. To some extent the question was just a standard form of automatic small-talk. Person A states, 'I'm pregnant.' Person B states, 'Congratulations! Boy or girl?' On many occasions people were shocked, uncomfortable and even frustrated that I did not want to know the gender of my child. Many people struggled to find the vocabulary to talk about the genderless baby. Others were stumped when buying gifts without knowing if it should be pink for a girl or blue for a boy. People asked what gender I wanted. It felt strange that I should have a preference based on gender rather than any other characteristic. I wanted a happy baby. I wanted a baby who would grow up and be happy with who they were. I didn't care which gender. I found it funny that imagining what my child would be like could be shaped by such binary ways of thinking about gender. I sometimes answered the question 'What are you having?' with the answer 'A human.' Then when probed to say a gender, I might say 'tomboy', 'princess boy' or 'don't care'.

I now have a baby who I would say currently seems to identify as 'happy' most of the time. I do use gendered pronouns to describe them when I need to but not always and I don't correct people who get anxious about (mis)gendering them. I'm hoping to allow them the space to grow into the person they are and not impose gendered, stereotyped and narrow possibilities on them. I wish they did not have to grow up in this binary gendered world. Even now, at such a young age, my baby is exposed to binary ideas about gender. We attend baby-singing groups and typically end up singing songs about male pirates and little girls who get scared of spiders. I think that being an 'outsider' I'm particularly sensitive to the ways that gender, as well as other identities, is both passively and actively policed. I want to encourage my child to navigate this binary gendered world and find their own place in it. As they grow, I aim to actively expose my child to wider notions of gender and attempt to reduce the impact of deeply embedded cultural binaries, such as the belief that only girls can be pretty and only boys are adventurous.

While the parent and baby groups have left me feeling disconnected from the motherhood club I'm assumed to be a part of, they have, however, made me more aware of the ways that many women feel alienated from the narrow societal expectations of motherhood. I've enjoyed those moments of solidarity with other parents when we can laugh about the impossible pressure to get it all right and the mostly contradictory information out there about how to 'get it right'. I find that I'm not the only one worried about the intensive blue and pink marketing to babies and their carers. I've found other queer parents who are also finding their own ways of resisting the influence of gender-normative culture on their children. My unique constellation of identities means that I draw on multiple communities for solidarity and parenting strategies. While I still feel like an outsider, these communities help me to define parenting for myself and to be comfortable with my own version of what it means to be a parent.

BIOGRAPHY

Eli has been an active member and community organiser in the queer community in the UK for almost a decade. They have an eclectic set of interests and skills. They are an artist, writer, community builder, workshop facilitator, and self-confessed geek with interests in graphic design, coding, programming and gadgetry. Their current visual art and writing projects engage with futurism, disability, and representations of the lives of queer and transgender people of colour.

Chapter 23

'Why Are We Using This Changing Room?'

Cal Orre

'Look at the dog. It must be really hungry. It's been standing there for ages!'

Rio is joking about the dog statue outside the swimming pool, like they always do when we pass it on our way to our regular Monday evening swim. We have tried to have Rio in swimming class, but it didn't work at all since Rio refused to do anything the teacher told them to. Instead they chose to stand in one corner of the pool, brooding. After a few times like this we gave up and realised we have to try and teach this child how to swim in another way. So now we go – just me and Rio –every Monday to the pool to be in water. Maybe, in a very distant future, they will learn how to swim.

The swimming pool is located in a suburb a few stops north on the subway line from where we live in Stockholm. It's not a fancy place; it feels kind of old and worn down, even if it was built fairly recently. We leave Rio's boots at the entrance and bring mine with us to the changing room. There is a sign on the door with a figure of a person in a dress.

'Why are we using this changing room?' Rio asks. 'Last time when I was here with Mina we used that one over there.'

I think twice before answering this question. It's extremely hard to explain the gender binary and the division of bodies and identities into different changing rooms. Especially it's hard to explain it to this kid, who does not even know the word 'ladies' and does not really have a clear understanding of norms around gender yet.

'Well, for some reason they divide people according to bodies into different changing rooms,' I try to explain, 'and ladies is another word for women. I guess they think that everyone with my kind of body is a woman.'

I have already lost them with this explanation. Ages ago. They started instead to think about things that are important in their world, like monster trucks, Moana and the evil coconuts, that Christmas is coming soon and about all the presents they will get, or that they need the bathroom. It just feels so sad having to explain this very disturbing system to a child who is not yet very affected by it and who clearly does not understand it.

Rio is five and, at least in this moment, non-binary. Very clearly so. They are very firm with wanting the pronoun 'hen' in Swedish, which is equivalent to 'they' in English. They often state that they are not a boy. Sometimes they say that they are a girl, but most often they say, 'I am not a boy or a girl.'

Loads of people misgender Rio. Loads of people really try using the right pronoun, but it's so uncommonly used in our language that even the ones who really try make mistakes a lot of the time too. It annoys Rio. For a while Rio had the strategy of not caring about the pronoun, saying that 'hon', 'han' and 'hen' ('she', 'he' or 'they') all work for them. It made their life easier because they did not have to correct people or get annoyed all the time. However, now they want most people to use 'hen'. They are five years old and already experience, every day, that people misgender them. Constantly. It must be really hard to have that already at that young age. They also get furious when people call them 'a boy'. It is very common that they need to state, 'I'm not a boy!' When I became a parent, I started noticing even more how much people gender kids *all the time*, and how most people treat kids very differently depending on the perceived gender of the child. Rio has always been ambiguous to people, so Rio has been quite randomly gendered and hence experienced the different ways people treat them in a very clear way.

In the fall we were in a big department store in the centre of Stockholm to buy a new bathing robe for Rio. The old one, the red one with pink hearts that Rio loved so much, had become way too small for them. Rio really didn't want to give it up, even though the robe was for a one-year-old and the sleeves now only reached to the bend of Rio's arm. We were in the department store for ages, looking at all the toys. The *Moana* merch (Rio really wants a Maui doll and a boat), the Lego® (here it's the big space ships and the cool racing cars that are the most desired) and all the other stuff that make Rio go 'ohhhh'. It was hard to drag Rio from all the cool and beautiful toys towards the clothes department, and it was even harder to find a robe that Rio would say yes to. They certainly did not want a black one. 'I hate black' is a very commonly used phrase. Rio is seriously not a fan of my style of clothing. They wanted the exact same robe that they had before, but that was not possible. There was not a big selection to choose from among the robes that were made of cotton rather than synthetic fabric. Rio was quite unsatisfied when they only got to choose between two different ones that were, since this world is very normative and binary, pink or blue.

Anyway, when we got to the register to pay for the robe, the person behind the counter started talking a bit with Rio. Rio is not the most communicative person when it comes to chatty strangers, so they were mostly quiet.

'Are you a boy or a girl?'

Rio didn't answer.

'Why do you want to know that?' I asked.

The person replied,: 'We have gifts for kids: football cards for boys and stickers for girls.'

'Why can't the child decide for themselves what they want, regardless of gender?' I continued, and the person seemed to get the point and showed both the glitter stickers and the football collector's cards to Rio. Rio chose the glitter butterflies stickers of course (who wouldn't?) and they were super happy.

On the way out of the store Rio said, 'The person thought that only boys can like football and only girls can like butterflies. That is not true.'

I gave an affirming reply and then Rio went on talking about all the toys they want for their birthday. It just makes me smile how this five-year-old can have a deeper understanding of gender stereotypes than most adults in this country.

One September afternoon I was in the kitchen making pancakes for Rio and their friend Robin, who lives in the building right next to ours. Robin's family is fairly normative. He has a mom and a dad and is quite happy being gendered as a boy, doing 'boys' stuff'. I don't know exactly what he or his parents think about our family with three non-binary parents, but the two children get along very well. I was, as usual, listening to one of my podcasts about either American politics or *Buffy the Vampire Slayer*, so I wasn't really paying attention to what was happening in the room where Robin and Rio were playing. I thought that they were probably playing thieves and police or something similar. When I left the kitchen to do something, I happened to overhear their conversation.

'There are boys and there are girls,' said Robin, 'and we are boys, and we are the best.' Here I hesitated. I didn't feel I could leave that statement unchallenged, even if it came from a five-year-old; however, I also didn't want to suddenly burst in and correct him. Luckily, I didn't have to think for very long about how to intervene, because suddenly I heard Rio respond, 'I am a girl.'

Robin, sounding surprised, replied, 'What? But you are the best!'

'Both boys and girls are the best. And I am the best, especially when I am wearing something beautiful.'

BIOGRAPHY

Cal Orre (they/hen in Swedish) lives in Stockholm, Sweden, with their child and their two co-parents, Mina and Zafire. They have worked in the field of LGBTQ rights for the last ten years at the Swedish Federation for LGBTQ Rights, RFSL. Their expertise is in HIV prevention, sexual health, trans health and political advocacy work. Cal and Zafire are currently recording Sweden's first podcast about queer parenting, gender neutral upbringing, polyamory and ways to make more feminist choices in one's family life.

Chapter 24

No Easy Answers

Daniel Morrison

'How did you get here?'

'I drove.'

'You drove?' There's suspicion and uncertainty in her voice. 'How long have you been looking after him?'

'His whole life. Eleven years.'

'Really? Have you got any ID on you?'

We're in A&E, in the middle of a short June night. My son is beside me, in his dressing gown, his face swollen and tears drying on his cheeks. I'm having to shout so the receptionist can hear me through the screen. She's seeing me as a teenage boy babysitter with a sick child and fake ID, and I can almost hear the child protection warning bells ringing in her head as she examines my driving licence and looks at me.

'Is this yours?'

I can see, reflected in the window between us, people starting to look. There's blood and boredom in this room, people whose night out ended badly, someone mumbling to herself in a corner. People look up from their phones, sensing a distraction. I move the boy in front of me, placing myself between him and the room without thinking. 'Yes, it's mine.'

'What's wrong, Mum?' he asks, sensitive to my moment of fear.

'Mum?' asks the receptionist, looking again at the name on my driving licence.

'Nothing's wrong,' I tell him. I don't want him to think there's anything secret or shameful about this. 'I think they're a bit confused about me because most mums are women.' I look back at her. 'I'm transgender. That means I used to be female but now I'm male. He still calls me "Mum". My legal name is the one on my driving licence. I'm 39 and I gave birth to him. How long's the wait tonight?'

Being non-binary means there's never an easy answer. What I told her wasn't true, but it was the quickest way to end the conversation. There are two binary boxes for gender, and I don't fit and don't want to. This means that life throws me into a variety of situations in which I have to tell a part truth or have a lengthy conversation. When a drunk guy put his face close to mine and asked if I was a fucking faggot, I said 'yes', because it was truer than 'no', and I wasn't willing to waste more than a word on him. There isn't a space in the world that fits, and so we make our own, or skip between the two permitted options, or make a space for ourselves, shaped by the edges of half-truths. In my work as a therapist, my lesbian client reads me as dyke, my young gay male client reads me as young gay man, and my trans client reads me as trans man. None of them are entirely wrong, and none are fully right. I don't contradict them or explain myself; to do so would be to centre my experience in the room and it doesn't feel necessary. They see the part of me they relate to, the aspect of my complex self that they want as a therapist. I exist in the space between this triangle of mirrors, shaped by what they need from me.

Even the word 'non-binary' is defined by what it is not. When I try to define what it is for me, I can't find the words. Inside, it's simple and easy, a spaciousness, a simplicity. When I try to explain it, I lose the sense of it in a tangle of communication. It's a freedom from restraint and expectations, and this more than anything is what I want to give to my children. My hope is that by living as I do, explaining to them as fully as I can, but mostly just by existing as my authentic self, I'll show them that there are no limitations on who and how they should be in the world.

When I first had children, I lost my name. They became not only the centre of my world but redefined me as an extension of theirs. I was in friends' phone books as 'Bobby's Mum'. Teachers, club leaders and people on checkouts called me 'Mum'. My whole identity vanished into a gendered monosyllable. The expectation is that you happily shed all individuality until 'Mum' is no longer the most frequent word you hear in a day, and only then is it acceptable to reclaim your self. Again, my identity is defined by their needs. This one dimension of a complex self is all the world sees and reflects back to me. I exist behind this mirror of people seeing what they expect to see, in a looking-glass world where nothing is concrete or simple. In the therapy room, I give myself to my clients for an hour, but to my children I give myself until they've built a self of their own. Does it matter that the self I'm rebuilding isn't the one I wore before they were born? Are they aware of this on some level?

Do they have a swirling shapelessness in their core where there should be something solid enough to build a self around? This 'un-selfing' of parenthood was the chrysalis I hid in while I took myself apart. Now they're older I'm emerging as a different person, more whole, more clear and authentic, and also less recognisable. That look of confusion and suspicion in the hospital is the closest I get to being gendered correctly.

The greatest gift of walking the world in the liminal spaces is seeing how things work. There are lines so embedded in our culture they're invisible, and yet I can see them, laser-like, and see the contortions people make to keep those lines intact. I can tell when people read me as Dad – usually when I'm with my youngest – because they tell me how great I am. I was never told I was wonderful for taking my kids to the park when I was read as female, although I was just as wonderful a parent then as I am now. The wonder that's in me is how this highlights the casual misogyny that's so ingrained, the unexamined assumptions of 'women's work' and different standards we're held to, depending on our sex assigned at birth. Two years of testosterone mean that now when I'm with my eldest, a strapping 5 feet 8 inches 14-year-old, we're read as two teenage boys and told we need an adult to come with us into the skate park. This is maybe the saddest of all – I can see how much fear and disapproval there is of teenagers, and I'm sorrowful that as my boys move into the adult world they are met with this.

It hasn't been easy for my eldest. His generation are striding forward with the undoing of gender, building on the foundations of those who went before, becoming more comfortable with their explorations and those of others, but this isn't the case everywhere. High school can still be brutally tribal, with young people scrambling towards adulthood by clawing and stamping on their peers. I see his burning need to fit in, and I keep my distance from his school, trying to give him the space to find his own story. When they started school at eight and ten, after the joy and slog that is home schooling, I didn't come out to their teachers. I wanted them to go in with only their own names and stories, not the reflection of mine. I told them it was their news, to share if and when they wanted. My eldest used it to win a game in a drama class, playing Two Truths One Lie: 'I like hot chocolate, my Mum's mostly a boy, and I want a Ferrari when I grow up.'

My youngest doesn't appreciate the shock value and can't remember how or when he's told people. It's not really news for him. He's lost me in the rumble of bodies leaving school, and stands by the gate, looking around for me. 'Your Mum's over there,' says his friend, 'or is that your Dad?'

'Oh, it's my Mum, but he's non-binary. You coming to the Land?'

'Later, I got to go and get changed. See you there at 4?'

Sometimes there are easy answers.

BIOGRAPHY

Daniel (he/him) is a writer, parent and therapist in North Wales and is currently studying an MA in Gender, Sexuality and Culture. He facilitates and supports workshops for the LGBTQIA+ community around consent, energy work and conscious connection.

BODIES, HEALTH AND WELLBEING

Chapter 25

On Borrowed Spoons

Alex Iantaffi

"Excuse me but this bathroom is for people with disabilities," says the usher. They're definitely talking to me. Not the other cis-appearing, feminine-looking white women in line with me; just me. I feel the familiar surge of anger as well as the collapse of exhaustion deep in my bones. I breathe and simply say, "I know," and do not move. The usher is relentless. "You know there are more bathrooms in the main lobby…" They are still pointedly looking only at me. I let the anger shoot clearly through the words now spilling from my lips, directly aiming at them. "Yes, I have been a patron of this theater for ten years. I know where the bathrooms are. Would you like me to provide you with my medical history, diagnoses, and how my disabilities impact me in front of everyone right now?" I am glaring. I am breathing. I am tired. I notice the space my anger creates between the usher and me, and all around me. A few people quietly leave the line. My anger, my directness, my very presence do not fit into this Minnesota (n)ice.

This is only one example of an experience of what might happen when I try to go to an accessible public bathroom as a visibly non-binary, queer person with invisible disabilities, and—once I open my mouth—an audible accent that does not belong where I live. Sometimes I can just pee. Some of these times, tears of relief spill from my eyes instead of anger from my mouth: the gratitude at being able to just pee unquestioned, or for a kind word by a member of staff or another member of the public, becomes overwhelmingly visible on this ableist, cis-normative tapestry. Sometimes friends or partners who do not share my experiences shake their heads and say emphatically, "It shouldn't be this hard to pee." I agree, but I could add so many things to that list: to get up, to shower, to breathe, to sit down, to stand, to go somewhere, to move, to lie down, to sleep, to exist.

I'm aware that I might be tipping into melodrama and self-pity right now. I hope to lightly lean into it and not fully descend into those territories, much as the melodramatic appeals to my Sicilian side (maybe some stereotypes have a kernel of truth). Those things are not hard all the time. That's part of the issue. I have lived with fibromyalgia for over 20 years now (and with complex post-traumatic stress disorder [PTSD] my whole life), as well as with asthma and probably with some as-yet-undiagnosed autoimmune issue. My queer brother calls me a "holy petri dish of mystery" sometimes. I wholeheartedly agree. Some days I can dance and laugh and do more than many people can in 24 hours. Other days I can hardly get out of bed. My symptoms are sometimes textbook for fibromyalgia and other times confounding, not only for me but also for my healthcare providers. New providers sometimes like to talk about my weight if they feel overwhelmed by their inability to help. I wish they had some more original responses than fatphobia. Doctors can be predictably patronizing and dismissive when faced with chronic illness and their own impotence.

In some ways my disabilities taught me how to live in the liminal possibilities of non-binary identities and experiences. My disabilities and being an Italian immigrant, first to the UK for 15 years, and then to the Dakota and Anishinaabe territories currently known as Minneapolis, Minnesota, USA, for the last ten years. In the middle of all that, I also came out as genderqueer after a few years of already identifying as a lesbian, then queer and bi, and later trans, and eventually trans and non-binary. The semantic landscape shifted under me as I got into deeper relationship with myself and my communities, while my sense of self and my experiences changed far less than the language used. One of the core clichés of these experiences was the eternal, existential questions: "Do I belong?"; "Where do I belong?"; "What if I'm faking it?"; "What if every terrible thing my trauma brain is telling me is true after all?"

I am sure that many people can relate with this part. After all, belonging is indeed an existential human need. As a therapist, I often dance with this need with my clients. It is a challenging dance: the tune and steps are similar yet different every time. However, the question of whether I am faking it is not purely "imposter syndrome," as I first thought. The more I've been able to immerse myself in communities of people who share experiences and identities similar to, or resonant with, mine, the more I have been able to realize that some of my fear of "faking it" might be a mix of one part developmental trauma to nine parts systemic oppression.

Being surrounded by dominant cultures where there are limited or no reflections of my identities, experiences, and even existence results not only in erasure but also in relentless, ever-present questioning of my own legitimacy as a person. It is challenging, if not impossible, not to internalize oppression in any form. The erosion of one's possibilities for being is exhausting.

At a recent occupational therapy appointment, a well-meaning, new-to-me provider says, "Well, at our age we start to have some of these challenges and physical decline." She is kind, so I try to be as patient as I can. I tell her I have had some of these symptoms since I was in elementary school, and that I was diagnosed with fibromyalgia in my twenties. She apologizes and discloses that her kid has invisible disabilities too. It is easy for any of us to fall into the trap of ableism: to believe that physical capacity is only impacted as we get older, that the norm is absence of pain, full mobility, and as many spoons as we need to get through the day to live our lives (for the uninitiated, spoon theory is Christine Miserandino's (2003) metaphor used to explain the amount of energy disabled people have available—equivalent to having a limited number of spoons and each task requires a certain number of spoons till eventually they are all gone).

I struggle with ableist internalized beliefs every day. For years I believed that maybe, if I did all the right things, I would run again. I loved running. It gave me a sense of agency and freedom growing up. I could literally run away—free, unencumbered—a thing I could not do in my everyday home life as a child. Also, because I had a pretty bad kidney infection around five years old, I needed to be still or else be in pain for many of my elementary school years. I had earned running, right? The sad truth is that nothing is owed to me, and that running—even gently, even for just a mile—will send me back to bed with a flare-up for days, or possibly weeks. Yet, every time, for years, when I felt better, when I was not in a flare, I would tell myself I could run again. Some days I still do. Because what if this is not real? What if this invisible disability—which many doctors don't even "believe" in, as if it were not a fact—is an invention of my own mind? What if I can will myself to be well? What if all the lies this ableist, capitalist, patriarchal, white supremacist, cisgenderist dominant society whispers to me every day are true? Could mind really be over matter? But, isn't my mind matter, part of my body, of me? Is there really any of me that is not physical existence, body? Yes, those questions keep me busy when I have nothing else to do but lie awake in pain at night, when all the sleep hygiene, physiotherapy, and medication are not enough to take the reality of my body's suffering away.

Other questions I often ask myself include: "Am I sick enough to spend this money on this treatment/to ask for this accommodation/to let other people do this physical labor instead of doing it myself?" And those questions are shaped by gender too. In my twenties, when I presented as feminine, I did not want to appear weak as a feminist, yet my body refused to be strong, or stronger than it was. Now, as a masculine-appearing person, I fear being seen as weak, because none of us can be truly free of toxic gender binary notions as long as they are pumped into the air we breathe, day in and day out. Even on better days, when I refuse to treat myself as a capitalist commodity and consider myself worthy of medical attention and treatment, I have to navigate the maze of gendered systems. Will people at this new clinic be at least friendly to me as a non-binary person? Will they use my name and pronouns? And, the eternal question: Will there be a safe place to pee? Of course there are more questions that touch on other aspects of who I am. Will they just reduce my problems to my BMI, even though literally there is blood in places where no blood should be found? Will they dismiss me because of my accent, my appearance, my weight, my (lack of) citizenship, my diagnoses?

I won't lie. Some days I dream of being cured, even though there is no cure, even though I have read as many nooks and crannies of critical disability studies as I can and love the incredible writing of Eli Clare in *Brilliant Imperfection: Grappling with Cure* (2017), which addresses tensions and complexities around the idea of cure as a disabled and trans person. Some days I also dream of just being trans masculine—or even better, just your average homo, being able to navigate spaces and pee in some peace wherever I go. Unlike what one of my tutors assumed when I was training to become a systemic therapist, my liminal identities and experiences, my differences, do not make me feel "special." In this world, where I live, they often make me feel alien and tired, very tired. Other days, most days, I dream of and work for deep self-compassion and self-acceptance in the midst of a world that views me as a commodity and a means of production. I dream and work for the restoration of communities that have survived settler colonialism and have decolonized not just our consciences but our practices, our relationships with land, self, and one another.

My own non-binary, liminal identities and experiences, and those of people around me give me hope. They remind me that no matter how bleak the landscape, weeds of restoration keep coming up again and again. I feel stronger, no matter how bad a day I might be having physically, when I remember that this is where I belong. I belong with my non-binary siblings, not just human ones, but also all the wonderful non-binary beings like clown fish and birch. I belong with all those who dance across the landscape of health, in all its locations. I used to think of us as weeds of resistance, but my dear queer sibling, Donald Engstrom-Reese, taught me that weeds do not resist, they restore. We, the people who live across, beyond, and between in many ways, are weeds of restoration. The days I can remember this, the pain seems more bearable, the cognitive fog a more amenable companion. I do what I can and leave what I cannot to someone else, to another day, or resign myself to it never being done, and I just go pee wherever I can, ignoring the looks and the "helpful" ushers.

BIOGRAPHY

Alex Iantaffi, PhD, (they/he) is a therapist and writer. Over the years, they have written about gender, disability, sexuality, bisexuality, polyamory, BDSM, deafness, education, sexual health, HIV prevention, and transgender issues. Alex is a trans masculine, non-binary, bi queer, disabled, Italian immigrant parent living on Dakota and Anishinaabe territories, currently known as Minneapolis, MN (USA). Alex has recently co-authored the books *How to Understand Your Gender: A Practical Guide for Exploring Who You Are* and *Life Isn't Binary* with Meg-John Barker (Jessica Kingsley Publishers).

Website: www.alexiantaffi.com

Twitter: @xtaffi

Chapter 26

Dahlia among Orchids

Neither a Boy Nor Girl 'on The Inside', but
Gender-Chaotic 'on The Outside'

S. W. Underwood

Gender is a ritual. Before birth, I was assigned male. Yet, as early as I recall, I remember being not-a-boy. The pronouns others used to refer to me didn't matter. I remember instead an internal sense of affinity with girls, and the play choices girls tended to make. But I never thought of myself as a girl. I knew I wasn't a girl—others told me so often!—but I knew also I was not a boy. I was somewhere in-between, outside, on my own.

When my mother took me and my siblings to the store to choose our own new bed comforters for Christmas, I unabashedly chose a blanket decorated with Ariel, the Little Mermaid. At the skating rink with my classmates, the skate rental representative asked me every time what my size was, followed by a hand-wringing and meek whisper, "I'm sorry, but are you a boy or a girl?" Internally, I was delighted that he asked, but I felt his own embarrassment in asking me pour as hot shame down my face and chest. When the Spice Girls became popular in the mid-90s, I fantasised about being Baby Spice. I remember lying in bed with Emma Bunton's face plastered on the back of my eyelids. I asked my parents if this was the sign of a crush that I could not stop thinking about her. They affirmed it. As I look back, this crush was different from every other crush that followed. My fantasies about Baby Spice involved me wearing her clothes, brushing my own (non-existent) long hair, styling it the way she did, and embodying that provocative sort of sexual white femininity.

All children experiment. Most children play around with gender at a young age and, absent from external pressure, most probably think nothing of it. As a young adult who once identified as a gay, cis man, it wasn't that unusual for other gay cis men to share stories of them loving 'feminine things' when they were young. My broad preference for feminine kid culture was paired with a profound aversion to masculine kid culture. I watched the 'other' boys playing hockey on the street outside, stood in the corner ignoring them when they played rough video games, and generally felt like an alien when stuck into groups of boys. No matter what we did, I always felt like an imposter, like I did not belong.

The pressure to Be a Boy grew stronger as adolescence loomed. I remember increasingly negative sanctions when I would express myself in feminine ways. The shoes—"unisex," my mother called them—I wore to elementary school were a target for the other kids. One morning, they encircled me in the schoolyard and made fun of me so vociferously for being a girly boy wearing girls' clothes that I left school and walked for an hour across the city to Mom's work just so I didn't have to be around them the rest of the day. At home, my decision to wear glitter in my hair angered my father. "He can't do things like this!" he shouted at my mom.

When I started to develop a sexual and romantic interest in men, I realized I was gay. I lay in bed at night with visions of cute boys as the new imprints on the back of my eyelids. These crushes were very different. As innocuous as fantasy is, the reality of my new sexuality fomented a deep shame. Not only was I a feminine boy, upsetting everyone around me for being who I was, now I was gay too.

The pressure to conform is perhaps greater at no point than in early adolescence. I responded to these pressures by doing something I'd never done before: I pretended to be a boy. I wore baggy jeans, massive t-shirts, and a big puffy black jacket that covered up my tiny body. I never raised my voice above a monotone and made sure I was never seen doing anything associated with femininity.

Though I fell in love for the first time with a boy and partnered with him for three years, I continued to repress myself. If the boy I loved also loved boys, then that was who I was going to be.

BLOOM

At 20 years old, I found myself single, facing adulthood, but so disillusioned with my life, a sense of pressing anomie separated me from my social world. The person I'd become was a lot like others expected me to be. Why, then, did I feel so alienated? No longer surrounded by other kids in public school, set free from my first three-year relationship with a boy, and uncertain about the person I would become in the next couple of decades, I left the city.

As my gender conformed to masculine expectations of me, so too grew my anxiety and despair. In retrospect, I knew nothing of the correlative link between my gender and mental health. I felt instead an inexorable need to rebel against everything about myself, to shed all symbolic and relational trappings that suffocated me. I dropped courses at college; I sabotaged my jobs by fighting with my employers; I cut out all friends from my adolescence. And though I didn't understand why at the time, I refused to date for another three years.

With a new friend, I spent the summer island-hopping along Canada's west coast. She was a misfit too, wrestling with her own cultural and ideational shackles. She was a straight, cis woman, but taunted for her towering height and muscularity, for her inability to conform to feminine gender expectations. I was drawn to her contrarian personality, her critical mind, her bravery in refusing to shave her legs and armpits, and even her refusal to wear anything to cover her breasts in public—after all, men could show their nipples, she argued, so why shouldn't she? Fuck it all, we declared.

We foraged what we could from the forests and scoured the mud flats at low tide to collect oysters. We befriended strangers everywhere and invited them into our nomadic nudist colony. In retrospect, I've never been so happy as I was during those summer months.

Every person who joined us shed with their clothes many of the markings of their social identities. Difference based on culture, class, and race seemed to matter less in these moments. Interacting skin-to-skin equalized us, and notably to us, it flattened gender. Interacting skin-to-skin increased our vulnerabilities; it exposed what we work to conceal every day. Here, we were humans first.

I observed then the artifice of our social identities. Symbols all but removed, I found something more essential. For the first time in my young life, I'd found myself. I was not the expectations others put upon me, nor the expectations I'd internalized myself. I was a person yearning to be free.

One of those summer evenings, clothing askance, I sat alone upon a cliff on the edge of an island. As I stared ahead, I focused on the evergreens around me, the susurrus of the wind rocking the trees lightly back and forth, the fading sunlight dancing on the ocean waves. I dreaded returning to the city, to my job, and to my everyday world, knowing that the peace I felt sitting on that cliff would dissipate.

I decided then that I would try to embody that feeling. I renamed myself Sol, to honor that moment of holistic connection I felt that evening on the cliffs of Vancouver Island.

When I returned to the city, I turned my wardrobe upside down. I tossed out all solid colors, all jeans and sweaters, and replaced them with gender-chaotic knickerbockers and billowing capes. I pierced my face and dyed my hair fiery blonde. Wherever I deemed my presentation normative, I subverted it.

Over the next few years, I ran nude along the beaches of the West Coast, disappeared into the forests of the Rocky Mountains, left college, and moved to India on a whim. All the privilege and opportunity the world handed me, I embraced…to any end.

NYCTINASTY

By 23, I returned to Canada a new person. My years of adventure and growth had transformed me in many ways, but I returned to a life of ashes. My education was in pieces. My professional growth—whatever that was—had returned to the dirt. And I had not dated since I was 20. I'd loved my years of growth, but I now desired to ground my life and build something permanent.

I met a boy. His focus, determination, and professional clarity infatuated me. I fell hard. He represented everything I'd lost in my years away from home, and I told him I needed him to be the rock that weathered my stormy seas. I needed him to show me how to rebuild my world.

The love that developed between us tethered me to him, and I felt overcome by my desire to please him. Without realizing what I was doing, I began to smother myself again. He hated my piercings. He hated my blond hair. He hated that I called myself Sol and wore gender-chaotic clothing.

I think he loved me. But not at all like I loved him. I was so desperate for his affection that I changed my name back. I let my natural hair color grow out. I turned my wardrobe upside down, bought new jeans and sweaters, and conformed to the type of boy he liked.

As I regressed, friends of mine began to come out as trans. Curious about his views on trans people, I asked my partner if he would ever date a trans person. "Absolutely not," he said. Deflated, and confused by my own pain in hearing this response—after all, I was not a trans woman, so why should I care—I asked him why not. His answer stupefied me; he regularly told me he would date women if the right one came along, though he had only dated boys. With no sophistication and with resistance to my asking, he asserted plainly that he did not find trans people attractive.

On his public blog, my partner wrote his views on why trans people were morally culpable if they did not disclose their history or status as trans prior to sleeping with a cis partner. My friends, outraged, insisted that I leave him.

His views mattered to me. I was entangled emotionally in what he thought of me because I wished he would love me the way I loved him. I kept my weight at 105 lbs throughout our relationship because he told me that he had never been as attracted to his ex—who had a flat tummy and protruding hip bones. My body, my gender, and everything I aspired to be, all became defined by whatever he needed to love me.

BLOSSOM

I never did leave him. He left me to do a PhD in another province. Though I could say I regret not having left him myself, I learned a lot about who I am, and that I don't regret. As I'd asked of him, he showed me how to finish college and get into graduate school. While I'd once again conformed to external expectations of my gender, I now had a purpose in life that kept me grounded: a PhD of my own in gender studies.

Within weeks of arriving in Toronto, I met a new man. Our relationship began polyamorous. He'd been with a partner for nearly a decade when he met me, and I soon became another of his partners. Though I dated other men, I fell harder for him, and for our relationship together built on shared friendship and small joys. We have the same sense of humor, of adventure, and of those vital domestic moments needed to recharge. This love was easy.

As the years passed, we found ourselves primary partners with no others. Faced with the choice to transform our relationship into a monogamous one, we saw no reason to do so—after all, we'd fallen in love while we each had other lovers and sex partners. Jealousy and possessiveness were never ingredients in our relationship's recipe. No reason to add them now, we agreed.

I feel a freedom in love I've never experienced before. His sexual satisfaction and my own are not determined by one another. Neither of us expects the other to fulfill all our romantic and sexual needs. He places no demands or expectations on me that constrain my autonomy. This emancipatory sexual politics, accidental though it is, is coupled with an ethic of care so genuine that I now feel I can be whoever I am, and he will still be there. To my disbelief, I regularly hear him say, "Cute boys are a dime a dozen. You are one in a million. Nothing will ever change that."

He'll never know what he's given me: the permission to live exactly as I am, to play, to explore, to grasp for mermaid blankets and glitter gel; to look in the mirror and see my own reflection, not the reflection of someone else's desires. At night, I lie beside him as he sleeps. I look forward, focused on the grey hair sprouting among the blond, the soft rasp in his restful breathing, the fading light on the lines around his eyes left by his smile. I feel myself upon that cliff on Vancouver Island again, with him by my side.

I never asked him to call me Sol. From stories of my past, he gleaned its importance and began to use it on his own. I never told him which pronouns to use, but he began cycling through all available when he referred to me. As my wardrobe becomes more feminine, I wait for his questions, left only to beam as he tells me how beautiful I look in my dress. As I grow my hair into a long, curly mane, and sweep my forehead with trimmed bangs, I look for signs that he will no longer love me. "Do you like my long hair?" I ask him. "I like you, Sol. I prefer short hair on girls, boys, enbies, on everyone, but I want you to do whatever makes you feel good," he responds with a kiss on my forehead. "Do you like my face without facial hair?" I ask after over a year of laser treatment. "I do," he responds. "I can see your gorgeous face more clearly." "How about my boobs?" "More of you to love."

For me, transition has not been a process of working towards a goal. It has been a ritualistic journey of discovering myself. Without the burden of norms and relational pressure, I drift evermore . . . perhaps not towards womanhood, at least not yet, but away from my assigned gender as male. With every choice I make, and most importantly, with every person who loves me as I am, I leave manhood behind, and feel lighter and freer because of it.

BIOGRAPHY

S. W. Underwood is a homebody and researcher at the University of Toronto. They live with their partner, three cats, and two birds in southern Ontario. They hope to become a mother in the coming years and to continue researching, teaching, and advocating about and for misfits everywhere.

Chapter 27

Is It Still a Body?

H Howitt

It's Spring 2018. A friend has bought two tickets to Travis Alabanza's trans writing workshop and texts me to ask if I want to come. It's something I might've done once. I might not have thought twice about it, once.

Squinting, I try to recall the past versions of myself that would have unquestioningly gone to such a workshop. I barely remember them. They are strangers. Naïve. Ignorant. No sense of what is coming. What is going. The loss that awaits.

Now I think: is that me? Am I a trans person? Am I a writer?

This version of myself has spent the past seven months consumed by chronic pain, immobility and fatigue. A period of ill-health that saw me mostly confined to my bedroom, culminating in an admission to a psychiatric hospital, just weeks before the invitation to the workshop.

These questions preside against a backdrop of the more haunting doubt that has been reverberating around my head since I left the hospital: *is it still a body?*

I want to go to the writing workshop.

I tell my friend that I have two black eyes (science brain shouts: BILATERAL SUBORBITAL HAEMATOMA!) and that I have some access requirements. I give silent thanks in the gaps between seconds to the disabled girlfriend who taught me how to be physically disabled, who taught me how to talk about access from a place of empowered entitlement, because we *are* entitled to it, because we are *not* an inconvenience. I ad lib to incorporate my mental health needs into the now more familiar language of physical access requirements. The friend is very accommodating of my needs, and so we go.

I don't know Travis super well, but what I do know is that they create spaces with love in them. This is evident as soon as I enter the room. There is love in here. In an ice-breaker go-round, we are invited by Travis to say our name, our pronoun, our relationship to writing, and what juiced drink we'd be today and why. I go last.

The people who precede me answer these questions with their gender at the forefront of their experience. I never knew that foregrounding my gender was a privilege that could be taken from me, just like I hadn't anticipated losing my knees. I've not been trans these past seven months. I've been sick. You can't be both. There has been no room for my gender. If there is one thing that has characterised disability for me, it is bureaucracy. Paperwork. Administrative forms and faceless institutions. The name that is used in the countless correspondences, called out in numerous waiting rooms, is my dead name: a name I have become once again accustomed to hearing and responding to. Even my spouse, who hasn't used the wrong pronoun for me in years, begins to slip up during the never-ending phone calls and appointments.

Am I a trans person?

I've had months and months of medical investigation, whereby my trans identity has no relevance. My gender is obfuscated by the medicalised lens my body is scrutinised through. I am a female patient. My radiographers enquire about my fertility and make assumptions about my sexuality. My rheumatologist is a misogynist who addresses my husband, not me. I am acutely aware of the womanhood he fixes me with, and I don't care. I am 100 per cent invested in making these doctors take me seriously; the last thing I'm going to do is tell them I'm trans. I am performing 'educated, sane, normal member of society who desperately needs to find out why they can't fucking walk'. I can't risk prioritising my gender feels. In fact: what gender feels? In these establishments I am what I need to be. A woman. Same goes for benefits. I selectively remove 'testosterone' from the bibliography-like list of medications on my application form to receive state disability benefits. Best not to complicate things. Come to think of it, am I even remembering to take it? My muscle tone is definitely on the slack, but I suppose the horizontal lifestyle will do that to you, hormones-be-damned. I haven't worn outdoor clothes much recently. It's too difficult to get jeans on and off, and too dehumanising to ask my loved ones to do it, even though they do, and they do so with as much integrity and honour as they can, imbuing the act with their respect for my humanity. I live in pyjamas. How trans can you be in pyjamas? The only people that see me are my housemates and my doctors. All we talk about now is my health. If a trans falls in the forest, and there is no one there to hear it, is it still a trans? Is it still a body?

It's my turn in the go-round. How can I answer these questions? Do I have a relationship to writing? If I do, it's a fraught one. We're on a break. Or is it terminal? I've not written or read a thing since I got ill. I babble something about being on hiatus from my PhD and skip to the juice question. I say I'm orange-flavoured Fybogel. The fibrous powdered husk that I have dissolved in a cup of water religiously, morning and night, since my doctor upped my codeine prescription: a feeble attempt to soften the cementing effects of opiates. A ritual prayer for a shit. *Please God, let me shit.*

What I don't say in the go-round is this: the opiates I was prescribed seven months earlier – the day after my girlfriend stayed up with me all night, as I sobbed and sobbed, in so much pain in my hips that I could not be still for more than a minute, a pain that would not subside no matter what I took or how I positioned my body – they numb more than my physical pain. It's not just my guts that are being cast like cement. ('*Drink a cup of cement,*' I recall my Australian aunt telling me, years ago – an unsympathetic jibe when you're being a wimp. It translates to '*Harden the fuck up*'.) I don't say that I too am hardening. Setting. That I am trapped in here. That I use this laxative to remedy the side-effects of a drug that functions in equal parts to suppress appetite, to suppress pain, and to suppress the gnawing knowing that grows despite these efforts: a knowing that threatens eruption, threatens war.

When I come to write this story, I can tell it two ways: I can either retrace my steps chronologically, in which case, it appears my physical health and mental health are distinct from one another, and the deterioration of the former precedes the annihilation of the latter. Or I can tell it with the wisdom of hindsight, which renders the articulation of these things as separate and linear ludicrous. I am a monist, after all, and so I can only portray the decline of my physical health as it happened, in messy entanglement with my mental deterioration. If I know that vital information lies at the nexus of these multiple levels, what else can be uncovered when I interrogate my fragmented experiences, and the liminal spaces that exist just outside of and in-between categories?

Allow me to expand on this lesser-known indication of opiates as knowledge-suppressors: pain meds, like most things, operate on multiple levels. On one level, I use opiates as analgesia – an orthodox treatment to a purely physical problem. The pain I am numbing is physical. Scans show serious degradation to my joints, some of which require major surgery. On another level, there is a deeper pain, a more urgent need for numbing. I am pharmacologically suppressing the emergence of something amorphous, hidden, not visible in scans, etched instead into the uncharted map of my emotional body. I know not, nor am I interested in, the linear question of cause and effect. All I know is this: the pain that erupts in my hips is attached to something. Something non-physical. Something ancient. Something put there a long time ago. And it is trying to tell me something.

I take opiates to kill the pain in my body, because that makes life more liveable. I take opiates because they muffle the growing, nagging knowledge that is trying to speak itself, and if I am forced to listen, life might be unliveable. It is this dual-function which I am both aware of and not-aware of that forces me to reconcile the seeming separate fragments of my experience, the physical and the non-physical. It forces me to challenge the very notion that our experiences ever fit neatly into discrete categories. That you can be both and neither. That conflicting truths can, and do, exist within us.

The seeming contradiction of knowing the unknown: you know, and you don't know. I'm sure that I am not the only trans person who can say in all honesty, 'I always knew' and 'I just didn't know!' We fear knowledge because it is often accompanied by its inconvenient friend: action-to-be-taken. It's why we don't quit smoking. We don't go vegan. We avoid getting our blood pressure checked. We avoid our bank balance. We know, and yet we don't know. It is the internal dilemma, when some part of us craves the forbidden fruit, and another tries to refuse it. Who knows what chaos will reign over our lives once we receive this knowledge? What hitherto unimaginable actions might be called for?

Sometimes there is a long period before the conscious knowing; a kind of demi-knowing. It's not not-knowing, but it's pre-*knowing*. I can draw a line of comparison between these months of bed-bound opiate use trying to block out the incessant call of my subconscious, to the months, many years earlier, that preceded my eventual acceptance that I wasn't a woman, and that I was probably going to have to do something about it. I recall the day I was in tears with confusion and indecision about my desire to start taking testosterone. I had not yet 'come out'. We didn't have a language then for my gender. I knew I wasn't a man, so why this urge to take masculinising hormones? My partner hushed my tears. 'Babe, if you were cis, you probably wouldn't be crying about this.' 'But I don't think I'm trans!' I replied. 'I don't feel "trapped in the wrong body."'

The Dominant discourse demanded I have a series of early childhood memories of 'wrong-bodied-ness' or 'difference', and a pathological repulsion of my genitals. Neither of these things described my experience – at least, not all of the time. I let out a diatribe attempting to relay my gendered experience to my partner. I am plural, dynamic, wishy-washy. I'm not trans, but I'm not not-trans either. I exist in the liminal space, between, or maybe even beyond these categories. Is there a liveable life for someone like me? What does it all mean? 'I think it means you can call yourself trans, babe, and you can start taking the hormones, if that's what you want.' My partner was right, and that was the day I finally let the knowledge of my transness into my consciousness. It was our culture of cisnormativity that acted as knowledge-suppressor, a culture that kept me in the borderlands of trans and not-trans. Now, with the advent of non-binary visibility and activism, I know that I am trans enough. I am not a man, and I am not a woman, but I am trans.

It took me just as long to claim the moniker *trans* as it did *disabled*. It was around the time I began to hear the words 'non-binary' more and more in queer spheres that I also started to notice how I couldn't manage the escalators on the Tube anymore. Convinced I'd just strained some muscles in my legs from too much dancing, I put off investigation until I couldn't walk.

I recall being acutely shocked when the orthopaedic surgeon told me he'd not seen knees like mine on anyone under 70 and asked what I'd done to wear them out to the extent that I had. He asked if I had been a long-distance runner my whole life. 'I won't even run for a bus,' I retorted. He informed me I had advanced osteoarthritis in both knees, irreversible damage that would require a double knee replacement within the next five years. I still didn't call myself disabled. It was our culture of ableism that acted as knowledge-suppressor. I'd been taught what a disabled person was: disability was an identity for those 'others', wheelchair users, people who were really fucked and had been forever. I'd been taught that life was unliveable for these people. If I am forced to acknowledge I am disabled, can life ever be liveable? Even after I qualified for my disabled parking badge and actually had to use a wheelchair, I resisted the identity.

I'd spent years in the liminal space of gender: both and neither cis and trans, man and woman. And now I was forced into the liminal space of disability: both abled and disabled, or worse, neither abled nor disabled; in the world and not in the world; too sick to work, to walk, but not sick enough to qualify for state support. In the final months prior to my hospital admission, my physical health had deteriorated to the point that my life became a blur of enforced bed-rest; prescription drug madness; constant doctor's appointments and MRIs; assessments by officials, sent by the state to assess my worthiness for support. (Get this: according to the soulless bureaucrat sent to my bedroom, I was not worthy.) They were dark months. I was in a liminal space, a hatching space, a birthing space. A kind of slow labour. They were months in which my awareness was gestating. Something was emerging. The arbitrary line that delineates sane from insane was wavering. Was it all in my head, or did my body keep the score? My knowing and my not-knowing were on a slow-mo, action movie collision course. Dihydrocodeine was no longer the effective barricade it once was; it was losing its efficacy as knowledge-suppressor. My subconscious knowing was now hammering at the door of my consciousness. My inner monologue pleaded: '*Go Away! I don't want to know. I don't want to know. Please, please, don't come in. If I am forced to receive this knowledge, how can I live? If what you tell me is true, is it still a body?*'

Know this: the army that you deploy to suppress the knowledge your subconscious is trying to deliver to you is not stronger than the will of that knowledge. You will weaponise everything you have at your disposal – more drugs, more self-harm – every day in an attempt to distance you from yourself, and you will lose. Such is the nature of what needs to be known.

On a dark afternoon in February, the army of my conscious will, knowing it was beat, employed its final strategy. I went blind. I dissociated so extremely that the not unfamiliar dark ring of my peripheral vision grew and grew until I could not see. *I could not see.* I was in my bedroom, the room I had barely left for months. The room that had held me, suspended, for all this time, so familiar, that I had begun to despise it and I could not see it!

Alarmed, my housemates sedated me with Valium and more codeine and put me to bed.

From the accounts of my loved ones, and from my medical notes, I know that I awoke in what I later came to identify as a flashback, a common symptom of complex post-traumatic stress disorder (cPTSD), which I would eventually be diagnosed with. The awful knowledge which had been battering on the door of my consciousness had finally broken through. Upon waking, I was flooded with images, noises, sensory experiences. The scratchy carpet-tiles of the office at the back of my dad's shop. Something to do with my sister. Things I cannot even write. Things I have never spoken of since. These scenes replayed as if in real-time, and though I have little recollection, I know that they erupted violently, and frightened the people trying to care for me. The community mental health team intervened, and I was hospitalised two days later.

'I thought I'd already lost everything I could,' I wept to my girlfriend, referring to the profound loss of trust in my physical body: the loss of my knees, the loss of my mobility, the loss of the life I'd had before pain. I had not been prepared to lose my mind as well. To lose my childhood. My family. I thought being confined to my bedroom was as bad as it could get, a final resting place; but it turned out to be just another interstitial space, a waiting room for hospital. Just when you think, 'Well, at least it can't any get worse,' the secret floor you thought was the basement bottoms out and you crash through the ceiling of the penthouse. I was left with a profound universal wisdom: there is always more to lose; you know not when it will be taken from you.

The emergency mental health team unquestioningly sought a bed on a female ward. Once admitted I even started wearing clothes made for women again. By this point, my existence had been pared down to the barest of bones: 'If all I can do is survive, that's okay. If all I can do is survive, that's okay,' I wrote from room 10. I cared not about the segregated placement. My cPTSD, I reflected, is grounded in a womanhood that I did not choose but was subjected to. My trauma happened because I was a woman. A girl, actually. Because I was a girl, I was traumatised, violated. I wanted to be with the other women on the ward. I craved the solidarity of womanhood, however ill-fitting. I spotted the other queers, the other gender traitors, the confusers. The fellow patients who were in *not-quite-the-right-ward* but *better-than-a-ward-full-of-men* ward. The patients who might reject this identity in one sense, but in another need it to make sense of the gendered violence that put them there. We eyed each other with shy recognition and solidarity.

During one of my ward rounds (a weekly meeting with the head psychiatrist and the staff team), the white cis man who was in charge of my care took umbrage at my history of sex work, and my non-monogamous 'lifestyle', implying that either I brought this illness on myself, or that these things proved I was damaged beyond repair. He turned to his team, as if I were absent, to piously inform them that my 'rage outbursts', as he put it, were a result of taking testosterone. He suggested I take up long-distance running and join an AA meeting, despite having neither knee joints, nor alcoholism. So, confused was he by my request for gender neutral pronouns, that he lost his grip on grammar entirely. 'So, H, do they drink often to cope with these rage outbursts?' He was unable to comprehend that I could be, all at once, trans, traumatised and disabled – one must take precedence. They must be 'treated' separately. Furious? It's the trans. Depressed? Not enough exercise. Disabled? We don't deal with that here – this is a psychiatric unit.

At this stage, I am under the care of three different NHS services: one for my mental health, one for my physical health, and a third to provide gender care. Unsurprisingly, none of them talk to each other. Imagine my chagrin, then, when I discover that the urgent psychiatric assessment with a trauma specialist that we've waited weeks for has been scheduled for the same day as my long-awaited appointment with the consultant psychiatrist at the Gender Identity Clinic (GIC). I don't think twice about rescheduling the GIC. This would have been the third appointment in a trio of psychiatric assessments that have fallen roughly annually, since my referral in 2014.

These appointments are a series of gates which trans people are required to pass through in order to receive the gender care sought. Two psychiatrists must independently agree: 'Yup, this one's a trans, let 'em have their way.' For tricky patients, like me, a third gate-keeper is required before any healthcare is offered. Why am I tricky? Firstly, like plenty of cis people, I don't uphold gender typical values. I am not a straightforward binary trans person. I am queer. I partner with people who complicate the homo and heteronormative assumptions about relationships. 'She [sic] has successful penetrative sex with her [sic] husband,' notes the first GIC psychiatrist, a kernel of doubt, a question mark over the validity of my gender, the subtext weighing it down heavily. Secondly, I am a survivor. I have been asked if my transness is because of childhood sexual assault. I perform 'educated, sane, normal member of society who desperately needs to access the fucking healthcare they deserve' by answering in my most measured tone that I think probably not. I think that people have genders, and also people are abused. No one questions cis people about their genders in the face of their trauma history, so why is my gender pulled into question? If trans was seen as morally neutral, rather than something to be avoided or explained away, then the reasons one might come to a trans identity would be irrelevant. When you cease to make being trans a pathology, 'discovering' an aetiology, or root cause, ceases to make sense. No doctor has ever trawled a patient's history to find the root cause of their cisness, or their straightness.

And what I really want to say in response to this line of question – no, shout, sob, is: 'Maybe it fucking well is! Maybe I detest my body and flee from it any way I know how because my girlhood was violently used to destroy me?! Maybe my sexuality is weird because how can sex ever be normal? And so what? So what if I'm trans because I was abused, who fucking cares the reason? We'll never know, because you can't go back and take it all away and see if I'd live life happily as a woman, so stop with the fucking thought experiment and give me the fucking care I deserve!' These are the doubts we never get to say aloud, so busy are we with the job of proving ourselves 'enough', legitimate, and deserving of care. Not for the first time, I wonder if I'd have received better treatment from each of the three health services if I'd lied by omission about the others. Seeking disability support? Don't mention the being mad or being trans! Need urgent psychiatric care? Best not disclose you take testosterone and have a pain condition – they won't believe you anyway. Want to transition? Well it'll take a hell of a lot longer if you're traumatised and physically unable to run the assessment gauntlet.

I am using my sane, measured voice when I phone the GIC to tell them that I can't make my scheduled third appointment due to the clash with the urgent mental health assessment. The person on the phone tells me the rescheduled appointment will be in February 2019. Eleven months. I beg mitigating circumstances, urging an earlier date. The receptionist suggests I try to move my psychiatric assessment instead. 'No,' I tell them, slightly less measured, sanity cracking. 'No, right now my mental health is more important than my gender, because without a mind, I can't have a gender. In fact, I don't even have a gender right now. I nearly died three weeks ago, and what use is a gender to a dead person? None! No use! So yeah, thanks for the suggestion, but I think I'll keep my mental health appointment. Go ahead and reschedule for 2019.' The receptionist sounds a bit baffled, tells me something about waiting lists, apologises that they can't do more, and hangs up.

Am I trans? Is it still a body?

That appointment clash fell nine days before Travis's trans writing workshop. Little wonder then that as I enter the room I am more than a tad apprehensive, heart thumping as each participant in turn introduces themselves in the juice-drink ice-breaker. My answer in the go-round is met with warm, knowing laughter, and Travis makes a beautiful joke about being for trans liberation so long as it's inclusive of trans babes suffering with irritable bowel syndrome. It's the perfect reception to my big vulnerable constipation share. A few others chip in with their own poo stories and I feel held. Consequently, I am able to immerse myself, my *selves*, in the workshop. In one of the exercises Travis invites us to use a prompt from their work. They ask us, 'If you could go back in time, to just before you left the house today, what would you say to yourself before you step outside?'

This is what I wrote:

Before you step outside...
Nothing about who you are is wrong.
Sharing your experiences is a two-way gift,
it's okay if you can't.
That voice that tells you you are attention-seeking to talk about illness?
That's your internalised ableism,
that's mum,
that's having to choose between being sick and being trans to access
the services you need
you deserve
you are righteously angry at not receiving.
You have a body. It is a trans body. It is a disabled body. It is a
traumatised body. And it is still a body. Don't let the institutionalised
compartmentalisation you are experiencing seep into your wholeness
and split you apart.

BIOGRAPHY

H (they/them) is a white, disabled, non-binary, trans identified, queer porn performer, sex educator, and PhD candidate. They are passionate about sharing skills to explore pleasure and intimacy, exploring tools to facilitate embodiment, and finding language that works to talk about gender and sexuality. H teaches and learns from a sex-critical, intersectional perspective that embraces our varied, plural and complex relationships with sex and our bodies. They believe that the cornerstones of this work are curiosity, consent and compassion. H researches trans sexualities at the University of Brighton, where they are reading for their PhD. Their project 'How We Fuck' explores the tools and practices trans people use to navigate bodies and sex.

Website: www.hhowitt.com

Chapter 28

Trans, Autistic, and a Lot More Besides

Sam Hope

I want to talk about what it is like to be a 'special snowflake' and to have spent a lifetime trying to be ordinary: trying to be less fragile, less unique, less sensitive to changes in the weather. Being altogether peculiar is generally not a comfortable place to be. And yet being someone I'm not – that's worse. Not only does it mean living with the agony of masking everything, it also betrays all the other people who are in the same boat.

My efforts to mask my autism, coupled with my ability to dissociate, helped me create a persona that seemed like a perfectly functioning cis neurotypical person. So how do I then convince the world that I am trans, that I am autistic, that I am struggling or suffering? And if the mask slips, then the switch from apparently functioning to hot mess chimes another false note, leaves me even less believed or supported. Invites judgements such as attention seeker, putting it on. Clearly you can cope better than this, we've seen you.

Masks are lies but wear them long enough and they become the truth. The psychic effort of being someone I'm not is enormous, but it's naïve to think I could just sift through my experiences and separate out what is 'real me' from what has been built into me by others. Because what is built is still real; effort has given it substance.

In other words, human beings are socially constructed; our habits and our social environment shape our brains as much as our brains shape our world.

There's a cumulative social impact to being different. For instance, trans kids are more likely to be bullied and abused, because they are more likely to be isolated, less likely to be defended, and less likely to be believed. If you're trans and autistic, that compounds the problem, as autistic kids are also more likely than others to be bullied and abused. In my case, being trans and autistic led to me being vulnerable to abuse, and led to me growing up with complex trauma and dissociation because of my childhood experiences.

I often find that people muddle up things that are part of my identity with things that are part of my trauma; for example, 'Your poor eye contact is from shame due to abuse.' Er, no, it's because I'm autistic. Stuff that should be understood as simply who I am is written off as 'damage'. Even my queer trans identity has been labelled as that by some.

At the same time, trauma has moulded me and shaped me in ways that, after a ton of therapy, I am cool with. It is still me and it's still okay, even if it was a later modification rather than 'factory fitted'.

Many of my experiences growing up did not match those of others around me, and were also quite contradictory. I was outdoorsy and physical but badly coordinated and rubbish at sports. I turned my ankle every other day and couldn't hold a pen properly – still can't – and yet I would happily spend time walking along the tops of fences, climbing trees, walking on stilts. I was academically bright, eventually, but incredibly slow, with poor attention. I could remember the most ridiculously precise things but never where I put anything. I was shy but chatty. I was highly perceptive but also quite oblivious at times. Now, I can trace these issues to my divergent brain and body. Then, I was just the super-weird kid, and in the 1970s that wasn't an okay thing to be.

Because I had so many quirks, the fact that I wanted to marry Lucy Mason as soon as I met her, aged five, was just another such difference among many. This was just one aspect of my ability to be so much better at replicating the stereotypical social messages aimed at boys than girls. I might have seemed not to follow the rules at all, but really, I followed 'boy rules' to the letter without even having to think about it. For me, it was an orientation towards whatever nonsense society was programming boys to do, because my gender identity tuned me into that wavelength. Given I came from a military family, it was mainly 'Toxic Masculinity FM'. I learned how not to cry at age six.

If I'd been raised in another time I'd have wanted powdered wigs, blush and embroidered waistcoats, I have no doubt.

The world, of course, had sly and brutal ways of trying to knock all this out of me.

I cannot claim my gender identity as some sort of radical or autistic non-conformity. I totally conformed. It's just that my whole gender orientation was pointing in the 'wrong' direction. Only years later, as an adult, did I painstakingly and consciously learn how to perform 'woman' with any semblance of skill, until she, too, became a part of who I am.

Only lately have I discovered a phenomenon that made so much sense of all my seemingly unrelated weirdness. My physical disability, autism, attention deficit hyperactivity disorder (ADHD), high sensitivity, queerness and gender incongruence. Here is the mind-blowing revelation, which I investigated when researching for the neurodivergence chapter of my book: when human beings are divergent in one way, this increases the statistical odds of them being divergent in other ways. A whole bunch of divergent traits cluster together in the population – non-heterosexuality, left-handedness, being 'double jointed' (joint hypermobility), being a genius, synaesthesia, myalgic encephalomyelitis (ME)/chronic fatigue syndrome/fibromyalgia, physical conditions like Ehlers-Danlos syndrome, gender divergence, particular face shapes, dyslexia, ADHD, high sensitivity, autism, dyspraxia and other body and brain quirks.

In other words, gay people are more likely to be left-handed, autistic people are more likely to be trans, neurodivergent and/or queer people are more likely to have joint hypermobility, and so on. Crucially, there is no evidence or much likelihood that these things are causally linked; it would be hard to imagine how, say, left-handedness causes autism or being gay makes you more likely to smell colours (synaesthesia). However, people will try, for example, to dismiss a physical disability as psychosomatic due to the stress of being gay, or an LGBT+ identity as a symptom of poor social understanding due to autism.

In other words, 'different' people tend to be different in lots of unrelated ways. It really is possible to be all of these things, or at least many unusual things all at once. What a relief it was to learn this, but what a challenge it is to carry all these quirks in one body.

In my lifetime the narrative around many of my differences has been continuously shifting. Left-handedness has, in 200 years, gone from being deeply stigmatised to wholly accepted. Consequently, nobody is going to ask a left-hander if they use their left hand because their autism makes it difficult for them to conform to right-handedness. Disability, neurodivergence and transness, on the other hand, seem to be going on a round trip, where currently we appear to be returning to the stigmatised point of origin, despite past gains in acceptance. I hope it is just backlash, but I fear we are going backwards.

I spent much of my life being told my ME/fibromyalgia, my gender/ sexuality and my autism/ADHD/sensory experiences were the result of my traumatised childhood and that enough therapy and self-exploration would 'fix' me into a physically able, normative, neurotypical person. Discovering that there's medical evidence that my brain and body just work a little differently was a key factor in learning to accept, even celebrate, myself as I am, and this has resulted in more substantial wellbeing than all my attempts to 'fix' myself. It's exhausting enough carrying these differences without believing they are somehow my 'fault' for not having sufficiently 'dealt with' the stuff I've been through. I spent much of my thirties trying to rid myself of physical disability through therapy and feeling like I must be doing it wrong. Self-acceptance has brought me so much peace.

Not that as a therapist I hold much store in the idea that people need to be 'fixed', whatever they have been through, but as a client it's an idea that has held too much power for me.

I keep having to remind myself that disability is not failure, but it runs contrary to the increasingly ableist messages I hear from the world around me. I live under a political regime that has achieved the deaths of thousands of disabled people through benefits cuts and sanctions without much public outcry; where people are only valuable if they are productive. And yet many of our differences are only disabling because of external conditions. For instance, a raft of recent research suggests the mental health of trans people is contingent on how we are treated, and the World Health Organization (1992) has decided to declassify gender incongruence as a mental illness, just as they did with homosexuality in 1990. This acknowledges that the way society treats trans people creates the conditions for extreme stress and trauma – society disables trans people, in other words.

Many people like to make connections and have neat formulations about everything. They love their binaries and they like to find patterns. So, when I was a loud, awkward, oddly dressed teenage 'girl' coming to college walking with a stick, of course it was all just proof of my 'attention seeking' behaviour. Of course, my gender and sexuality were seen as just another example of how 'messed up' I was. The messages of my youth were designed to dismiss or reject everything about me and confuse and conflate all the divergent parts of my identity. The psychic pressure of having so many differences ignored, conflated, stigmatised or dismissed was immeasurable, even without the abuses that happened as a result.

Trying to discover my 'true self', amid all the noise telling me everything about me is damage, was not an easy task. I just turned 47. I came out as non-binary at 42. Now I exist as an out non-binary trans person. I can't hide the fact that my ME/fibromyalgia and chronic migraines physically limit me. I am open about the fact that I have (diagnosed) autism and ADHD, and that I'm an HSP (highly sensitive person), a phenomenon there is also now increasing research evidence for. I now (reluctantly) speak about the dissociation and complex post-traumatic stress disorder (cPTSD) I have experienced because of childhood trauma, and the depression and anxiety I experience because of, well, everything else. Then there's the eating issues and dermatillomania that might just be stims (self-stimulatory behaviour common in autistic people) that have got out of hand, but they caused their own amount of turmoil before I understood them.

I say I exist because it is important to know that trans people exist, non-binary people exist, whether people want us to or not. But I don't just exist. I live a full and interesting life, working as a writer, a trainer, a therapist/supervisor and a community organiser. It turns out that I am not just a collection of 'deficits', I have unique talents. I am deep, empathic and clever, good at making connections and distilling complexity. Any sense of 'failure' I might have about who I am is external. The culture I was raised in may see me as just a collection of problems, but I am so much more than that, and I am whole and enough, just as I am. Oh boy, did it take a lot of hard work to be able to say that!

Alternative perspectives, different senses and experiences have the capacity to remind us that every bit of our experience is deeply subjective. I have learned, mostly by surrounding myself with braver people than myself, just how much non-binary, autistic, creative, divergent people, if allowed to thrive, if celebrated in all our inherent non-conformity, can open worlds of possibilities for all of us.

In permaculture, there is a saying that growth happens in the margins. The saying holds true as much for people as it does for plants. The margins are an exciting/creative place to be but also a terrifying/unsafe place to be at times, particularly times in which the political ideology of sameness and 'one true way' dominate and difference is characterised as a threat.

Perhaps it's the fearful conservative in all of us that gets in the way of humanity reaching its potential. Individually we fight to be less on the margins instead of making the margins our home and celebrating together what can be accomplished there. For me personally, some of the most important choices I have made have been the risks I have taken to move away from the centre and the safety of 'passing' for 'normal'; to build bridges and networks outwards and neglect the paths to the centre. And some of the biggest betrayals to myself and others have been in trying to preserve my safety and status – for example, by coming out as lesbian instead of trans because it affected my career less if I hid my transness. Ten years of my life passed living as a lesbian, hiding my transness and my bisexuality in a small-town community that depended on sameness for cohesion and secure borders.

This act of writing is a process of self-marginalisation, and that seems appropriate to me. It is a reminder to myself to cease assisting the ongoing quest to storm the centre ground. I sometimes wonder whether if we all flocked to the margins and accepted the fragility, vulnerability and beautiful weirdness that is inherent to our existence, would we perhaps learn to tread more carefully with each other? For myself, I am now discovering that the things that are best about me are the very things I have tried hardest to school out of myself.

When people use 'snowflake' as a negative term, the emphasis is clear: don't be vulnerable, don't be fragile, don't be unique. I have attempted to crush or abandon all my snowflakey qualities, but I now discover they are absolutely the best thing about me.

BIOGRAPHY

Queer, trans, disabled, neurodivergent and non-binary, Sam Hope (they/them) is a writer, trainer, and therapist/supervisor who lives on a low income near Nottingham, UK with their partner and a collection of rescued cats. Sam runs the Facebook page *Trans Inclusive Feminism* and is the author of *Person-Centred Counselling for Trans and Gender Diverse People* (Jessica Kingsley Publishers). They are also an enormous nerd and have been known to waste ridiculous amounts of time reading and writing obscure fanfiction.

Chapter 29

Fleshing Out Non-Binary

Francis Ray White

My fat is an affront to binary gender. I know that's a bold opening statement, but a vague disclaimer is nobody's friend. I'm not here to give you a rundown of all the ways being fat makes being non-binary harder or different (different from what?) – like the two things can be separated. No, I want to explain how my fatness *is* non-binary and how thinking of it like that helps me carve a liveable life out of being things that I am frequently told should not and cannot exist. There are, of course, infinite ways to be non-binary, and whether we describe it as an identity, a feeling, or a general sense of who we are, we can't get away from the fact that we also have to live it, in a body. As humans we are embodied beings. We move through the world in, and as, particular bodies: bodies that shape how we are perceived and interacted with by others, but that also shape who we are and what we can be in return. I've never been non-binary in/as a thin body, just as I've never been non-binary in/as a racialised minority, working-class or disabled body, and my experiences reflect how this has enabled me to fit and succeed in some ways, and to not fit (sometimes literally) and fail in others. This is the story of a work in progress, of trying to make space for the messy intersections of my body, gender and identity, and of really over-thinking it in the process.

So yeah, I'm fat. That's not an insult, it's a description, though being able to say that is part of the story here. My whole life, a continual anti-fat drizzle in the cultural ether has let me know that my body is 'wrong'. Wrong, as in: 'No one will ever fancy you.' Wrong, as in: 'What about your health?' Wrong, as in: 'We don't make that in your size.' Perhaps the most insidious message instilled in me at a tender age was the one saying I couldn't stay fat and needed to do something about it ASAP. The implication was that life could only properly start once I'd lost weight.

Until then I was expected to exist in a holding pattern of deferred joy consisting largely of endless dieting and crushing self-surveillance. There is no permission in wider society to imagine a future in which you are still fat, let alone one in which you are still fat *and* have access to all the goodies thinness alone is meant to confer (popularity, wellbeing, sex, fashionable outfits). Learning this deeply entrenched, deeply fatphobic mentality is easy. Unlearning it, and finding out what else might be possible, is where things start to get interesting.

As a baby queer I was already starting to realise that life could pan out in exciting ways no one bothered to tell me about growing up. Then I got into gender studies at university and as a result gained a pretty robust critique of the patriarchal bullshit designed to make me feel crap about my body. I proudly rejected feminine norms of beauty and appearance on the grounds that a) it was the feminist thing to do, and b) my favourite bands didn't wear skirts or make-up, so why should I?

However, my immersion in feminist/queer worlds failed initially to dislodge my internalised fatphobia (possibly because mainstream feminist critiques of the body and beauty are not that great when it comes to talking about actually being fat). So, I still took it for granted that being fat was bad. I still wanted to lose weight and I was still envisioning a future for myself where I was no longer fat. When I eventually found fat activism in my mid-twenties, it was an absolute revelation. It was the early 2000s and I fortuitously fell in with a bunch of queer fat folk who were on the periphery of a DIY feminist festival I was helping to organise. Though I couldn't pinpoint a specific moment my life changed, getting to know people who laughed in the face of diets and who were (to my eyes) the coolest people on earth, gradually helped me let go of the fantasy that if I could just fit into smaller trousers my life would be immeasurably better. This aspect of fat activism was genuinely transformative. Fat was no longer a blight, or weight a 'problem', and instead I began to be able to imagine entirely new ways of living the relationship between my fat body, my gender non-conformity, and what I would eventually come to name as being non-binary.

At this time my politics of gender non-conformity were squarely aimed at stretching the category of woman to accommodate people like me: butch-ish blobs with zero interest in femininity. My fat body was suited to this project in ways it had never been suited to anything, and that felt like cause for celebration. Even clothing stores supported my programme of gender subversion by failing to provide 'correctly' gendered clothing in my size – although I was not 'super fat', I was fat enough to be sized out of most high-street 'women's' clothes. To me this was proof of the narrow confines of current gender formations, and also a jolly good excuse to go shopping in the 'men's' section where (in some shops) clothes do come in slightly more generous sizes. I'm not saying they fitted well, but if I could get into anything, I counted that as a victory. Thus, my low effort, queer/masc drag aesthetic was born at the intersection of subversion, convenience and the absence of many other viable options. It's mostly about ill-fitting trousers, stretchy, collared t-shirts paired with fabulous vintage polyester neckties and sleeveless knitwear – it's not a look that's ever been fashionable, but it works for most occasions so it's one less thing to think about.

I started to rethink my fat as an asset, or at least a useful resource for undermining gender norms. Being fat, I literally could not embody the kind of feminine daintiness required to be fully, and heteronormatively, 'ladylike'. I did not go in and out in the right places. I mostly just went out and then out some more. I'm blessed with fat in a typical 'male' distribution around my middle (waist, what waist?) rather than in the 'female' hips/ass/thighs areas. Had I been thinner, I would have been more unmistakably female-shaped, but my fat seemed to blur it out, edging me towards more liminally gendered spaces. Yes, I also had an impressively matronly chest, but at times even this could read as extra belly – I still got the occasional 'sir' in shops if I was wearing the right coat. However, if I was beginning to think of fat as something that troubled gender, this wasn't always what more visible kinds of fat activism reflected back to me. Fat activism as a whole, and the very popular 'fatshion' (fat-fashion) arm of it in particular, has developed with a cis, and usually femme-presenting, woman in its mind's eye. The movement is dominated by such women, and understandably, given they experience a particularly pernicious mix of misogyny and fatphobia, with racism, classism, ableism and heterosexism thrown in for good measure.

But this wasn't my experience of being fat and I increasingly felt excluded by that type of fat activist discourse. I didn't want pretty underwear in big sizes, or to be told that 'real women have curves'. I wanted to use the challenge fatness posed to the category of woman to stretch that category to breaking point, not to double-down on some pretty traditional notions of femininity in order to be included in it. It seemed like fat activists were expending a lot of effort trying to gain access to a group your genital arrangements are supposed to get you free membership to (isn't that how it works?). I could no longer understand why they were bothering.

It wasn't just this aspect of fat activism that was causing me problems. A lot of fat political rhetoric avows that if you can somehow get over your own fatphobia then the payoff is a feeling of being 'at home' in your body; but that wasn't working for me, mainly because I was starting to think I was trans. I already had one foot outside the category of woman on account of my fatness and queerness, so I began to wonder why *I* was bothering with it, and whether I wanted out altogether. Becoming more and more uncomfortable with being assumed to be a woman on the basis of how my body was being read, it got harder to feel 'at home' in that body. The old sensation that maybe life would be better on the other end of a bodily transformation started to rear its head again, but this time my fatness was playing a slightly different role.

Coming out as trans for me mostly meant changing my name and asking for 'they/them' pronouns. I didn't use the term 'non-binary' at first because it wasn't on my radar back in 2011, but later, as the term gained traction, it became a useful way to shorthand my desire to refuse (binary) gender. I didn't initially change anything about my appearance, but soon felt the spectre of not feeling 'trans enough' creeping up on me. Increasingly, being read as female despite my efforts at non-feminine gender presentation didn't just irritate me, it hurt. I was frustrated that I didn't seem to look as ambiguous and unreadable as other non-binary types and started to wonder if it was because I was fat.

For a while my fatness had been the head cheerleader for my embodied gender non-conformity because it de-feminised me, but now it seemed to do the opposite. My soft rolls and lack of hard edges put my body at odds with the artful black and white images that illustrate the answer to the question 'What does non-binary look like?' Those bodies are invariably thin. Skinny even. They are also almost always white, able-bodied and clad in expensive looking tailored menswear (shirt unbuttoned almost to the waist to expose tantalising lack of tits, of course). While rationally I know it's nigh on impossible for anyone to be consistently read as non-binary, it was tempting to wonder whether if I were closer to this fat-free model of genderlessness I could cut a more ambiguous figure and thus be (mis)gendered less often.

Here we arrive at the crux of the fat/gender/body dilemma. The proposition that losing weight might be the solution to my lack of gender recognition could not have sat more awkwardly with my hard-fought-for fat politics. But something else was wrong with the logic of it: how could being thinner be the key to making me both more and less gendered? A 'properly' feminine body is thin, otherwise why would fat women have to work so hard to be considered feminine? A 'properly' masculine body is also thin – just look at the advice offered to transmasculine people that emphasises minimal 'female' fat, a narrow waist and broad shoulders as the key to being successfully read as male. Now to top it off, to have a 'properly' genderless/androgynous body you have to be, guess what? Thin! So, as a fat person who doesn't hate being fat or want to be thin, what the hell are you meant to do to live an embodied non-binary life in/as a body that feels like yours and that other people read in ways that vaguely respond to how you feel?

I wish I had the answer, but ultimately I have come to this: fat doesn't have a gender, or at least, not a binary one. It creates feminine softness *and* masculine bulk. Despite what a lot of cis female fat activists have argued, being fat does makes me less of a woman, but it also fails to make me a man. By sticking out and refusing to fit in, literally and metaphorically, fat both shapes bodies into binary forms, and subverts that same binary. I'm taking that as conclusive proof that fat is non-binary! This doesn't mean you cannot, or should not, change aspects of your body or appearance to better embody who you are; doing so will enable you to be, or to do, new things in all sorts of new ways. Bodies and selves are capable of incredible change, but when we are told that certain bodies are 'wrong', or that only certain bodies can 'be' certain things, our ability to be present in the world diminishes. That's why I will not defer life for the sake of a future that is always out of reach. Rather, I will be defiantly present right now in the fatness that has enabled me to be non-binary and the non-binaryness that has enabled me to be fat.

BIOGRAPHY

Francis Ray White (they/them) is a queer, white academic who lives and works in London. They are a senior lecturer in Sociology at the University of Westminster where, for the past 12 years, they have had the privilege of teaching gender and sexuality studies to undergraduates. When they're not teaching, Francis researches and writes on questions of fat and trans embodiment. Outside academia, Francis volunteers as a speaker and occasional youth worker for the organisation Gendered Intelligence. Francis also enjoys participating in various kinds of queer cultural activism and has made many zines and posters for Unskinny Bop, London's fattest/queerest disco.

Email: f.r.white@westminster.ac.uk

Chapter 30

Nursing whilst Non-Binary

Drew Simms

I'm a psychiatric nurse working with adolescents who have eating disorders. I'm also genderqueer. On the surface it may seem that these two aspects of my life are unrelated, but I wouldn't be at the stage I am now (that is, six months on hormones) without my job being what it is, and I wouldn't be the kind of nurse I am (one who advocates for the care needs of LGBT youth) without my experiences of gender.

Let's rewind for the origin story. Something in me rebels against any attempt to formulate a comprehensible narrative out of gender development, as it is near impossible to do so without simplifying and cherry-picking 'the signs' if you are to have the vaguest hope of being understood by anyone who is not trans or a gender theorist. Having said this, here is my personal history of gender as best as I can summarise it:

Recently my father informed me that my parents knew I 'wasn't straight' (their understanding of my 'difference') from a very early age but did not know what to do about it, so did nothing. There were plenty of worse options they could have gone with than burying their heads in the sand, so I don't hold it against them. There were a couple of incidents in my early childhood that I recall, the most memorable being when I confidently told my classmates about how excited I was for my voice to break and the resulting confusion and disappointment when I was roundly ridiculed.

It wasn't until I was 15 that the thought crystallised in my mind that I was not a girl. However, this being 2003, and the internet not being what it is now, I had no frame of reference for what I was feeling. I was going through a George Orwell phase at the time and viscerally resonated with the concept of stealing people's power of thought by shrinking their vocabulary. I had no language for who I was, so I could not exist.

When I look back on this time now, I invariably think of *The Well of Loneliness* (Hall 1928), which I also read at this age. (It turns out that teachers would leave you alone if you conspicuously read lesbian literature whilst Section 28, a homophobic piece of legislation that resulted in teachers being unable to acknowledge LGBT existence as 'a pretended family value' on pain of dismissal, was still in the process of being phased out.) I know that sounds pretentious, and whilst I was insufferably obnoxious, as is only right when you are 15, it links into how language creates the space that identity is given to fit into. Scholars speculate on whether Radcliffe Hall was a trans man or a butch lesbian, which is an unanswerable question because at the time the only language available was 'Invert': a conflation of gender and sexuality.

It was for similar reasons that I tried to live up to the label of 'butch lesbian' as the closest thing I had heard of to what I was feeling. I got most of my reading from charity shops and picked up a copy of *The Female Eunuch* (Greer 1970). All this book did was make me feel guilty about my sense of gender, which according to the line of Greer's argument must be down to unresolved internalised misogyny. It took many years for me to reason out a counter-argument to this, given that I loved women and spent a long time wishing my uncomfortable feelings would go away so that I could embrace being a girl with the same ferocious intensity that my friends seemed to. In the end I did what many do: I balled it all up and threw it to the back of my mind in the junk drawer of 'things I can't work out and have too much going on to deal with'.

I have very few memories of the next decade. I had chronic untreated depression: a fog I saw no way out of until the sheer mass of all the things I'd pushed to the back of my mind caused a breach and exploded. I burned my entire life to the ground and started again.

I began work as a health care assistant and applied for a nursing degree in London, 150 miles from the city I was living in. I had a psychology degree but due to the economic crash, combined with my own mental fog, I'd been stuck in retail for four years. I was desperate to do something that helped people and I wanted to use the knowledge that I'd gone into debt for. I was excited to move to London, a place where I could be anonymous but also engage with a queer scene that felt like a small, wonderfully strange and drama-filled village.

Because I was essentially starting adulthood again from scratch – and the floodgates had opened – I was also thinking about gender constantly. My new friends were teaching me a new language, sharing writing with me that was less than 40 years old and contained voices that rarely see mainstream print. I started using 'they/them' pronouns amongst those close to me, and over the next two years eased out of the closet in more and more situations.

During this time I was completing my required hours of clinical experience in a range of services. In almost every placement setting I encountered patients who were trans or otherwise questioning their gender, and I saw the approach my colleagues took to their care. A typical interaction with a colleague about a trans client involved them using psychoanalytic speculation about the client's parental relationships or experiences of abuse, in an attempt to explain their presentation, and me trying to explain how such theorising undermined the validity of their gender and went against evidence and advice for best care. Mostly people were willing to learn, but sometimes this did not make me popular.

From knowing them, I'm sure these people's intentions were good; they'd just never really had to think about it before and they hadn't had great training in the subject. I felt like I could fill a need here, that I could develop a resource library for the people I worked with and be an advocate for trans people in mental health services. This would become the driving focus of my career.

The summer before my final year I had the opportunity to spend a day with a gender services clinician who will remain nameless. I thought this would be a great way into my desired career path: becoming a trans practitioner specialising in the mental health of trans people. It was with a hopeful heart that I informed the doctor I was spending the day with that I was non-binary. Instead of encouragement, or even bland acceptance, the doctor immediately launched into a speech that began: 'The problem with non-binary people is...' Even the most innocent summer child knows nothing good is going to follow that. Along with a range of inappropriate statements that I am unwilling to write here, I was informed that the only way a person can successfully live in a non-binary gender is if they are 'a professor of gender studies at a liberal university in Brighton'. Numbly I sat through the rest of the day, saving my tears for the train home. This experience also left me feeling that my needs would never be met by those currently in control of NHS gender services.

I later heard that this doctor is somewhat in the habit of going rogue and it seems that it is not only his patients that despair of him. My experiences since then have led me to believe that most doctors in Gender Identity Clinics (GICs) are patient-focused and good at listening, but I did not have these good examples for comparison at the time.

I qualified as a nurse in 2016 and began working with young people. I found I was good at it. I'd introduced myself with my new name and nobody batted an eyelid but I was not sure enough of my footing to tell people my pronouns. I also had more money coming in than I'd ever had before in my life. That's not to say nursing is objectively well paid, it is just well paid in comparison with how I was living before and it took some getting used to. It was months before I realised I could now afford to get the dental work done that I'd needed since 2010. That's a big part of why it took me so long to realise I could go to private gender services: I didn't trust that the money would keep coming in. I also didn't trust the doctors and processes in gender services, thanks to the gentleman described above and horror stories I'd heard from friends, languishing on years-long waiting lists. Why spend money to be told I can't really exist the way I feel I need to?

Then, there was this boy. I work on an eating disorders ward, and I knew we would get trans young people being admitted at some point (research suggests that trans people are more prone to disordered eating than their cisgender peers). When this boy came into our services, I introduced myself with my pronouns: something I'd never had the courage to do in a professional setting before. In that moment he went from watching me to actually looking at me. We had as good a conversation as can be had with a child who's just been admitted to hospital far from home, and then I got on with my shift. I realised later that when he spoke to the other young people and the staff, he was going to realise that I wasn't out at work. I felt uncomfortable about this for several reasons. First, it's not good to have a secret between oneself and a client, particularly if the secret is yours rather than theirs; I worry about boundaries a lot and I'd inadvertently raised one of my own red flags. Second, I wanted this boy to look at me and see hope for the future, not someone twice his age who's still hiding and who's given up hope of being recognised.

Then I thought, why? Why have I done nothing about this for so long? Why aren't I doing something about it now?

The latter question was the one I couldn't answer. I would never judge someone for not being in a position where they felt safe enough to transition, so I had to extend that compassion to myself. Now though, I had all sorts of privileges and security that I wouldn't have dreamt of five years ago.

So, I sent an email. There was a consultant I'd heard good things about from my non-binary friends and he saw private patients as well as working for the NHS. I got an auto-response warning of long waiting lists and telling me what I'd need to do once I got an appointment. Then there was a last-minute cancellation slot and suddenly there I was, three months after I'd sent the first email, being told by a very nice man that all things being equal, I could start HRT within a month.

One of the first things I did was get drunk at a work party and come out to as many people I could at once. It wasn't the healthiest strategy, but it did the trick. This helped. It explained why I'd been so invested in the way the trans boy was treated, and why I thought I was such an expert on it. I was no longer the condescending better-ally-than-thou for making a 'misgender jar' (a swear jar for when anyone got the patient's pronouns wrong); rather, I was someone who saw their own pain in his, and was trying to intercede in it.

Shortly after this I had an abstract accepted to give a lecture about the care needs of trans youth at a conference for people who work in child and adolescent mental health. I was elated but also terrified; I had never addressed this many people before for any reason, never mind on the topic closest to my heart. The day itself was a realisation of my greatest hopes. My peers were desperate to learn: they inundated me with enquiries about resources; they told me stories of trans young people they were trying to help, and wanted my opinion on whether they were doing the right thing; they asked if I could visit their site to deliver training. Needless to say this was overwhelming for one person, and mostly I validated their efforts and referred them on to organisations better placed to help. I had spent weeks mentally running simulations of people asking me hostile questions accusing me of pushing an agenda, only to find that my expectation of the proportion of people who would have a transphobic bias had been wildly inflated by the volume of exposure such people get in the media. This was a lovely surprise and a rare blow to my pessimistic world view.

At the time of writing I have been on hormones for six months and, as you can probably guess, my experience at work has been a mixed bag. My colleagues seem to exist in a delicate state of simultaneously knowing and not knowing. I am still regularly asked whether I have a cold and I explain no, my voice is breaking. In terms of my pronouns, the young people I work with effortlessly made the switch without question; my colleagues are having a harder time. I must accept some responsibility for this as I don't like to correct people and, although I'd have every right to, the idea of consistently correcting everyone is exhausting.

I recently met another non-binary nurse for coffee to compare experiences and offer mutual support about being out at work. We had a laugh-or-cry realisation, which we opted to laugh at: we set the bar so low that anything short of outright rejection and/or aggression fills us with a gratitude that makes it hard to demand more. The truth is that whilst the proportion of people who meet my existence with good will appears to be much higher than I originally expected, the way I function in society is still heavily influenced by fear of the minority who would do me harm. I think you would be hard-pressed to find a trans person who does not have this fear, but there is a specific edge to it when you work with people classed as a vulnerable group, such as children with mental health issues.

Lucy Meadows was a teacher who was hounded by the national press until she completed suicide. The entirety of the news story was that she was a trans woman who was also a teacher. This happened in 2013. Whilst in recent years the press seem to have switched focus to trans youth themselves as some sort of imagined risk to their peers, I still find myself fearing that it would only take one parent to go to a reporter on a slow news day and that would be my life over.

And so I am torn between wanting to protect trans youth and wanting to keep myself safe, between hope and fear. I have decided to conduct myself as if the best-case scenarios are true, and deal with the consequences if they are not. This is the only way I can see of continuing my work. On the days I cannot do this for the sake of myself, I do it for the sake of the young people who are forever inspiring me with a level of resilience they should not have been forced to develop to survive.

I choose to believe that although the road to trans health equality is long, we are on it, and I will continue to contribute to every painfully slow step for as long as I am able, because progress is not a natural side effect of the passage of time – it is a struggle with many casualties, and the retention of gains is not guaranteed.

BIOGRAPHY

Drew (they/them) is a psychiatric nurse working in Child and Adolescent Mental Health Services (CAMHS) eating disorder services in London, where they live with their partner and an unhealthily large stash of yarn. They are currently doing a research MSc in child and adolescent mental health at King's College London and would love to liaise with other trans researchers.

Contact them at drew_simms@outlook.com or see pictures of their knitting and their views on popular culture at @MxDrewSimms

Conclusions

When we embarked on this project, our hope was to bring together a collection of personal narratives that presented some of the diversity of what it is like to be non-binary, as well as challenging the limited ways in which non-binary people are often represented – if they are represented at all. In this final section we will review some of the themes in the book, discuss the context that has been present during the time we have been working on this project, and share some of our hopes for the future.

We have been personally moved and touched by the stories that have been shared, and are grateful to all of the contributors who have been part of this process. Authors have shared stories of coming home: of finding places in themselves where they can celebrate who they are, and communities where they feel safe. They have shared their stories of movement, change, and transformation over time: journeys they have been on and those they have met along the way. Narratives of joy, sadness, frustration, celebration, and fear have been told, with authors connecting with their own vulnerability in doing so. We have heard about the importance of our histories and backgrounds in forming who we are, the perspectives we take, and the possibilities that are open to us, as well as those which are not.

Various themes stood out for us as editors: themes that were present across multiple aspects of identities. Many non-binary people spoke of the sense of not quite belonging: the experience of being an outsider. For many, this feeling was not limited to their experience of gender, but was present within their families, schools, communities, and/or countries of origin. For some, this sense of not belonging drove a need to find spaces where they did belong, where they were seen, held, and could flourish. Contributors shared the importance of the development of strength and resilience, and how this was often found within the self, personal relationships, and further intersecting identities.

Another common theme was a sense of having to strategically choose when to foreground – or background – different aspects of identity, and the sense of pain and freedom constrained which could go along with this. Several authors spoke of foregrounding their masculinity, femininity, androgyny, or other gender expressions in different spaces in order to remain safe-enough or to survive. They also reflected on foregrounding their transness, queerness, or non-binary-ness in some contexts, and keeping these hidden in others, again often in order to be safer or to access vital services. Such experiences intersected with other vital aspects of their being; for example, keeping non-binary-ness hidden in order to access disability services or healthcare, or recognising that only certain non-binary expressions were available – in certain contexts – to somebody of their body, race, or class.

There was also a theme about how many aspects of our lives, beliefs, experiences, and identities are non-binary, and/or fluid. Contributors not only experience their gender as non-binary, but identities and histories relating to nationality, sexuality, class, health, and spirituality were also not easily put into boxes or seen as either/or. It seemed that this was coupled with the idea of multiple selves: different selves that are brought out in different contexts, different places, and with different people (or alone). The idea of multiple, fluid, shifting selves is a concept that we connect with, and one that we embrace when we consider how we take care of ourselves and also celebrate the multifaceted nature of being a human being.

CHALLENGING TIMES

The process of editing this book has – in some ways – been a mirror of the wider context and times of the last two years in what has been called 'the trans moral panic'. In the UK we have seen a rise of interest in the topics of trans and gender diversity in both the general public and the media. Some argue that this is linked to the increase in the number of referrals to gender services in recent years and also related to the UK government's review of the Gender Recognition Act. The media has latched onto – and, in some instances, driven – political narratives drawing on emotive discourses: trans women have been depicted as a threat to cis women, trans men have often been invisible or accused of 'corrupting young lesbians', and non-binary people have been depicted as mad, confused, and deluded, and are often objects of ridicule.

These stories that are told about trans, non-binary, and gender diverse people serve to invoke narratives of fear. It is not surprising therefore that we frequently hear of the harassment, hate crimes, and discrimination that gender diverse people in the UK are facing at present. We have had authors pull out of this project due to a decline in their mental health in relation to being physically attacked or persistently harassed simply because of their gender. Others have said that they do not feel happy to share their stories at present, even under a pen name, for fear of being targeted. We as editors have also not been immune to this context, even finding ourselves caught up in social – and mainstream – media panics due to our work in these fields. While there are flickers of hope, particularly in relation to the increased visibility of gender diversity, non-binary support networks, and role-models, during this period, it has overwhelmingly been a time where it has been tough and risky indeed to be trans or non-binary, and to work in these areas.

In challenging times self-care, resilience, and reflection becomes even more important. In the process of editing this book we have given ourselves permission to breathe, step back, and review. In consumeristic, capitalistic, production-driven cultures the pressure to keep going, to keep producing, to keep working is ever present. Coupled with challenging times and activist movements where the narratives of keeping on fighting, keeping on campaigning, and keeping on pushing are ever present, self-care, self-compassion, and days off can seem like foreign principles. This is a theme that several authors have picked up in their chapters as they have shared their own ways of challenging and managing this culture. We will now share some of the ways we take care of ourselves.

TAKING CARE

The concept – or value – of balance is vital across multiple areas of our lives, interestingly echoing the non-binary theme as it's often a matter of finding the both/and, the in-between balance point, or the way of navigating a paradox.

For example, for many of us there's a vital self-care balance to be struck between engaging outwards and inwards. Connecting with others is central to our lives: friends, partners, colleagues, passing acquaintances, and even those whom we have never met but who are present in our lives through books, music, films, and other kinds of stories. Being embedded within community gives a clear meaning and purpose to our work, as do our clients, students, and readers. Yet, as well as looking outwards, to connections in the world with others, life would be a struggle without solitude and time for individual self-care and reflection. The outer and inner are interconnected as self-care requires systems and structures of support to enable us to have the time and resources to prioritise it. We also have to cultivate community cultures of care and consent in which it is expected and invited that we will look after ourselves, give ourselves time, and help others to do so too, particularly within a wider culture that does the opposite.

We all face another balance or tension as people who work in these areas which are so hugely personally relevant to us. On the one hand, it can give a great sense of meaning to be (hopefully) contributing to the communities we are part of ourselves, potentially offering support to those – readers, clients, students, etc. – who have struggled in the ways we have struggled. On the other hand, the professional, personal, and political being so intertwined means that there can be little retreat or rest from this, and difficulties in one area can echo through the others. It is fragile indeed, for example, to stand up and give a talk on non-binary experience or the trans moral panic, or to work with a client or student who is struggling around gender, when this is our everyday lives and when we ourselves bear the brunt of the media onslaught, everyday misgendering, and transphobic discrimination and hatred.

In difficult times it is important for us to also notice what is going well, a further balance to strive for. What are we proud of? What are we looking forward to? What is perfectly fine just as it is right now? What aspects of our lives are we thankful for? Can we appreciate the wealth of beauty that exists around us? What are the small simple things in life that give us joy or pleasure? Who cares for, loves, and respects us, and is there for us when we call? There is much to be grateful for.

Lastly, and most relevant to this collection, it is important for us to connect with the aspects of ourselves where we do hold privilege. We may have more opportunities, choices, and freedom than we might otherwise if some of our intersections were different. At times these can work to buffer some of the challenges; however, this reflection can also come with pain and an awareness of how much more work there is to be done. In what areas can we work to share our privilege and what does that look like? Where should we step back and allow others a voice? Where should we step forward and take up room ourselves? How much should we focus on the communities we connect with directly? How much with more marginalised communities we may not be part of ourselves? Where can we most compassionately – and effectively – engage our time, energy, and resources? These are all complex questions that are worth continuing to ask, not with the aim of finding a definite solution, but with the knowledge that the answers will likely shift and change over time as we – and the wider world – do.

LOOKING FORWARD

The collection of chapters here shows a snapshot in time. Some of them have mentioned the political challenges that trans, non-binary, and gender diverse people face at present; others have mentioned specific aspects of current queer/trans communities, culture, and services, such as Open Barbers, Bar Wotever and ClinicQ in the UK. If we were to embark on a similar book in 10 or 20 years' time, the stories people would share would be different, as the culture, time, and narratives told about us would also be different.

It is difficult to predict what the future might bring. When we look back on our communities' histories, the notion that time passing equates to progress in terms of inclusivity, quality of life, and LGBTQI+ rights is tempting. However, unfortunately we don't need to look very far to see that life for queer and trans people can get worse far more easily than it can get better, that progress is not a simple linear process, and that rights can be taken away by governments and organisations just as they can be given. (Even the use of the words 'given' and 'taken away' shows how power operates in these processes.)

There is also the difference between laws and rights that people have – or are fighting for – and how these can be quite separate to the culture and thinking that is present in a particular country. As we saw in the chapter by Ludo and Mina, who are from Malta, living in a country with a self-declaration model of gender recognition does not necessarily equate to a more inclusive culture for gender diverse people. At the time of writing, in the UK we are waiting for the outcome of the government's review of the Gender Recognition Act, with questions around whether a model of self-declaration could be implemented and also whether non-binary people will get legal recognition. Yet, as detailed above, this process of review has led to various other 'debates' about trans people coming to the foreground, which has resulted in the UK becoming less, rather than more, safe for gender diverse people.

This demonstrates the significance of how stories that are told about us, often without us, impact directly on our lives. One of our hopes for the future, and even the present, is for more positive, rich, vibrant, and diverse stories about trans and non-binary people to be shared, meaning increased visibility of gender diverse people's lives. We can think of examples where this is happening: some celebrities have spoken about their own gender identities and experiences; non-binary characters are starting to emerge in films and TV shows like *Billions* and *Trans Parent*; social media hashtags are used for everyday visibility, such as #ThisIsWhatNonBinaryLooksLike; and websites such as Beyond the Binary have increased the visibility of diverse non-binary experience. However, at present the predominant image of non-binary people (if one does an internet image search, for example) is of a young, white, slim, wealthy, non-disabled person who is more likely masculine or androgynous than feminine in gender expression. Clearly being visible comes with risks and it is often safer for those who hold more privileges to be openly non-binary. Also, those who are relatively privileged are often more able to partake in activism and creative projects due to having greater time and resources to do so.

We hope that this collection will form part of the emerging breadth of narratives about gender diverse people's lives. We believe in the power of mirrors: of seeing ourselves in the eyes and lives of others and having parts of ourselves accurately reflected back to us, supporting the development of a solid, multifaceted, positive, and integrated sense of self. If you are a non-binary person who picked up this book with a sense of curiosity, we hope that you enjoyed this collection. But, more than that, we hope that you have found parts of yourself here in these stories: that you have found a sense of connection, reflection and a sense of belonging to those who also share part of your story.

References

Ahmed, S. (2006) *Queer Phenomenology: Orientations, Objects, Others*. Durham, NC: Duke University Press.

Alabanza, T. (2018) 'When your body doesn't meet society's expectations, dressing for the heat can be dangerous.' *Metro* 26 June. Available at https://metro.co.uk/2018/06/26/as-a-queer-gender-nonconforming-trans-person-dressing-for-the-heat-can-be-dangerous-7661419, accessed 18/09/19.

Barker, MJ & Iantaffi, A. (2019) *Life Isn't Binary*. London: Jessica Kingsley Publishers.

Barker, MJ., Vincent, B. & Twist, J. (2018) 'Non-Binary Identity.' In C. Burns (Ed.) *Trans Britain*. London: Unbound.

Clare, E. (2017) *Brilliant Imperfection: Grappling with Cure*. Durham, NC: Duke University Press.

Confucius (circa 480 BCE) *The Analects*. Available at https://manybooks.net/titles/confuciuetext02cnfcs10.html, accessed 16/08/19.

Crenshaw, K. (1990) 'Mapping the margins: Intersectionality, identity politics, and violence against women of color.' *Stanford Law Review 43*, 1241.

Greer, G. (1970) *The Female Eunuch*. London: MacGibbon & Kee.

Hall, R. (1928) *The Well of Loneliness*. Garden City, NY: Sun Dial Press.

Haza, O. (1982) 'Gesher Tzar Me'od', *Li-Yeladim (Songs for Children)*. [CD]. Tel Aviv: Hed Arzi Music.

Hill-Collins, P. & Bilge, S. (2016) *Intersectionality*. Cambridge: Polity Press.

hooks, b. (2014) *Ain't I a Woman: Black Women and Feminism*. New York, NY: Routledge.

Iantaffi, A. & Barker, MJ (2017) *How to Understand Your Gender: A Practical Guide for Exploring Who You Are*. London: Jessica Kingsley Publishers.

Kessler, S.J. & McKenna, W. (2000) 'Gender construction in everyday life: Transsexualism.' *Feminism & Psychology 10*(1), 11–29.

Law, B. (2019) *Growing Up Queer in Australia*. Carlton, VIC: Black, Inc.

Lorde, A. (2007) *Sister Outsider: Essays and Speeches*. London: Crossing Press.

Miserandino, C. (2003) *Spoon Theory*. Available at https://cdn.totalcomputersusa.com/butyoudontlooksick.com/uploads/2010/02/BYDLS-TheSpoonTheory.pdf, accessed 18/09/19.

Muñoz, J.E. (2009) *Cruising Utopia: The Then and There of Queer Futurity*. New York, NY: New York University Press.

Tanis, J. (2018) *Trans-Gender: Theology, Ministry, and Communities of Faith*. Eugene, OR: Wipf and Stock

Woolf, V. (1928/2004) *A Room of One's Own*. London: Penguin Books.

World Health Organization (1992) *International Classification of Diseases and Related Health Problems* (10th edition). Geneva: WHO.

Editors' Biographies

Jos Twist (they/them) is a White British genderqueer person who occupies many in-betweens. They work as a psychologist supporting gender diverse youth in London. Their clinical, academic and research interests include diversities and intersectional identities, narrative approaches and ethics. They are involved with a variety of community projects and activities, and also enjoy cycling in the woods, reading, and going on adventures with their partner.

Ben Vincent (they/them) is an academic sociologist, currently working at the Open University, looking at the integration of trans healthcare provision. They are the author of the book *Transgender Health: A Practitioner's Guide to Binary and Non-Binary Trans Patient Care*, as well as a range of other pieces on gender diversity. They enjoy gaming, playing the piano, and painting.

Meg-John Barker (they/them) is the author of a number of popular books on sex, gender and relationships, including *Queer: A Graphic History*, *How To Understand Your Gender*, *Life Isn't Binary*, *Enjoy Sex (How, When, and IF You Want To)*, *Rewriting the Rules*, and *The Psychology of Sex*. They've also written a number of books for scholars and counsellors on these topics, drawing on their own research and therapeutic practice. In their spare time they love – er – doing more writing, and drawing comics, and taking long walks with friends.

Websites: rewriting-the-rules.com, megjohnandjustin.com

Twitter: @megjohnbarker

Kat Gupta (they/them) is a queer, genderqueer, British-Indian academic and researcher living in the UK. They have researched and written about the British suffrage movement, newspaper representation of transgender people, and online erotica. Their activism focuses on LGBTQ+ Black and minority ethnic inclusion. They are interested in too many things, including but not limited to bodies, consent, minority representation, and how we use language to create, sustain and communicate identities.

Website: http://mixosaurus.co.uk

Twitter: @mixosaurus

NOTE
Any royalties that the editors would have received for their work on this book will be donated to Transgender Europe: https://tgeu.org

Life Isn't Binary
On Being Both, Beyond, and In-Between
Meg-John Barker and Alex Iantaffi
Foreword by CN Lester

Paperback: £14.99 / $19.95
ISBN: 978 1 78592 479 8
eISBN: 978 1 78450 864 7
240 pages

Barker and Iantaffi have written the book we all need for this moment in time. – CN Lester

Much of society's thinking operates in a highly rigid and binary manner; something is good or bad, right or wrong, a success or a failure, and so on. Challenging this limited way of thinking, this ground-breaking book looks at how non-binary methods of thought can be applied to all aspects of life, and offer new and greater ways of understanding ourselves and how we relate to others.

Using bisexual and non-binary gender experiences as a starting point, this book addresses the key issues with binary thinking regarding our relationships, bodies, emotions, wellbeing and our sense of identity and sets out a range of practices which may help us to think in more non-binary, both/and, or uncertain ways.

A truly original and insightful piece, this guide encourages reflection on how we view and understand the world we live in and how we all bend, blur or break society's binary codes.

Meg-John Barker is an internationally recognised and hugely influential writer, therapist and thinker on gender, sex, relationships and mental health.

Alex Iantaffi is an internationally recognized independent scholar, speaker and writer on issues of gender, disability, sexuality and mental health. They are also a licensed marriage and family therapist, sex therapist, somatic experiencing practitioner and supervisor.

How to Understand Your Gender
A Practical Guide for Exploring Who You Are

Alex Iantaffi and Meg-John Barker
Foreword by S. Bear Bergman

Paperback: £14.99 / $19.95
ISBN: 978 1 78592 746 1
eISBN: 978 1 78450 517 2
288 pages

For anyone who's ever wished they had a smart, kind, friend with whom they could calmly and safely discuss gender issues: this most excellent book is that kind of friend. – Kate Bornstein, author of *Gender Outlaw*

Have you ever questioned your own gender identity? Do you know somebody who is transgender or who identifies as non-binary? Do you ever feel confused when people talk about gender diversity?

This down-to-earth guide is for anybody who wants to know more about gender, from its biology, history and sociology, to how it plays a role in our relationships and interactions with family, friends, partners and strangers. It looks at practical ways people can express their own gender, and will help you to understand people whose gender might be different from your own. With activities and points for reflection throughout, this book will help people of all genders engage with gender diversity and explore the ideas in the book in relation to their own lived experiences.

Alex Iantaffi is a licensed marriage and family therapist, supervisor, sex therapist, scholar and Editor-in-Chief of the Journal of Sexual and Relationship Therapy. He is also adjunct faculty at the University of Wisconsin-Stout, a parent and active community organizer. @xtaffi on Twitter

Meg-John Barker is a writer, therapist, and activist-academic specialising in sex, gender and relationships. They are a senior lecturer in psychology at the Open University. @megjohnbarker on Twitter.

Transgender Health
A Practitioner's Guide to Binary and Non-Binary Trans Patient Care
Ben Vincent, PhD
Foreword by Dr Stuart Lorimer

Paperback: £15.99 / $22.95
ISBN: 978 1 78592 201 5
eISBN: 978 1 78450 475 5
208 pages

BMA MEDICAL BOOK AWARDS FINALIST

The number of people coming out as transgender continues to rise, and this book shows healthcare and medical practitioners how to deliver excellent primary and secondary care to gender diverse patients.

This guide provides accessible and practical advice on tailoring the social and ethical aspects of practice to the needs of each individual. Beyond setting out how clinical procedures should work for gender reassignment, it explains how to use language and pronouns in a respectful way, provides information on transgender services and resources, and offers insights into the challenges commonly faced by transgender people in both medical and social contexts. Based on cutting edge research and the lived experience of the author as a non-binary person, this is essential reading for all those working to meet the needs of transgender people in healthcare settings.

Ben Vincent holds a PhD in Sociology and Social Policy from the University of Leeds. Ben specialises in transgender identity, community practices, and transgender healthcare.

Person-Centred Counselling for Trans and Gender Diverse People
A Practical Guide
Sam Hope

Paperback: £22.99 / $32.95
ISBN: 978 1 78592 542 9
eISBN: 978 1 78450 937 8
248 pages

Trans clients are frequently doubted, misunderstood, infantilised and judged by professionals, and this book presents an approach that ensures psychological wellbeing and trust is built between counsellor and client. This person-centred, affirmative approach is based around unlearning assumptions about gender and destabilising professionals' ideas of 'knowing better' than, and judging the client, so that they can forge a relationship and connection that is on an equal footing. The book explores a range of topics such as the overlap of gender diversity and autism, sex and sexuality, intersectionality, unconscious bias and reflective practice. Essential reading for professionals that want to support trans people's mental health and social wellbeing.

Sam Hope is a non-binary trans therapist with many years' experience of working with the LGBT community. Sam is a BACP-accredited trauma therapist and delivers training to counsellors and third-sector professionals on trans issues. They run the *Trans Inclusive Feminism* Facebook page; run their own blog; and write for *Beyond the Binary and The Queerness*.

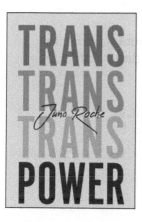

Trans Power
Own Your Gender
Juno Roche

Paperback: £12.99 / $18.95
ISBN: 978 1 78775 019 7
eISBN: 978 1 78775 020 3
256 pages

Staggeringly visionary. – Attitude

Essential reading. – Charlie Craggs

Bold and ground-breaking. – Owl

'All those layers of expectation that are thrust upon us; boy, masculine, femme, transgender, sexual, woman, real, are such a weight to carry round. I feel transgressive. I feel hybrid. I feel trans.'

In this radical and emotionally raw book, Juno Roche pushes the boundaries of trans representation by redefining 'trans' as an identity with its own power and strength, that goes beyond the gender binary.

Through intimate conversations with leading and influential figures in the trans community, such as Kate Bornstein, Travis Alabanza, Josephine Jones, Glamrou and E-J Scott, this book highlights the diversity of trans identities and experiences with regard to love, bodies, sex, race and class, and urges trans people – and the world at large – to embrace a 'trans' identity as something that offers empowerment and autonomy.

Powerfully written, and with humour and advice throughout, this book is essential reading for anyone interested in the future of gender and how we identify ourselves.

Juno Roche is an internationally recognised trans writer and campaigner, and Founder of Trans Workers UK and the Trans Teachers Network. On the Independent's Rainbow List 2015 and 2016, she is a patron of cliniQ and received the 2015 NUT Blair Peach Award for her campaign 'Why Trans Teachers Matter'. She regularly contributes to publications including *Diva, The Guardian* and *Vice* and is the author of *Queer Sex* (Longlisted for the Polari First Book Prize).

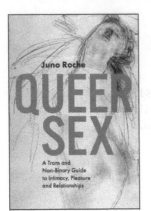

Queer Sex
A Trans and Non-Binary Guide to Intimacy, Pleasure and Relationships
Juno Roche

Paperback: £12.99 / $18.95
ISBN: 978 1 78592 406 4
eISBN: 978 1 78450 770 1
168 pages

LONGLISTED FOR THE POLARI FIRST BOOK PRIZE 2019

Queer Sex is simply phenomenal. – Bitch Media

A gift to anyone looking to open their minds and fall in love. – CN Lester

In this frank, funny and poignant book, transgender activist Juno Roche discusses sex, desire and dating with leading figures from the trans and non-binary community.

Calling out prejudices and inspiring readers to explore their own concepts of intimacy and sexuality, the first-hand accounts celebrate the wonder and potential of trans bodies and push at the boundaries of how society views gender, sexuality and relationships.

Empowering and necessary, this collection shows all trans people deserve to feel brave, beautiful and sexy.

Juno Roche is an internationally recognised trans writer and campaigner, and Founder of Trans Workers UK and the Trans Teachers Network. On the Independent's Rainbow List 2015 and 2016, she is a patron of cliniQ and contributes to publications including *Diva*, *The Guardian* and *Vice*.

Written on the Body
Letters from Trans and Non-Binary Survivors of Sexual Assault and Domestic Violence
Edited by Lexie Bean
Foreword and additional pieces by Dean Spade, Nyala Moon, Alex Valdes, Sawyer DeVuyst and Ieshai Bailey

Paperback: £13.99 / $19.95
ISBN: 978 1 78592 797 3
eISBN: 978 1 78450 803 6
216 pages

LAMBDA LITERARY AWARD FINALIST – LGBTQ ANTHOLOGY

Written by and for trans and non-binary survivors of domestic violence and sexual assault, *Written on the Body* offers support, guidance and hope for those who struggle to find safety at home, in the body, and other unwelcoming places.

This collection of letters written to body parts weaves together narratives of gender, identity, and abuse. It is the coming together of those who have been fragmented and often met with disbelief. The book holds the concerns and truths that many trans people share while offering space for dialogue and reclamation.

Written with intelligence and intimacy, this book is for those who have found power in re-shaping their bodies, families, and lives.

Lexie Bean is a freelance writer for *Teen Vogue* and a performer. They have edited two previous anthologies of letters, *Attention: People with Body Parts* and *Portable Homes*. They are based in New York.

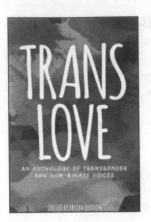

Trans Love
An Anthology of Transgender and Non-Binary Voices
Edited by Freiya Benson

Paperback: £14.99 / $19.95
ISBN: 978 1 78592 432 3
eISBN: 978 1 78450 804 3
296 pages

SELECTED AS A 2019 LGBT BOOK OF THE YEAR BY DAZED AND MS. MAGAZINE

A ground-breaking anthology of writing on the topic of love, written by trans and non-binary people who share their thoughts, feelings and experiences of love in all its guises. The collection spans familial, romantic, spiritual and self-love as well as friendships and ally love, to provide a broad and honest understanding of how trans people navigate love and relationships, and what love means to them.

Reclaiming what love means to trans people, this book provokes conversations that are not reflected in what is presently written, moving the narrative around trans identities away from sensationalism. At once intimate and radical, and both humorous and poignant, this book is for anyone who has loved, who is in love, and who is looking for love.

Freiya Benson is a trans woman and an experienced writer, and has written for magazines and websites, including the *Huffington Post*, and *Vice*.